D1795644

Palgrave Studies in Animals and Literature

Series Editors
Susan McHugh
Department of English
University of New England
Auburn, ME, USA

Robert McKay
School of English
University of Sheffield
Sheffield, UK

John Miller
School of English
University of Sheffield
Sheffield, UK

Various academic disciplines can now be found in the process of executing an 'animal turn', questioning the ethical and philosophical grounds of human exceptionalism by taking seriously the nonhuman animal presences that haunt the margins of history, anthropology, philosophy, sociology and literary studies. Such work is characterised by a series of broad, cross-disciplinary questions. How might we rethink and problematise the separation of the human from other animals? What are the ethical and political stakes of our relationships with other species? How might we locate and understand the agency of animals in human cultures?

This series publishes work that looks, specifically, at the implications of the 'animal turn' for the field of English Studies. Language is often thought of as the key marker of humanity's difference from other species; animals may have codes, calls or songs, but humans have a mode of communication of a wholly other order. The primary motivation is to muddy this assumption and to animalise the canons of English Literature by rethinking representations of animals and interspecies encounter. Whereas animals are conventionally read as objects of fable, allegory or metaphor (and as signs of specifically human concerns), this series significantly extends the new insights of interdisciplinary animal studies by tracing the engagement of such figuration with the material lives of animals. It examines textual cultures as variously embodying a debt to or an intimacy with animals and advances understanding of how the aesthetic engagements of literary arts have always done more than simply illustrate natural history. We publish studies of the representation of animals in literary texts from the Middle Ages to the present and with reference to the discipline's key thematic concerns, genres and critical methods. The series focuses on literary prose and poetry, while also accommodating related discussion of the full range of materials and texts and contexts (from theatre and film to fine art, journalism, the law, popular writing and other cultural ephemera) with which English studies now engages.

Series Board
Karl Steel (Brooklyn College)
Erica Fudge (Strathclyde)
Kevin Hutchings (UNBC)
Philip Armstrong (Canterbury)
Carrie Rohman (Lafayette)
Wendy Woodward (Western Cape)

Candice Allmark-Kent

Literature, Science, and Animal Advocacy in Canada

Practical Zoocriticism

Candice Allmark-Kent
Devon, UK

ISSN 2634-6338   ISSN 2634-6346   (electronic)
Palgrave Studies in Animals and Literature
ISBN 978-3-031-40555-6   ISBN 978-3-031-40556-3   (eBook)
https://doi.org/10.1007/978-3-031-40556-3

© The Editor(s) (if applicable) and The Author(s), under exclusive licence to Springer Nature Switzerland AG 2023
This work is subject to copyright. All rights are solely and exclusively licensed by the Publisher, whether the whole or part of the material is concerned, specifically the rights of translation, reprinting, reuse of illustrations, recitation, broadcasting, reproduction on microfilms or in any other physical way, and transmission or information storage and retrieval, electronic adaptation, computer software, or by similar or dissimilar methodology now known or hereafter developed.
The use of general descriptive names, registered names, trademarks, service marks, etc. in this publication does not imply, even in the absence of a specific statement, that such names are exempt from the relevant protective laws and regulations and therefore free for general use.
The publisher, the authors, and the editors are safe to assume that the advice and information in this book are believed to be true and accurate at the date of publication. Neither the publisher nor the authors or the editors give a warranty, expressed or implied, with respect to the material contained herein or for any errors or omissions that may have been made. The publisher remains neutral with regard to jurisdictional claims in published maps and institutional affiliations.

This Palgrave Macmillan imprint is published by the registered company Springer Nature Switzerland AG.
The registered company address is: Gewerbestrasse 11, 6330 Cham, Switzerland

Paper in this product is recyclable.

For all in Canada, whether human or nonhuman,
and for Barbara and Henry.

Acknowledgements

I am deeply grateful to Robert McKay for inviting me to submit to the Palgrave Studies in Animals and Literature series all those years ago. Thank you for greeting my intermittent progress updates with kindness and patience. This volume would not have been possible without Susan McHugh or John Miller either. Thank you for supporting this project. I would also like to express my gratitude to the rest of the team at Palgrave Macmillan, especially my editor Allie Troyanos and my reviewer(s). Thank you for bringing this book closer to what it ought to be.

This project grew out of my PhD thesis, although it has expanded considerably. Some similarities remain in the analytical frameworks I propose and the literary interpretations they produce. Yet most of this volume is new material. What should have been a straightforward revision became increasingly ambitious as I uncovered the fascinating history described here. Still, I remain indebted to my PhD supervisors in the English department at the University of Exeter, Jane Poyner and Sinéad Moynihan. Without Jane's willingness to support my burgeoning interest in fictional animals, this book would not exist. In addition, I am extremely grateful to the staff and students at Carleton University. You expanded my thinking and reinvigorated my passion for literature. Just one year at Carleton changed the trajectory of my life.

I cannot express the gratitude I feel towards everyone who has offered encouragement along this journey. There are too many of you to thank by name. As family and friends will know, this project consumed me for several years. You watched me disappear into it for months at a time, but you always met me with love and grace when I resurfaced. This book would not have been possible without your support. For all my absences, you never told me to quit.

Much of this project was completed independently and without institutional support. As a result, I owe an impossible debt to the people closest to me. Lewis, you shared your home and became a patient ear to my excitement and frustration (depending on the day). Sophie, you always knew how to pick me up when I was down. Your belief made me feel unstoppable. Louise, you gifted with me a lifeline of support that carried me to the finish. Gene, you kept an eye on the big picture and reminded me that there would be life beyond this project. Thank you for seeing me as I want to see myself.

Tom, I could write an entire book about what you have done for me. You brought me into the sunshine from the depths of my PhD research and you have been a light in my world ever since. This project was built on the bedrock of your love, support, and patience. Thank you for waiting for me. Maybe now we can get on with our lives.

Of course, there are no words for my debt to Barbara and Henry. None of this could have happened without them. Neither this book nor my PhD thesis would exist if they had not been behind me. I am deeply privileged to have such a support system. Thank for carrying me to the end. I kept going for you.

Finally, I would like to thank all the nonhuman animals I have known. I wish I could make a better world for each of you. From my earliest memories, your gentle company taught me empathy, kindness, and a deep curiosity for other minds. All of you have challenged my expectations and kept me learning. I am grateful for it all. Even now, I would love to know what you were thinking.

CONTENTS

1   Introduction   1

Part I   Emergence   27

 2   1860s–1900s Contexts   29

 3   1860s–1900s Texts   45

Part II   Adaptation   79

 4   1900s–1950s Contexts   81

 5   1900s–1950s Texts   95

Part III   Divergence   131

 6   1950s–1980s Contexts   133

 7   1950s–1980s Texts   145

Part IV   Survival   181

  8   1980s–2000s Contexts   183

  9   1980s–2000s Texts   195

  10   Conclusion   245

Appendix: Questions for Practical Zoocriticism   255

Index   257

About the Author

Candice Allmark-Kent is an independent scholar. Born in the United States and raised in Great Britain, she studied at the University of Exeter (England) and Carleton University (Canada). She has published and presented papers on the relationship between literature, science, and animal advocacy. She has also taught British and North American literature and history. Her interdisciplinary interests span animal cognition, environmental history, animal ethics, science communication, the politics of representation, and storytelling in games. Currently, she is interested in how narratives can be used to improve public understanding of underrepresented species. Her next project explores the connection between stories and empathy.

CHAPTER 1

Introduction

This book charts 150 years of ideas about animals in the north of Turtle Island, also known as Canada.[1] It is an animal history filtered through human eyes. It is also inherently colonial. In this book, I restrict my focus to Euro-Canadian settler-colonial culture because, historically, this has been the dominant factor shaping the nation's animal laws. As we will discover throughout this book, Canada's conservation and animal protection policies were often created to serve the interests of upper- and middle-class white men. Consequently, this history skews towards the voices of those white male scientists, writers, naturalists, conservationists, advocates, and policymakers influencing these laws. This approach, albeit narrow, exposes complex legacies of settler-colonial thinking that make the history of Canadian-animal relations a rich area of study.

As a product of colonization, the nation's policies towards animals have been framed through a highly specific lens. These attitudes towards

---

[1] Many Indigenous peoples identify the continent of North America as Turtle Island, based on similarities between creation myths across different cultures. This book's focus on federal animal laws and government conservation policies requires references to the nation of 'Canada' throughout. Nonetheless, the events described in this book take place in the traditional territories of Indigenous peoples. Descriptions of 'wilderness' or seemingly 'empty' natural environments still refer to land stolen by European settlers during the colonization of Turtle Island.

© The Author(s), under exclusive license to Springer Nature Switzerland AG 2023
C. Allmark-Kent, *Literature, Science, and Animal Advocacy in Canada*, Palgrave Studies in Animals and Literature, https://doi.org/10.1007/978-3-031-40556-3_1

wildlife reveal the surprising longevity of early European ideas about a vast, 'pristine' landscape of many animals and few people. Myths of *terra nullius* (no-one's land) and superabundant wildlife encouraged a simultaneous impulse to both celebrate and annihilate. Successive governments have been caught in this tension between, what Neil Forkey (2012) terms, the "need to exploit" and the "desire to protect" (3). At heart, this relationship with animals has been (and continues to be) a colonial one shaped by a process of 'discovery,' categorization, 'ownership,' exploitation, eradication, and remedial 'preservation.'

If we imagine 'Canada,' some iconic wildlife may come to mind. Settler-colonial symbolism in Canada abounds with the furred and feathered bodies of the moose, bear, beaver, loon, and goose. They can be found on everything from postcards and coins to beer cans and clothing brands. Canada is rich with images of and ideas about wild animals. Indeed, literary scholar Gaile McGregor (1985) asserts that "Canadians are fascinated by animals" (192). Likewise, Margaret Atwood (1972) proposed that the entire nation sympathized with animals because they saw themselves reflected in the eyes of vulnerable creatures (79). Yet, the reality of Canada's lax and ineffective animal cruelty laws offers a stark contrast to these claims. Despite the nation's apparent affinity for animals, Canadian law leaves them almost entirely unprotected from violence. This means that the nation's beloved moose, bears, beavers, loons, and geese can be brutally attacked, cruelly tortured, or viciously killed for no reason.

A report by the International Fund for Animal Welfare (2008) ranked Canada at the bottom of a list of thirteen nations. In all areas of animal protection, Canada was found lacking. Initially, these laws had been a source of national pride when they were first put in place. Canada had existed as a confederated nation for only two years before enacting its first federal anti-cruelty legislation. The *Cruelty to Animals Act* of 1869 reflected the aspirations of a new country and promised the ethical and moral standards by which it would conduct itself. As Darcy Ingram (2013) observes, it set Canada on a path towards a "modern, progressive, respectable" identity to which it still aspires today (222). The problem is that there has been little meaningful progress since. Over the intervening years, the nation's animal cruelty laws have remained virtually untouched. It is no exaggeration to say that Canadian animal protection is stuck in the Victorian era.

Part of the issue is that, uniquely, Canada classifies animal cruelty offences as crimes against 'property.' When anti-cruelty laws first entered the Canadian Criminal Code in 1892, they focused on protecting cattle from mistreatment. As a result, they were placed under the property section of the code. Despite many attempts to move them, this is where Canadian animal protection laws remain today. In legal terms, even the most horrific acts of animal abuse are essentially property damage. Canada is "the only country that makes it virtually impossible to prosecute cases of neglect" (IFAW 2008, 5). Moreover, by only defining animals as property, all non-captive animals are excluded. Thus, wild or feral animals have no legal protection from cruelty. In 1898 the famous Canadian writer and naturalist, Ernest Thompson Seton, wrote "Have the wild things no moral or legal rights?" (357). Sadly, 125 years later the answer remains, irrefutably, *no*.

So, why has Euro-Canadian settler-colonial culture developed this specific relationship with other animals? Why is there such a discrepancy between *animal protection* and *animal representation* in Canada? Certainly, there is nothing inherent within the nation or its diverse populations to cause this situation. Nor, indeed, is there any specific 'Canadian psyche' at work. Instead, as John Sorenson (2010) puts it, we "tend to overlook that our present relationship with animals" is "not a natural or historical constant;" it is simply a "social construction" (12). To unpack these changing ideas about animals, this book brings together an interdisciplinary history of literature, science, and animal advocacy in Canada between 1860 and 2010.

What emerges from this book is a fascinating story of innovation, debate, transition, controversy, and hypocrisy. As indicated by the words of Ernest Thompson Seton, plenty of Canadians have spoken out on behalf of other species. Indeed, many have been at the forefront of scientific studies of animal minds, advocacy for animal protection, and creative efforts to engage with animals imaginatively. But they have also faced serious criticism and provoked significant backlashes. Moreover, public responses to their efforts have been inconsistent and governments have failed to enact substantial changes.

Over the next eight chapters of this book, we will learn that what we 'know' about other animals has changed radically over time. Whilst we might expect a steady trajectory in a single direction, what we find more closely resembles a series of pendulum swings. Recurring ideas, concerns, and questions ebb and flow throughout these pages. Questions about whether we can *ever* know other animals emerge at different times in science, literature, and philosophy. Belief in the existence of animal minds and emotions rises and falls and rises again. Public interest in nature, wildlife, and animal behaviour fluctuates throughout the decades. Government attitudes to animals oscillate between protection and exploitation. Anxiety about what makes us different to other animals remains a perennial concern. Likewise, the stigma of anthropomorphism continues to haunt writers, researchers, and advocates alike. Meanwhile, persistent debates about who has the right to speak on behalf of other animals are never fully resolved.

KNOWING OTHER ANIMALS

This book is about how we know other animals. On the surface, this might seem relatively straightforward. Yet, we humans bring a lot of baggage to our encounters with other species. Competing ideas from the arts, sciences, religion, philosophy, politics, and popular culture are constantly shaping and reshaping our beliefs about other animals. A scientific advancement, a compelling argument for animal protection, or a moving piece of literature can all cause a shift in our thinking. Together, these forces influence whether we see another animal as a threat, a friend, a meal, a trophy, or a pest. They also shape our expectations about an animal's intelligence, their ability to feel pain, or their capacity for emotion. Ultimately, whether accurate or not, these beliefs determine our opinions about how other species ought to be treated.

In this book, I introduce *practical zoocriticism* as a framework for studying how different forces interact to shape our ideas about other species over time. This book focuses on the relationship between three specific methods of communicating on behalf of nonhuman animals: literary representations of animal characters, the scientific study of animal minds, and advocacy for animal protection. I have chosen these three areas because each one promises to give us something uniquely compelling: an insight into the unseen, otherwise inaccessible, inner lives of other animals. Science studies how animals perceive, process, and comprehend the world. Animal advocacy considers the qualitative experiences of other animals, such as their wellbeing, pain, or trauma. Meanwhile, literature can imagine both sets of topics from the animal's *own* perspective. For instance, an author might speculate about what it feels like to experience the world through echolocation or to suffer the violence of human cruelty.

Against the dominant forces of science and animal advocacy, fiction would seem to have little bearing on our relationships with other species. Yet, the stories we tell do shape our attitudes. They can reinforce myths that cast different species as noble, innocent, cruel, or disgusting. They can play to human fears or flatter our egos. They can appear to widen the human-animal divide until it seems an insurmountable gulf. Or they can remind us that we are all inherently related on the Darwinian family tree. Although some writers may seem to legitimize our supremacy over other species, others do try to write on behalf of the animals themselves. Such stories can have a powerful influence over our ideas about nonhuman beings. As Joan Dunayer (2001) observes, the "way we speak about animals is inseparable from the way we treat them" (9).

In the opening decades of the twenty-first century, as urban populations rise and wildlife numbers dwindle, humans are interacting with fewer species. We invite a select group into our homes: cats, dogs, perhaps a hamster or guinea pig, a few tropical fishes, or the odd caged bird. At the weekend, our leisure activities might bring us into contact with more animals. Occasionally, we might visit a zoo or aquarium. Day-to-day, though, most of us see a wider variety of animals on screens than we do in person. Indeed, we may pay more attention to the animals we encounter in books, on television, or in video games than those we eat for dinner or wear upon our bodies. Given the current state of human-animal relations, it makes sense to take these imaginary animals more seriously. This is particularly important for wild animals whose habitats are remote or inaccessible to us. For my part, I have certainly spent more time with fictional sharks, tigers, or elephants than with real members of their species.

More than at any other time in human history, we are disconnecting from other species. Yet, everywhere, animals are in crisis. We are in the midst of a global mass extinction, in which hundreds of unique species have already disappeared since 1900 and many more remain at risk. At the same time, we continue to kill individual animals in their trillions every year through agriculture, fishing, experimentation, fur farming, hunting, sports, 'pest' control, and countless other means. The scale of the problem is almost incomprehensible when described in these terms. We may feel numb to such an enormous loss of life. As Paul Slovic (2007) puts it: "Our capacity to feel is limited" (90). Humans simply cannot empathize with trillions of individuals at once. Instead, we need to understand the problem on an *individual* basis. "When it comes to eliciting compassion," Slovic writes, "the identified individual victim, with a face and a name, has no peer" (86). Yet, in most cases of animal suffering, this can be hard to achieve. Here, we can see the potential power of fiction.

Unlikely as it may seem, some writers do make a sincere effort to depict the lives of other species as faithfully as possible. In essence, this is an attempt to know animals through fiction. It is the difficult task of placing readers inside the minds of other animals. Such writers do not just interpret or describe; they imagine and speculate. In other words, they strive to show us what observation alone cannot. The ways in which authors approach such a feat can tell us a lot about contemporary perceptions of animals. Some may strive for greater accuracy through extensive research and the latest scientific evidence. Others may ground their story in the current survival struggles of the species by engaging with animal advocacy. In each case, these fictional animals have a significant role to play in shaping our understanding of their real-life counterparts.

This book traces the evolution of various attempts to know animals through fiction in Euro-Canadian settler-culture. Undoubtedly, the most important development was that of the nineteenth century *wild animal story*. Co-created by two Canadian men, this form of writing prioritized the experiences and perspectives of nonhuman animals. These characters were not allegories or metaphors, but realistic individuals who existed in ecological networks of many different species. Crucially, these animals were the protagonists of their *own* stories. If humans appeared, they were usually antagonists or, at best, bystanders. Although the accuracy of these stories has been debated, their innovative approach created a legacy that remains today. The wild animal story changed the role of fictional animals because they were not just stories *about* animals; they were designed to help readers know real animals better.

One purpose of practical zoocriticism is to find the best methods of communicating on behalf of other animals. By studying how literature, science, and animal advocacy interact over time, we discover both an interwoven history and the future potential for reciprocal exchange. Insights from writers can help scientists and advocates engage the public more effectively. Meanwhile, fiction offers another branch of communication for both. Writers can use contemporary scientific information to improve public understanding or illustrate current issues within animal ethics. In turn, fiction can also raise questions that stimulate future research or illuminate new issues that need to be addressed. Throughout this book, we find many individuals who have sought such exchanges, as well as some rare figures whose own work straddles all three topics. All too often, however, these efforts were met with distain. For much of the twentieth century, the divisions between researchers, writers, and activists grew further apart. Now, it is time to set aside such short-sightedness.

Animal Studies

Understanding human-animal relations requires a holistic approach. No traditional academic discipline can present the whole picture. The task always requires some measure of interdisciplinarity. Animal studies is a cross-disciplinary endeavour to study human-animal relations in the broadest possible terms. There is no dominant approach, theory, or methodology. It is interdisciplinary, multidisciplinary, and even transdisciplinary.[2] Under this broad umbrella thrives many diverse approaches to studying nonhuman animals. This all-encompassing attitude means that more specialized fields have also emerged, such as anthrozoology, critical animal studies, and animality studies.

Anthrozoology is associated with the social sciences and emphasizes human-animal interaction. Topics might include anthropological studies of humans and companion animals or sociological investigations into the links between animal abuse and domestic violence. By contrast, critical animal studies is more explicitly concerned with advocacy and addresses the intersectional oppressions of both humans and other animals. Alternatively, animality studies focuses on the cultural study of animals without making any explicit commitments to advocacy or demands for equality.

So far, the work of animal studies has been conducted largely by researchers who began in other fields. (We are currently awaiting the first generation of scholars who have been trained exclusively in animal studies.) Each discipline brought to the table changes the flavour of animal studies a little. Now, within this broad spectrum, new subfields have begun

[2] See Derek Ryan (2015,14).

to coalesce. These emerging areas of research blend the foundations of a traditional discipline with the interdisciplinary frameworks of animal studies. This book contributes to two subfields: literary animal studies and animal history.

We have spent the past few decades describing animal studies as 'new,' 'emerging,' and 'fast-growing.' It seems safe to say now that the substantial field of animal studies has arrived—and it is not alone. Instead, it is the various subfields of animal studies that we should now call new, emerging, and fast-growing. A current priority for scholars tending to these fresh areas of research is the creation of theories, definitions, concepts, and methodologies. Of course, the same also holds for animal studies itself, which is by no means mature. Undoubtedly the sheer multiplicity of approaches to animal studies indicates the vitality of the field. Yet, it also exacerbates the difficulty of setting out new subdivisions. One such issue arises when the agenda of a parent discipline seems to conflict with that of animal studies. For literary animal studies, this problem has been particularly acute.

Literary studies was one of the last disciplines to heed the so-called animal turn. This was despite some clear invitations, such as the one made in Kenneth Shapiro's (1993) editorial introduction to the first issue of *Society & Animals*: "more studies are needed in the area of animals in the popular culture, particularly of animals in literature" (2). The delay was not unusual. Whilst the social sciences were driving the earliest developments in animal studies, many subjects in the humanities were held back by an implicit anthropocentrism.[3]

Glen Love (2003) puts it well when he remarks that the history of literary studies serves as a "textbook example of anthropocentrism" (23). Indeed, there is a widespread assumption that nonhuman beings are generally irrelevant to literature. 'Important' literature sheds light on humanity, illuminating the complexities of human characters and human concerns. By contrast, works about animals are seen as frivolous, naive, or amateurish. In Love's words, it is "one of the great mistaken ideas of anthropocentric thinking" that "society is complex while nature is simple;" that "nature is dull and uninteresting, while society is sophisticated and interesting" (23).

Fuelling the marginalization of animals in literary studies is the belief that no significant literature about animals exists. The truth is that these

---

[3] The term 'anthropocentrism' refers to a human-centred view of the world. It prioritizes human perspectives, as well as human interests.

texts are abundant, but we have been ignoring them. For a long time, the practice of literary studies has been that, when faced with animal characters, the reader must interpret them as *human*. In this way, certain works of literature could be made 'worthy' of academic study by interpreting their animal characters as allegories, symbols, metaphors, or simply stand-ins for humans. Of course, this habit reinforces the assumption that all animal literature is highly anthropomorphic. This is not to say that anthropomorphic or allegorical literature does not exist. However, there is a self-fulfilling prophesy here that ignores the existence of literature that sincerely attempts to represent nonhuman animals for their own sake.

For too long we have been ignoring or misrepresenting the work of authors who wish to write about animals *as animals*. By marginalizing all texts that prioritize nonhuman beings, or by distorting them until they seem to be about humans, literary studies creates and maintains the belief that all animal literature is only ever highly anthropomorphic and anthropocentric. In turn, this strengthens the idea that literature may only ever be about humans. Ultimately, animal literature is either overlooked or made 'important' by not being about animals at all.

Scholars of literary animal studies have begun the task of taking fictional animals more seriously. Yet, there is still some hesitation about how much anthropocentrism we are willing to shed. As this new field grows, the uncertainty about how to approach the question of animal ethics becomes increasingly apparent. There is no consensus about what our relationship with or duties towards real animals should be. The majority of animal studies work tends to suggest, at the very least, some form of allegiance towards improving human-animal relations. Within literary animal studies, however, the relationship between academia and advocacy seems more tenuous.

One perspective may state that the mere expansion of our analysis to nonhuman beings should not imply any call to advocacy or demand for equality. Another adds that, as literary animals are human constructs, they bear no relationship to real animals at all. An alternative stance may hold that we can never truly know other animals, only what we perceive them to be. This means that any claims we make on their behalf are inherently invalid, including those made by the sciences or animal protection movements. Consequently, this means that collective advocacy becomes problematic.

At present, there are a few ways to categorize attitudes towards real animals in literary animal studies, though none are conclusive. Julie Ann Smith (2001) describes differences between "pro-animal" and "pro-use" positions, as well as between "modernist" and "postmodernist" approaches. The "pro-animal" stance assumes that animals are knowable to humans, whilst "pro-use" argues that they are only what we "construct" them to be (295). Smith's "modernist theorists" operate from a position established by "animal rights philosophy" that the evolutionary continuity between humans and animals enables us to make certain "authoritative statements about animal pain and pleasure" (296). These scholars tend to be engaged in "animal-rights and animal-rescue work" (296). Alternatively, the post-modernists argue that "animal-rights philosophy reinscribes animals as lesser human beings, failing to imagine a radical egalitarianism" (296). They also seek a "corrective to the modernist tendency to domesticate the alterity of animals through language," which inevitably serves to reinforce the "human enterprise of colonizing the other" (297).

Along similar lines, Steve Baker (2000) has outlined animal-endorsing and animal-sceptical perspectives. Even though Baker proposed these terms as a way of categorizing representations of animals in art, they can also serve our purposes. This is because Baker took his inspiration from Kate Soper's (1995) classification of academic discourse as either nature-endorsing or nature-sceptical. However, it is worth noting that Soper does not align her concepts with modernism or postmodernism as easily as Baker. According to him, animal-endorsing perspectives will "tend to endorse animal life itself (and may therefore align itself with the work of conservationists, or perhaps of animal advocacy), rather than endorsing cultural constructions of the animal" (Baker 2000, 9). Whereas the animal-sceptical stance is sceptical not of animals themselves, but of "culture's means of constructing and classifying the animal in order to make it meaningful to the human" (9). Although they do not correspond perfectly, these positions evidently have much in common with the categories outlined by Smith.

If we merge Smith's and Baker's ideas together, we are left with two groups: "modernist," "pro-animal" endorsers and "postmodernist," "pro-use" sceptics. The first group takes a scientifically informed and advocacy-orientated approach. It argues that there are certain things we can know and attempt to represent about animals in order to advocate for their ethical treatment. These depictions may be imperfect but are important for pragmatic public engagement. This is because the way we represent animals influences how other humans see them and, ultimately, how they treat them. In this way, even fictional animals can contribute to our overall attitudes towards other species. Included within these attitudes are our beliefs about what kinds of treatment those animals deserve. We might expect this group to value "modernist," "animal-endorsing" creative work.

The second group posits that because animals are fundamentally unknowable, they resist our attempts to categorize, study, depict, or interpret them. All that we can ever know are our own constructions and these are inevitably anthropocentric and anthropomorphic. Therefore, claims made on behalf of animals by scientists or animal advocacy campaigners are inherently suspect. Ethical relationships with other animals require a complete dismantling of anthropocentrism in all its iterations. We can work towards this by deconstructing the ways in which human representations of nonhuman beings reinforce human supremacy. Yet some types of fiction can also help us to imagine alternative ways of being and more radical forms of egalitarianism. Unsurprisingly, this group would tend to dismiss "animal-endorsing" representations in favour of more "postmodernist," "animal-sceptical" texts.

So far, literary animal studies has operated through a broadly animal-sceptical perspective. This may be due to the approaches, theories, and concerns we have carried with us from literary studies. Glen Love (2003) points out that ideas about nature in literary studies have been dominated by nature-sceptical thinking (8). From this standpoint, animal-endorsing methods might seem too invested in human authority or making claims on behalf of other species. In animal-sceptical analysis, the radical alterity of the nonhuman is used to interrogate, challenge, or re-evaluate dominant forms of knowledge. However, I perceive two dangers in this strategy: fetishization and immobilization.

When conducting animal-sceptical analysis, it is possible to become too focused on the animal's subversive, anti-anthropocentric presence to the point that all connection to the fleshy realities of living animals is forgotten. The animal becomes a fetishized symbol of alterity. As such, it can be inadvertently abstracted into a prop for human meaning once again; a tool with which we can continually dismantle 'the human.' For those animal-sceptics engaged with animality studies, this is perhaps not an issue. However, literary scholars who wish to offer contributions to advocacy-orientated work in animal studies can become immobilized by the animal's ability to demonstrate the fallibility and insufficiency of human knowledge. Moreover, by becoming lost in this type of deconstruction, we may end up distancing ourselves from the engaging, innovative work of the broader, multidisciplinary, animal studies project.

Love (2003) highlights the issue by identifying a kind of anthropocentric solipsism in literary studies. He describes "a subjectivism [that] intimates no reality, no nature, beyond what we construct with our own minds" (26). All of us working in literary animal studies need to consider whether we are still operating under the legacy of such thinking. For instance, Charles Bergman (2001) describes conferences in which "actual animals seemed almost an embarrassment, a disturbance to the symbolic field" and "virtually nothing" was said about how our representations might affect them (np). He concludes that we may need to remind ourselves that animals are "not texts that we produce" but "living beings;" that we must "care as much for the worlds of being as we do for the worlds of meaning" (np). In a similar vein, Steve Best (2009) expresses fears about what will happen to animal studies within academia and whether the realities of living animals and their exploitation will become lost in abstraction and "buried in dense theoretical webs" (11).

Up to this point, literary animal studies has remained largely disengaged from the rich interdisciplinarity that is characteristic of animal studies. Interactions between literary and scientific researchers have been particularly rare. Even the substantial growth in research about the relationship between literature and science tends not to give serious attention to other animals. With such an obvious point of contact, it seems surprising that there has not been more engagement between the sciences, animal studies, literary animal studies, and the study of literature and science. This is particularly regrettable as the scientific study of animal minds has become much more open to interdisciplinary methods.

In the field of cognitive ethology, researchers are beginning to note the ways in which narratives, anecdotes, and storytelling can be used to identify unusual animal behaviours, communicate current findings to the public, or even postulate future hypotheses. I suggest that the current lack of interaction between literary and scientific researchers exposes some of the disciplinary biases, anxieties, and prejudices that have remained at work despite our common ground. On both sides, there may be an assumption that the other has little to offer.

PRACTICAL ZOOCRITICISM

Practical zoocriticism is animal-endorsing, advocacy-orientated, and scientifically informed. It takes inspiration from Glen Love's *practical* ecocriticism, Graham Huggan and Helen Tiffin's postcolonial *zoocriticism*, and Marion Copeland's work on *zoocentric* literature. I drew on Love's use of the word *practical* for its connotations of an engaged, pragmatic interdisciplinarity. In *Practical Ecocriticism*, Love (2003) argues that ecocriticism must be interdisciplinary to fulfil its most important work (47). I hold that the same is true of literary animal studies. Taking animals seriously means learning something about them. We must learn about their current status in the world: what threats they face and what protections they are offered. It also means learning something scientific about them: what we know about their biology and ecology and what we currently understand about their psychology.

As Love (2003) points out, the sciences are not just another cultural construction. They are "our best human means for discovering how the world works" (8). With so much at stake, it makes sense to imbue our work as "teachers," "scholars," and "literary citizens" with greater attention to the "biological and ecological context than has been previously evident in dominant nature-sceptical thinking" (7–8). Whilst such work might seem problematic to the sceptics, Love observes that the nature-endorsers gain credibility by being drawn to real problems and in offering advocacy and analyses that contribute to broader solutions (8). Thus, the word *practical* also conveys a commitment to nature-endorsing, advocacy-orientated work.

I borrow the term *zoocriticism* from Huggan and Tiffin's *Postcolonial Ecocriticism* (2010). They outline the need for "a broadly materialist understanding of the changing relationship between people, animals, and the environment" (12). Crucially, they note that this materialist understanding would still require attention to the "politics of representation" (12). For instance, conservation legislation tends to "depend on public response to representation rather than to the animals themselves or to their environments since, for most urban voters, there has been little or no experience of the 'real thing'" (139). Hence, they emphasize the reciprocal relationship between cultural representations of animals and the real-world, material status of living animals. Their notion of "zoocriticism" is not just concerned with "animal *representation*," but also with "animal *rights"* (17–8 emphasis original). I use *zoocriticism* to designate animal-endorsing, advocacy-orientated literary analysis.

Copeland (1994) defines "zoocentric texts" as "literature in which nonhumans appear not as the agents of social satire or of allegory but as characters in their own life stories" (277). She adds that such texts use "a variety of literary techniques, including anthropomorphism, to interpret the stories of other living beings for human readers who cannot, unaided, hear the words of the furred, feathered, scaled, or finned" (277).

Copeland expanded upon this definition in a joint editorial for *Society and Animals* with Kenneth Shapiro (2005). They proposed that zoocentric representation would present an animal character not as a symbol or a reductive stereotype, but simply as "him or herself" (344). The animal appears "as an individual with some measure of autonomy, agency, voice, character, and as a member of a species with a nature that has certain typical capabilities and limitations" (344). Thus, they suggest that we might evaluate zoocentric literature based on the degree to which it presents "the animal 'in itself,' both as an experiencing individual and as a species-typical way of living in the world" (345). At present, the details of how we would make such a judgement are unclear. I would argue that it requires interdisciplinary knowledge about what those "individual" and "species-typical" animal experiences might look like.

A further question we might ask is whether the individual is depicted as the *subject of a life*. This term was introduced by the American animal advocate, Tom Regan, in his book *The Case for Animal Rights* (1984). To be the *subject of a life* is to have inherent value. Regan identifies a range of characteristics, such as "perception, memory, and a sense of the future;" "an emotional life together with feelings of pleasure and pain;" "a psychophysical identity over time;" and "an individual welfare in the sense that their experiential life fares well or ill for them" (245).[4] Crucially, though, one either is a *subject of a life*, or one is not. All those who are, are so equally (245). Though Regan used the term as a criterion for ethics, it can also help us to judge an animal's literary representation.

Often the imaginary animals in our books, films, and video games are little more than objects. They have no desires or interests of their own; they usually exist to serve human ends. To help identify when an animal is

---

[4]For a full list of Regan's (1984) extensive criteria, see *The Case for Animal Rights*.

not being presented as the *subject of a life*, I propose another term: the *object of utility*. From my observations, this phrase best describes the reductive or disrespectful use of animals in fiction. It can apply to common situations in which animals are seen or treated as objects. Yet it also refers to highly anthropomorphic depictions used to convey human messages or morals. In each case, the animals do not exist for their *own* sake. Thus, whether animals appear as complex allegories or simply as part of the human protagonist's lunch, they are still *objects of utility*.

When judging an animal's representation, we can ask ourselves a series of questions. Species-typical questions might include: How has the author presented the animal's sensory experiences? Do these experiences result in any subjective inner states, such as pleasure, distress, or curiosity? What degrees of cognitive, emotional, or social complexity are being demonstrated? How does this species interact with other animals (including human beings)? By contrast, individual questions might include: Is this animal the *subject of a life* or an *object of utility*? Are they a distinct individual or a species stereotype? Do they have a biography? Have they been shaped by these experiences? Do they have a personality? Does the animal perceive the world through a unique, individual perspective? I have drawn up a list of questions we can apply to any animal representation (see Appendix). For anyone wishing to begin zoocriticism, this is a good place to start.

KNOWING ANIMALS IN FICTION

Writers in Canada have offered varied responses to the question of knowing other animals. Assumptions about whether animals are 'knowable' or not have wide ranging consequences. Questions about whether we can ever truly *know* other animals have shaped the scientific study of animal minds and stirred major debates about animal welfare and ethics. As we have seen, this topic even affects literary animal studies. Where one falls on the spectrum between animal-endorsing and animal-sceptical has a lot to do with one's stance on the 'knowability' of other animals.

I have identified four modes of animal representation based on degrees of 'knowability.' These are: the *indifference to knowing*, the *fantasy of knowing*, the *failure of knowing*, and the *acceptance of not knowing*. As these approaches are based on fundamental questions about knowing other animals, they affect more than just the representation of individual animal characters. They can shape plot, themes, and all human-animal relations in the text.

The *indifference to knowing* the animal describes a lack of interest in knowing other animals. Often coming from an anthropocentric perspective, it can be speciesist and may produce reductive or objectifying depictions.[5] In most forms of literature, nonhuman beings are not the subjects of their own stories. They may have no existence at all beyond what they provide for humans. Instead, they are *objects of utility* in human narratives, typically appearing as: decorations in a natural landscape; aggressors in a story of human survival; stand-ins for humans in a moral tale; trophies of a hunt; saviours, companions, transport, entertainment, or assistants for human characters; or simply an absence when human characters consume their bodies. As such, there is little interest in knowing the animals themselves. These representations tend to be distorted by either high anthropomorphism or mechanomorphic objectification. [6]

The *fantasy of knowing* the animal assumes that animals are knowable to some degree. Authors may try to encapsulate what it might be like to be another species by attempting to present them as accurately as possible. Or they may acknowledge the difficulties in attempting to depict animal minds by emphasizing the speculative nature of the work. We can refer to these as the *realistic* or *speculative* styles. Commonly, there is a sincere attempt to know the species involved and a sustained commitment to imagining their inner lives. Because of this, authors may choose to associate their work with science or animal advocacy. It is worth bearing in mind, though, that a *fantasy of knowing* is no

---

[5] Coined by Richard Ryder in 1970, the term 'speciesism' describes a prejudice based on the criteria of species. It can refer to the ways in which humans prioritize the interests of our own species above those of all other animals. Or it can describe our bias towards some nonhuman animals compared to others. For instance, consider the unequal treatment experienced by cats, cows, and cockroaches.

[6] We can think of mechanomorphism as the counterpart to anthropomorphism. Rather than seeing animals as humans, it involves seeing them as machines. This can apply to describing their actions through mechanistic language or even thinking of animals as mindless 'automatons.' Both anthropomorphism and mechanomorphism are equally inaccurate. However, it is worth noting that mechanomorphism does not carry the same stigma as anthropomorphism.

guarantee of a respectful depiction. Such stories may still perpetuate harmful stereotypes.

The *failure of knowing* the animal presupposes that animals are fundamentally unknowable. In fiction, these narratives tend to centre on a human's unsuccessful attempts to know or form a relationship with a nonhuman character. Often, the human character begins with their own *fantasy of knowing* but realizes the error in their thinking. This tends to arise through a dramatic or violent act in which the animal's unknowability is suddenly impressed upon the human. In such narratives, we tend to learn little about the animals themselves. This can be due to either unreliable human narrators or elusive animal characters. As a result, even respectful representations of animals can be somewhat limited. Generally, these narratives offer a pessimistic view of human-animal relations.

The *acceptance of not knowing* the animal explores the productive possibilities of rejecting the idea that we can ever know other animals. These texts may celebrate (rather than lament) our collective failure to know other animals. By assuming that all human knowledge is suspect, authors are free to challenge anthropocentrism, undermine speciesism, explore radical nonhuman existences, and reject species boundaries. These animals may not be 'animals' at all, but rather trickster figures or beings that straddle the natural and supernatural. Sometimes these individuals are unknowable because their intelligence exceeds our own. Such characters may undermine human supremacy by reminding us that we are vulnerable animals too.

Other than the *indifference to knowing* the animal, each of these styles is reflected in the core texts addressed in this book. It is important to note, however, that this selection is heavily weighted towards the *fantasy of knowing*. This because these narratives focus on animal protagonists in their *own* stories. As a result, they are also more likely to engage with real world debates around animal protection or animal consciousness. *Failure of knowing* narratives present limited depictions of enigmatic or elusive animal characters; we are often left to glean an impression of the animal from a distance. By contrast, the *acceptance of not knowing* can offer more potential for zoocentric representation. However, this becomes complicated when the 'animals' of the text blur the boundaries between humans, animals, and supernatural beings (such as spirits or mythological creatures). Sometimes the animal characters involved have no living counterparts.

Overall, *failure of knowing* and *acceptance of not knowing* texts tend to be more established within the Canadian canon. Indeed, most of the better-known books addressed in this volume are from these two categories. Marian Engel's *Bear* (1976) and Yann Martel's *Life of Pi* (2001) are *failure of knowing* novels, while Timothy Findley's *Not Wanted on the Voyage* (1984) and Margaret Atwood's *Oryx and Crake* (2003) are *acceptance of not knowing*. Their nuanced relationship to knowing other animals means that they are more favoured by animal-sceptical approaches. As such, texts from these categories have already received significant critical attention. Other well-known examples of the *failure of knowing* include, Robert Kroetsch's *Studhorse Man* (1969), Graeme Gibson's *Communion* (1971), and Margaret Atwood's *Surfacing* (1972). The *acceptance of not knowing* is less common, but could be applied to Thomas King's *Green Grass, Running Water* (1993), Lee Maracle's *Ravensong* (1993), Tomson Highway's *Kiss of the Fur Queen* (1998), and Douglas Glover's *Elle* (2003).

I am hesitant to apply my model too broadly to the work of Indigenous authors, however. Of course, the diversity of First Nations, Inuit, and Métis cultures means that there is no single 'Indigenous' attitude towards animals, just as there is no single 'Canadian' perspective. Yet crucial differences lie in our cultural constructions of the human-animal divide itself. Western ideas about other animals are built on anthropocentrism, hierarchy, and human supremacy. The authors addressed in this book (mostly white and male) persistently wrestle with questions of anthropomorphism or whether animals have feelings. These zoocentric *fantasies of knowing* are significant because they exist in a cultural context of objectifying animals and treating them as property. Such stories may seem reductive when understood through cultural contexts in which animals are already fellow persons (or even our family members) with their own agency, independent purpose, and nuanced relationships to humans (Robinson 2020).

Realistically, a far larger study would be required to give a full comprehensive understanding of animal fiction published in Canada. Even so, it would be difficult to do justice to such an approach. Recent scholarship has outlined the pitfalls of trying to understand Indigenous relationships with other animals through Western models, including those put forth by animal studies itself.[7] It is unlikely that the frameworks I use here would hold much relevance. Although this book attempts to encompass a broad timeline of 150 years, its focus on interactions between literature, science, and animal advocacy is relatively narrow. I prioritize *fantasy of knowing* texts because they are, generally, most applicable to the topic. Unfortunately, this often means favouring texts written by the middle-class white men whose voices were most prominent in contemporary debates around conservation, animal protection, science, and nature writing at the time.

CHAPTER OVERVIEW

I have organized this book chronologically with each chapter covering a period of a few decades. The historical scope of this book stretches from the 1860s to the 2000s. During this time, there were several significant upheavals in Canadian-animal relations. These local and global developments in animal protection and scientific studies of animal minds often found expression in contemporary literature. To help tell this story, the book is divided into four parts: "Emergence," "Adaptation," "Divergence," and "Survival." Each part contains a pair of chapters: one "Contexts" chapter, giving an overview of relevant historical contexts, and one "Texts" chapter, offering literary analysis of a few core texts from that period.

The first part of this book, "Emergence," spans the 1860s to the 1900s. Chapter 2 addresses the emergence of several significant historical developments. These include: the publication of Charles Darwin's *On the Origin of Species* (1859); growing public interest in animal intelligence; the new science of comparative psychology; the professionalization of the sciences; Henry Salt's theories of animal rights; the rise of Canadian humane societies; the *Cruelty to Animals Act of* 1869; and early developments in Canadian wildlife conservation. These events established important debates, ideas, and concerns that run throughout the rest of this book. They also shaped the creation and reception of a new form of writing: the wild animal story.

In Chap. 3, I examine the wild animal stories of Ernest Thompson Seton and Charles G. D. Roberts. Their work introduced the *fantasy of knowing* the animal to Canadian fiction. The wild animal story was

---

[7] See Koleszar-Green and Matsuoka (2018); Belcourt (2020); Brighten (2011); and Kymlicka and Donaldson (2015).

enormously popular, but surprisingly controversial. Seton and Roberts blurred the boundaries between science and storytelling in their work, which led to a well-publicized debate known as the Nature Fakers controversy. It began with an article published by the eminent American naturalist John Burroughs in 1903 and ended when President Theodore Roosevelt joined the discussion in 1907.

The second part of this book, "Adaptation," covers a period from the 1900s to 1950s. Chapter 4 explores a shift in ideas about animals at the beginning of the twentieth century. The science of comparative psychology had become increasingly concerned with avoiding anthropomorphism. This led to a greater emphasis on objectivity, experimentation, and external observation. As a result, speculations about animal minds, consciousness, or emotions were to be avoided. Two new branches of science developed in response, European ethology and American behaviourism. Whilst different in their approaches and methodologies, both fields favoured mechano-morphic language in an attempt to avoid anthropomorphism.

This shift in attitudes towards animals also found expression in conservation and the new science of ecology. As Canadian wildlife management became increasingly centralized and bureaucratized, there was a growing emphasis on efficiency. Suddenly, the language of economics, machinery, and productivity had entered conservation. From this perspective, wildlife was a natural resource and habitats could be improved to optimize their 'yield.' Unsurprisingly, this atmosphere of mechanistic attitudes towards animals meant that humane societies made little significant progress during this period. As a result, there were no meaningful improvements to Canada's anti-cruelty laws.

Chapter 5 explores the ways in which authors adapted the wild animal story in the wake of the Nature Fakers controversy. Here, we see the *fantasy of knowing* the animal split into the *realistic* and *speculative* styles. Both Roderick Haig-Brown's and Fred Bodsworth's realistic *fantasies of knowing* reproduced the wild animal story's style in *Return to the River* (1941) and *Last of the Curlews* (1955), respectively. However, they were much more cautious than Seton and Roberts in the claims they made on behalf of other animals. Both were more ecologically conscious as well. Haig-Brown (1941) depicted environmental destruction, pollution of waterways, and the impact of dam-building on Pacific Salmon migration. Meanwhile Bodsworth (1955) described the extinction of the Northern Curlew.

Alternatively, Frederick Philip Grove introduced the speculative *fantasy of knowing* in *Consider Her Ways* (1947). Whilst the book retained many core elements of the wild animal story, it evaded questions of fact or accuracy through a set of literary devices (such as layering first-person narration). Although Grove wrote about ants, he also offered a rare condemnation of animal agriculture by depicting the slaughter of a pig. Despite their different styles, all three texts maintained the wild animal story's engagement with both science and animal advocacy.

In the third part of this book, "Divergence," I address the 1950s to 1980s. Chapter 6 outlines a period of social, cultural, political, and scientific transformation. In North America, behaviourism had dominated the study of animal psychology. From the 1950s, however, the cognitive revolution swept through the sciences, social sciences, and humanities. In the 1970s, it reached the animal sciences and triggered a flurry of new theories, methodologies, and approaches. In 1976, Donald Griffin published *The Question of Animal Awareness* and established the new field of *cognitive ethology*. In so doing, he reintroduced the topic of *animal consciousness* to the sciences. This also enabled the new science of animal welfare to develop in the 1980s. Equally influential were the twentieth-century animal protection movements. During this period, Canadians demonstrated increased concern for animals in farms and laboratories, as well as animals in the wild. This led to the international campaign to ban seal hunting in Canada, which would hold disastrous repercussions for Inuit communities. In the 1970s, for the first time in decades, the idea of animal having *rights* also returned to the dialogue around animal protection.

In Chap. 7, I focus on the ways in which animal representation diverged from the *fantasy of knowing* and into the *failure of knowing* and *acceptance of not knowing*. Marian Engel's *Bear* (1976) made the most overt departure by explicitly rejecting the wild animal stories of Seton and Roberts. Even though her book was not the first *failure of knowing* narrative, it is a particularly strong example. In questioning whether humans could know anything about other animals, the novel does not engage with contemporary scientific developments or animal advocacy debates. In contrast, Timothy Findley's *Not Wanted on the Voyage* (1984) condemned animal exploitation, particularly medical experimentation. Yet, in this *acceptance of not knowing* narrative, the line between humans and other animals becomes complicated. As a fantastical retelling of the biblical flood myth, humans and other animals intermingle with angels, demons, mythical creatures, and human-animal hybrids. Alternatively, Andy Russell's *Adventures with Wild Animals* (1977) represents the continuation of the wild animal story and realistic *fantasy of knowing*. As a collection of short stories, they hold all the core characteristics of Seton's and Roberts's work. Indeed, all of the texts addressed in this book are novels, apart from those by Seton, Roberts, and Russell. Yet for all his efforts to incorporate science and animal advocacy into his stories, Russell was unusually dismissive of both scientists *and* animal campaigners.

The final part of this book, "Survival," begins in the 1980s and ends in the early 2000s. In Chap. 8, I address the twelve unsuccessful attempts to improve Canada's anti-cruelty legislation between 1999 and 2010. The government's reluctance to make even minor amendments can be traced to a backlash against the animal rights movement after the anti-sealing and anti-fur campaigns. Over the decades, the dialogue around this topic became increasingly extreme. Where some argued that Canada's reliance on animal industries meant that animal protection was a threat to the economy, others accused the animal advocates of terrorism. As a result, even minor amendments to the law were rejected by parliament. At the same time, however, astonishing discoveries were being made in the field of animal cognition. Topics that had been rejected as anthropomorphic at the beginning of the century had now returned to the realm of serious scientific investigation. Moreover, Griffin's own field of cognitive ethology continued to build evidence for animal consciousness.

Chapter 9 demonstrates the survival of each form of animal representation: the realistic *fantasy of knowing*, the speculative *fantasy of knowing*, the *failure of knowing*, and the *acceptance of not knowing*. R. D. Lawrence's *The White Puma* (1990) and Barbara Gowdy's *The White Bone* (1998) show that the core characteristics of the wild animal story survived a century after Seton and Roberts created them. As a field biologist, Lawrence represents the merging of science and literature to which Seton and Roberts aspired but lacked the scientific authority to fulfil. Lawrence presents a realistic *fantasy of knowing* that illustrates contemporary issues in cougar conservation. In *The White Bone* (1998), Barbara Gowdy offers a speculative *fantasy of knowing* that constructs complex African elephant societies, similar to those of Grove's ants in *Consider Her Ways* (1947). Although fantastical in parts, Gowdy grounds the work in contemporary conservation issues and scientific studies of elephant herds.

In *Life of Pi* (2001) Yann Martel creates a quintessential *failure of knowing* narrative through the relationship between Pi and Richard Parker. In a similar way to Engel, Martel offers a pessimistic view of human-animal relations. He condemns anthropomorphism, offers little engagement with science or advocacy, and presents an idealized celebration of zoos. Margaret Atwood's *Oryx and Crake* (2003) presents a stark contrast to the magical realism of *Not Wanted on the Voyage* (1984), even though both demonstrate the *acceptance of not knowing* the animal. Whereas Findley celebrates his unknowable animals, Atwood presents a future in which 'nature' has become unrecognizable. Genetic engineering has blurred species boundaries, upending our previous knowledge about other animals and toppling human supremacy. *Homo sapiens* have become an endangered species, whilst various hybrid lifeforms compete for dominance in the postapocalyptic landscape. In *Oryx and Crake* (2003), the survival of 'nature' itself and every recognizable animal species, including humans, is brought into question.

By the end of this book, we will find that the ideas addressed at the beginning have come full circle. Cognitive ethologists, animal advocates, and contemporary writers at the turn of the century are all engaged in similar pursuits to their earlier counterparts. Whilst Seton and Roberts were thoroughly criticized for attempting to contribute to science, a century later we find many scientists who welcome contributions from writers. However, although there is increased concern for animals, it seems that a desire to police the boundaries between humans and other species remains ever-present. Indeed, we find that many of the prejudices and issues of an earlier age have survived into the twenty-first century. Despite over 150 years of evidence and arguments to the contrary, Western cultures continue to pursue and protect human supremacy.

References

An Act Respecting Cruelty to Animals, Statutes of Canada 1869, c. 27.
Atwood, Margaret. 1972. *Survival: A Thematic Guide to Canadian Literature*. Toronto: Anansi.
Baker, Steve. 2000. *The Postmodern Animal*. London: Reaktion.
Belcourt, Billy-Ray. 2020. An Indigenous Critique of Critical Animal Studies. In *Colonialism and Animality: Anti-Colonial Perspectives in Critical Animal Studies*, ed. Kelly Struthers Monford and Chloë Taylor, 19–28. Oxon: Routledge.

Bergman, Charles. 2001. Making Animals Matter. *Chronicle of Higher Education*, March 28. https://www.chronicle.com/article/making-animals-matter/.

Best, Steven. 2009. Rise of Critical Animal Studies: Putting Theory into Action and Animal Liberation into Higher Education. *Journal for Critical Animal Studies.* 7 (1): 9–52.

Brighten, Andrew. 2011. Aboriginal Peoples and the Welfare of Animal Persons: Dissolving the Bill C-10B Conflict. *Indigenous Law Journal.* 10 (1): 39–72.

Burroughs, John. 1903. Real and Sham Natural History. *Atlantic Monthly.* 91 (545, March): 298–309.

Copeland, Marion. 1994. Review of *Animal Victims in Modern Fiction: From Sanctity to Sacrifice. Anthrozoös.* 7 (4): 277–290. https://doi.org/10.2752/089279394788609065.

Criminal Code, SC 1892, c C.29.

Dunayer, Joan. 2001. *Animal Equality: Language and Liberation.* Derwood: Ryce.

Forkey, Neil S. 2012. *Canadians and the Natural Environment to the Twenty-First Century.* Toronto: University of Toronto Press.

Huggan, Graham, and Helen Tiffin. 2010. *Postcolonial Ecocriticism: Literature, Animals, Environment.* London: Routledge.

Ingram, Darcy. 2013. Beastly Measures: Animal Welfare, Civil Society, and State Policy in Victorian Canada. *Journal of Canadian Studies.* 41 (1): 221–252. https://doi.org/10.3138/jcs.47.1.221.

International Fund for Animal Welfare. 2008. *Falling Behind: An International Comparison Of Canada's Animal Cruelty Legislation.* Accessed November 28 2018.

Koleszar-Green, Ruth, and Atsuko Matsuoka. 2018. Indigenous Worldviews and Critical Animal Studies: Decolonization and Revealing Truncated Narratives of Dominance. In *Critical Animal Studies: Towards Trans-species Social Justice*, ed. Atsuko Matsuoka and John Sorenson, 333–350. London: Rowman & Littlefield International.

Kymlicka, Will, and Sue Donaldson. 2015. Animal Rights and Aboriginal Rights. In *Canadian Perspectives on Animals and the Law*, ed. Peter Sankoff, Vaughn Black, and Katie Sykes, 159–186. Toronto: Irwin Law.

Love, Glen. 2003. *Practical Ecocriticism: Literature, Biology and the Environment.* Charlottesville, University of Virginia Press.

McGregor, Gaile. 1985. *The Wacousta Syndrome: Explorations in the Canadian Landscape.* Toronto: University of Toronto Press.

Regan, Tom. (1984) 1988. *The Case for Animal Rights.* London: Routledge.

Robinson, Margaret. 2020. Veganism and Mi'kmaq Legends. In *Colonialism and Animality: Anti-Colonial Perspectives in Critical Animal Studies*, ed. Kelly Struthers Monford and Chloë Taylor, 107–114. Oxon: Routledge.

Roosevelt, Theodore. 1907. Nature Fakers. *Everybody's Magazine.* 17 (3, September): 427–430.

Ryan, Derek. 2015. *Animal Theory: A Critical Introduction*. Edinburgh: Edinburgh University Press.

Seton, Ernest Thompson. 1898. *Wild Animals I Have Known*. New York: Charles Scriber's Sons.

Shapiro, Kenneth J., and Marion W. Copeland. 2005. Toward a Critical Theory of Animal Issues in Fiction. *Society and Animals*. 13 (4): 343–346. https://doi.org/10.1163/156853005774653636.

Shaprio, Kenneth J. 1993. Editor's Introduction. *Society and Animals*. 1: 1–4.

Slovic, Paul. 2007. 'If I Look at the Mass I Will Never Act': Psychic Numbing and Genocide. *Judgement and Decision Making*. 2 (2): 79–95.

Smith, Julie Ann. 2001. Conference Report – The Representation of Animals. *Society and Animals*. 9 (3): 293–297.

Soper, Kate. (1995) 2000. *What Is Nature?* Oxford: Blackwell.

Sorenson, John. 2010. *About Canada: Animal Rights*. Black Point: Fernwood.

PART I

Emergence

CHAPTER 2

1860s–1900s Contexts

This chapter examines new ways of knowing animals across literature, science, and animal advocacy at the end of the nineteenth century. These changes include: the emergence of the theory of evolution, growing public interest in animal minds, the science of comparative psychology, the rise of Canadian humane societies, the establishment of federal animal protection laws, the creation of the wild animal story, and the Nature Fakers controversy. This was a period of intense debate regarding the differences between human and nonhuman animals. Whilst some may have embraced narrowing the divide between species, others fought strongly to reassert human uniqueness. As we will find throughout this book, the ideas, disputes, and concerns established in this chapter would ripple and rebound through the twentieth century.

Comparative Psychology

In 1859, Charles Darwin published *On the Origin of Species*. It initiated, what Marian Scholtmeijer (1993) identifies as, the beginning of the modern period in thought about animals (7). The concepts of evolution, natural selection, and human-animal continuity all had a profound impact on previously established Western ideas about the origins of life on earth—and humanity's position within it. Darwin expanded upon this work in

© The Author(s), under exclusive license to Springer Nature Switzerland AG 2023
C. Allmark-Kent, *Literature, Science, and Animal Advocacy in Canada*, Palgrave Studies in Animals and Literature, https://doi.org/10.1007/978-3-031-40556-3_2

The Descent of Man (1871) and *The Expression of the Emotions in Man and Animals* (1872). Together, these texts triggered an immense cultural upheaval. Darwin's writing inspired excitement, curiosity, and considerable debate. The widespread impact of his work cannot be overstated. One of the most important consequences was a profound shift in perceptions of other animals, particularly regarding their intelligence.

Obviously, human curiosity about the minds of other animals did not originate with Darwin's work. Nevertheless, it is fair to say that the theory of evolution injected greater energy and urgency into the topic. For the evolutionary continuity between humans and animals to be accepted, the apparently enormous divide between 'animal instinct' and 'human reason' demanded explanation. The thrilling implications of Darwin's theories galvanized nascent public curiosity about the inner lives of other animals. During the 1860s and 1870s, the question of animal minds suddenly gained immense popularity. Robert Boakes (1984) describes the countless letters that flowed into both scientific and popular periodicals "reporting striking observations of animals that suggested unsuspected mental abilities" (25). Both experts and amateurs alike had anecdotes to share.

As part of his work, Darwin had amassed a collection of observations (both first- and second-hand) that indicated the existence of intelligence and emotions in animals (Morell 2013, 11). Before his death in 1882, he gave this collection to his protégé and successor, George Romanes. Born in Kingston, Ontario, to Scottish parents in 1848, Romanes had moved to England as a child and met Darwin at the University of Cambridge in the 1870s. In *Animal Intelligence* (1882) and *Mental Evolution in Animals* (1883), Romanes used the observations collected by Darwin (as well as his own) to attempt the monumental task of determining the intellectual and emotional capacities of each species (Morell 2013, 12; Boakes 1984, 25). It was the beginning of a new scientific field called comparative psychology.[1] This early form of animal psychology had a distinct evolutionary slant, which often involved drawing comparisons between the cognitive, emotional, and social capacities of human and nonhuman beings. Both men believed in mental continuity between humans and other animals, which meant that the distance between human and nonhuman intelligence was only a matter of degrees. In Romanes's (1883) words, there was no

---

[1] Within the context of this book, it is worth noting that histories of comparative psychology rarely recognize that its founder was born in pre-confederation Canada.

difference in kind between "the act of reason performed by [a] crab and any act of reason performed by a man" (337).

Darwin's and Romanes's beliefs in mental continuity meant that they inherently accepted the idea of animals having 'minds.' Romanes (1882) opens *Animal Intelligence* with his intention to study the "phenomena of mind throughout the animal kingdom" (1). It is worth acknowledging that his criteria for having a mind is quite broad. Romanes asks: "Does the organism learn to make new adjustments, or to modify old ones, in accordance with the results of its own individual experience?" (4). Along similar lines, he defines "reason" as the "intentional adaptation of means to ends" (17). Whilst his language might strike us as anthropomorphic, the actions he describes do not necessarily require the levels of complex self-awareness that we might associate with terms such as 'mind' or 'reason' today. In *Mental Evolution,* Romanes (1883) published a table illustrating the cognitive and emotional development of each species. According to this, the 'lowest' species capable of reason are: 'higher' crustacea (crabs and lobsters), reptiles, and cephalopods. Consequently, this means that he identifies reason in all mammals and birds, as well as hymenoptera, which includes wasps, bees, and ants.

It is crucial to recognize that belief in animal minds (or animal 'mentation') would be absent from the scientific community for most of the twentieth century. Bernard E. Rollin (2007) explains that, from the time of Darwin to the early years of the twentieth century, the "existence and knowability of animal mentation was taken as axiomatic" (258). Yet, this would change with the rise of behaviourism in the 1920s (see Chap. 4). After this point, any discussion of the existence and knowability of animal minds would be met with profound scepticism. We will see the repercussions of this transition throughout the rest of this book. (We have already seen its consequences in the 'animal-sceptical' perspectives described in Chap. 1) Margaret Floy Washburn (1908) summarized the issue in her textbook, *The Animal Mind.* By emphasizing the fundamental differences between human and nonhuman brains, she argued that if another human's brain is inaccessible to us, "how great is the mystery which looks out of the eyes of a dog?" (2).

In fact, Romanes (1882) had already addressed the difficulty of knowing other minds in *Animal Intelligence.* He accepted that we can "only infer the existence and nature of thoughts and feelings" in other individuals (1). But he proposed that, by using what we know "subjectively" about the operations of our own minds, we can use "analogy" to determine the "mental processes" lying beneath the "observable activities of other organisms" (1–2). At the time, this was known as the 'introspective' method. Early comparative psychologists observed, recorded, and interpreted the activities of other animals. Through analogies with human psychology, they drew conclusions about the cognitive, emotional, or social experiences of that individual. Then, they applied those capacities to the rest of that species. This is what we now describe as anecdotal cognitivism. Dale Jamieson and Marc Bekoff (1992) define it as the attribution of "cognitive states to many animals on the basis of observations of particular cases rather than controlled experiments or manipulations" (111).

Perhaps because *Animal Intelligence* verified many readers' perceptions of animals, it was extremely popular with the public. In the minds of some of his peers, however, Romanes's reliance on anecdotal evidence associated him too closely with the unreliable and unscientific popular writers. Despite his sincere attempts to establish comparative psychology as a scientific discipline, Romanes was lumped together with the same writers he condemned in the preface to *Animal Intelligence* as "anecdote-mongers" (1882, vii). Ironically, it was Romanes's own protégé, Conwy Lloyd Morgan, who would ensure the field's scientific credibility.

In *An Introduction to Comparative Psychology*, Morgan (1894) offered a rule to help prevent anthropomorphism when observing animal behaviour: "[i]n no case may we interpret an action as the outcome of the exercise of a higher psychical faculty, if it can be interpreted as the outcome of the exercise of one which stands lower on the psychological scale" (53). This was known as Morgan's Canon and would become the central tenet of behaviourism in the twentieth century. In moving comparative psychology away from Romanes's methods, Morgan finally enabled the field to gain full acceptance.

The problem for Romanes was that the sciences had been undergoing a process of specialization and professionalization for several decades. When Darwin published *On the Origin of Species* (1859), the word 'scientist' had existed for less than thirty years. 'Natural philosopher' had been the preferred term until Reverend William Whewell made the new suggestion during a meeting of the British Association for the Advancement of Science in 1833 (Chapple 1986, 3). Initially, 'scientist' was unpopular because it seemed too restrictive. At that time, divisions between academic disciplines were less concrete (3). Science and literature were printed side-by-side in the popular press (Otis 2002, xvii). As scientific and tech-nological advances opened up new areas of research, however, a gradual process of specialization began.

The creation of new fields and sub-fields made boundaries between disciplines more distinct. As a modern, professional body of scientists began to establish themselves, they raised new questions about the nature of scientific investigation. Bernard Lightman (2007) explains that those "who could claim to speak on behalf of science" gained "immense cultural authority and intellectual prestige," as well as the responsibility for shap-ing and defining 'science' itself (5). Consequently, policing the boundaries of science became an increasingly pressing matter for those with the neces-sary power—as well as excluding those who seemed 'unfit' for the responsibility.

In *Animal Intelligence*, Romanes (1882) had recognized that the study of animal minds lacked scientific authority. Having "constituted so much and so long the theme of unscientific authors," the question of animal intelligence seemed "well-nigh unworthy of serious treatment by scientific methods" (vi). In his words, the new field of "Comparative Psychology" had been "virtually excluded from the hierarchy of the sciences" before it had a chance to develop (vi). By the end of the century, however, Morgan's seemingly more 'objective' approach reflected everything valued by mod-ern science at the time.[2] It enabled comparative psychology to become a respected discipline at last.

Edward A. Wasserman (1981) notes that "Morgan's canon, coupled with his insistence upon the collection of observable and reliable evidence of animal intelligence, helped to move the psychological study of animal behaviour from the parlour into the laboratory" (242). Rather neatly, it coincided with both the rise of laboratory science and the final acceptance of 'scientist' as a professional title. As we will see in Chap. 4, it also laid the foundation for North American behaviourism, which favoured more mechanistic perceptions of animals. This meant that, in the scientific com-munity, any discussions of animal 'intelligence' or 'emotions' would be taboo for most of the twentieth century.

---

[2] See Eileen Crist's (1999) *Images of Animals* for analysis of the mechanistic language that became associated with behaviourism and its application of Morgan's Canon.

CRUELTY TO ANIMALS

Just as Darwin's work had inspired a new public interest in animal minds, it also motivated related concerns about their abilities to feel and suffer. It is no coincidence that the Canadian animal protection movement arose in the 1860s. The influence of Darwinism combined with wider nineteenth-century social reform efforts, as well as the need to develop a positive national identity. Indeed, it was only two years after Confederation that the new nation of Canada established the *Cruelty to Animals Act* (1869). Darcy Ingram (2013) notes that the timing was not a coincidence; the act stood as a "statement of ethics and principles," indicative of a new "modern, progressive, respectable" national identity (222). In the same year, the Canadian Society for the Prevention of Cruelty to Animals (CSPCA) was established in Montreal. Given the new atmosphere of interest in animal minds and welfare, the *Cruelty to Animals Act* received strong support.

Building on this momentum, the act was successfully expanded in the 1870s to ban dog- and cock-fighting and to include standards regarding the transportation of cattle. However, progress soon stalled. Ingram (2013) observes that, throughout the 1880s and 1890s, "proponents of new legislation and policy initiatives" found themselves "repeatedly frustrated by lengthy debates" (242). New bills were obstructed as their progress through parliament slowed to a halt. Out of nine attempts to improve the legislation, only one bill passed. This set a pattern that has been repeated ever since. From the 1880s onwards, it became increasingly difficult to make even minor improvements to animal welfare. Today, over a century later, efforts to ensure modest animal protection laws rarely succeed (see Chap. 8).

In 1892, a slightly amended *Cruelty to Animals Act* became the backbone of the first federal animal cruelty laws. Today, Canada's anti-cruelty provisions remain largely unchanged. Subsequent amendments have been relatively minor and, for the most part, have merely expanded or reworded existing legislation. The problem is that the first Canadian Criminal Code listed "Cruelty to Animals" under "Title VI: Offenses Against the Rights of Property" (*Criminal Code*, SC 1892, c.29, s.512–515). This means that, uniquely, the Criminal Code of 1892 established the legal status of animals in Canada as *property*. By contrast, laws prohibiting violence to humans appeared under "Title V: Offences Against the Person" (s.209–302). Canada's first federal animal protection laws lay alongside such offenses as theft, receiving stolen goods, fraud, and forgery. In fact,

"Cruelty to Animals" stood directly between "Mischief" and "Offences Connected with Trade and Breaches of Contract" (s.481–511; s.516–526). Beyond their placement within the code, the wording of the laws themselves also reinforced the status of animals as property. Section 512 (a) states that anyone is guilty of an offence who "wantonly, cruelly or unnecessarily beats, binds, ill-treats, abuses, or overdrives or tortures any cattle, poultry, dog, domestic animal or bird" (*Criminal Code*, SC 1892, c.29, s.512). The types of animals and situations listed are clearly designed to protect a person's 'property' (such as cattle or dogs) from 'damage' by a third party. Moreover, the careful wording of "wantonly, cruelly or unnecessarily" ensures leeway for owners themselves to continue exploiting their own animals (s-512). The abuses inherent in animal agriculture, for instance, would be deemed 'necessary' and, therefore, legal. Other laws addressed the transportation of cattle and property damage done by the animals themselves when being moved, such as during cattle drives.

The only mention of wild animals is in 512 (c), which prohibits encouraging, aiding, or assisting in the fighting or baiting of "any bull, bear, badger, dog, cock, or other kind of animal, whether of wild or domestic nature" (*Criminal Code*, SC 1892, c.29, s.512). However, the Criminal Code was slightly amended by the only successful anti-cruelty bill of the nine proposed during 1880s and 1890s. In 1895, section 512 (a) was expanded to include "any wild animal or bird in captivity" (*An Act Further to Amend the Criminal Code, 1892*, 1895). These were the only protections afforded to wild animals. To borrow the wording of the legislation, this meant that it would be entirely legal to wantonly, cruelly, or unnecessarily beat, bind, ill-treat, abuse, or torture any non-captive wild animal. Not only did Canada's first Criminal Code establish the idea that animals are property, but that animals only deserve protection *as property*. This set a precedent that continued for over a century.

Evidently, Canada's first animal laws were designed with human interests in mind (namely those of upper- and middle-class white men). These laws were more about protecting the valuable property of cattle ranchers from careless employees than ensuring the wellbeing of the animals themselves. Likewise, prohibitions against urban blood sports, such as organized animal fights, were part of wider nineteenth-century social reforms also concerned with issues such as gambling and drinking. The wealthy white supporters of these movements may have condemned working-class cockfighting rings in the city while seeing nothing wrong with their own countryside fox hunts at the weekend. This inherent contradiction explains the stagnation of Canada's animal welfare movement (together with the lack of protection for wild animals hunted for sport). Fundamentally, Canadian humane societies remained more conservative than their British or American counterparts because their members depended on animal exploitation to a greater degree (Ingram 2013, 222–3).

Across the water, the work of English writer and campaigner Henry S. Salt offers a stark contrast.[3] In the same year that the Criminal Code classified the torture of animals alongside fraud, theft, and damages to personal property, Salt (1892) was arguing that animals have inherent rights. In *Animals' Rights*, he recognized "universal rights" in "all intelligent beings" (35). Leaving little room for hypocrisy or conflicts of interest, he wrote that to "take advantage of the sufferings of animals, whether wild or tame, for the gratification of sport, or gluttony, or fashion, is quite incompatible with any possible assertion of animals' rights" (37–8). He extended this same logic to meat-eating, arguing that the "transit and slaughter of animals are necessarily attended by the most atrocious cruelties" (48). Crucially, Salt recognized universal rights in both wild and domesticated animals, although he acknowledged that the latter have a "special claim on man's courtesy and sense of fairness" in their unique position as "his fellow-workers, his dependents, and in many cases the familiar associates and trusted inmates of his home" (35).

Notions of establishing rights for animals may have been too radical for nineteenth-century Canadian humane societies. Ingram (2013) emphasizes the nation's "high dependence on animals as resources, sources of labour, and objects of sport," compared with the United Kingdom or United States (223). With "sportsmen," "vivisectionists," "cattle ranchers," and "owners of carting agencies" amongst the membership of

---

[3] Salt's books, which also include *The Plea for Vegetarianism* (1886), *The Logic of Vegetarianism* (1899), and *The Creed of Kinship* (1935), were published on both sides of the Atlantic. In his preface to the 1980 edition of *Animals' Rights*, Peter Singer describes the book as "the best of the eighteenth- and nineteenth-century works on the rights of animals" (1980, viii). It was not the first, of course, but the most complete. Indeed, modern animal rights theories "have been able to add relatively little to the essential case Salt outlined in 1892" (viii). Yet, whilst the book went through multiple prints, it had little impact "outside humanitarian and vegetarian circles" (ix). In part, this was due to Salt's secluded, rural lifestyle. Nonetheless, he did maintain friendships with a range of important artistic, literary, political, and philosophical figures of the day, including Mahatma Gandhi. Whilst Salt himself remains relatively unknown, his ideas tended to reach the public through the influence of his friends (vi).

humane societies, it should be no surprise that the Canadian movement did not develop more "complex interpretations of animal welfare" (223). This tension between exploitation and protection can be found throughout most early animal protection efforts, including wildlife conservation. In times of economic need, the financial value of nature can be exploited; in times of prosperity, its inherent value may be protected. Inevitably, this oscillating attitude produced inconsistent efforts in all areas of animal advocacy.

CONSERVATION

Janet Foster (1998) observes that several factors delayed and obstructed the development of formal wildlife conservation in Canada. In the nineteenth century, these issues included: myths of superabundant wildlife and an uninhabited frontier; the National Policy's emphasis on development and exploitation of nature; the terms of the British North America Act, which placed natural resources under provincial jurisdiction; and a fundamental lack of knowledge about wild animals (4–12). The establishment of Canada's first national park reveals the government's attitude at the time. In the United States, Yellowstone National Park was established in 1872 to preserve both 'wilderness' and wildlife. In 1885, when ten acres of land were set aside around the Banff hot springs, it was to preserve a "valuable natural resource that could be exploited in the interests of the government and the railway" (20). Two years later, when Banff Hot Springs was protected as the country's first national park, it was not a wildlife sanctuary, but a tourist resort (20, 25). Of course, preserving 'wilderness' was a colonial endeavour. To establish a national park required the relocation of Indigenous peoples already living there.

For most of the nineteenth century, conservation consisted of scattered local practices for managing populations of wild animals. Whether formal or informal, local or state-sanctioned, these strategies involved determining the types and numbers of animals that could be killed for consumption or recreation. Tina Loo (2006) notes the government's limited involvement, which amounted to little more than setting "seasons, bag limits, and bounties" (6). Yet, the need for more comprehensive wildlife conservation was becoming increasingly clear. Wild animals were being "pushed, parched, burned, starved, and blasted out by European settlement" (17). They were hunted to feed hungry settlers or gunned down by labourers bored and exhausted from railway construction, mining, or forestry (16). Still, the government showed little concern. Ultimately, there was greater interest in the protection of natural resources, than the protection of 'nature' itself.

The government's limited approach to conservation was restricted to two categories of animal: 'game' and 'vermin.' According to Loo (2006), even the word 'wildlife' was rarely used (2). The category of 'game' was a changing and seemingly arbitrary assortment of animals, some of which were not native and had been introduced to the region by sportsmen as "exotics" (14). Using Nova Scotia's statute books as an example, she notes that in 1816 the only listed game were snipe and woodcocks. Moose became game in 1843, pheasants and robins were added to the category in 1856, followed by caribou in 1862, then non-Indigenous elk in 1894, and finally "*animals valuable only for their fur*" in 1896 (14, emphasis original). Alternatively, 'vermin' were a more stable collection of mammals—mostly wolves, bears, coyotes, and cougars—chosen for their predation of both wild and domesticated animals (14). In other words, vermin were targeted because they threatened the animals who humans might want to kill. Evidently, Canada's early efforts to protect animals, whether wild or captive, were shaped more by concerns of wealthy white men than the needs of the animals themselves.

Animal Fiction

The First Peoples of Turtle Island have been telling stories about animal persons with individuality, agency, and consciousness for hundreds of years. Yet the same cannot be said of European storytelling in Canada. Indeed, until the end of the nineteenth century, English-Canadian literature paid little attention to the lives of animals.[4] Given that settler-colonial interest in both their minds and welfare was only articulated from the 1860s onwards, this makes sense. Indeed, prior to 1850, animals rarely even appeared as distinct individuals. Two new genres increased the presence of individual animals somewhat: the children's animal story and the animal biography. The former originates with Catherine Parr Traill's collection of essays and stories *Afar in the Forest* (1850) and the latter with

---

[4] For a more comprehensive history of animals in early Canadian literature, see Alec Lucas's "Nature Writers and the Animal Story" in *Literary History of Canada: Canadian Literature in English* (1977).

Susanna Moodie's *The Little Black Pony and Other Stories* (1850). Both are significant because they focused on animals as individuals for the first time. When animals had appeared in other forms of writing, such as nature essays or travel accounts, they were more-or-less indistinguishable 'objects.' Their presence was, quite literally, short-lived.

The nature writing of early European settlers expressed an intensely anthropocentric relationship with nature and a profound lack of restraint when it came to killing. It was as though these writers worked with a pen in one hand and a gun in the other, often describing animal deaths with light-hearted humour. As Christoph Irmscher (2009) puts it, they "regarded Canada as a kind of gigantic self-serve store where they could hunt, shoot, and fish to their heart's content" (151). This attitude even extended to early amateur naturalists. Irmscher describes some who appeared to conduct their work with "an axe, not the dissecting knife," and others who seemed to use a knife and fork: "merrily eat[ing] his way through the Canadian fauna" (152–3). These writers remained fixed in this early settler thinking well into the nineteenth century. Despite the emerging evidence of species loss, they continued to reinforce popular myths of a boundless landscape abundant with wild animals. In such acutely anthropocentric forms of writing, nonhuman beings are objects to be stalked, caught, and consumed.

Even writers with a more benign attitude rarely engaged with wild animals as individuals. The children's animal stories of Traill's *Afar in the Forest* (1850) were didactic and highly anthropomorphic. Meanwhile, Moodie's animal biographies in *The Little Black Pony and Other Stories* (1850) focused on domesticated animals and were published in a volume otherwise dedicated to human stories. It is important to recognize that, in both genres, animals still tend to have a utilitarian value. In other words, they are always put to some use: as domesticated companion animals for humans or as anthropomorphic literary devices to teach morals to children. Simply put, there just seems to have been little interest in the lives of individual wild animals at this point. This can be understood through a general lack of knowledge about wildlife, an absence of concern for their treatment, and broader anthropocentric trends across contemporaneous literatures in the United States or United Kingdom. Thus, for most of the nineteenth century, wild animals were held at a distance in nature writing; they were a more or less indistinct mass of 'wild life.'

In the 1880s and 1890s, two men changed the history of Canadian literature. Separately—yet almost synchronously—Ernest Thompson

Seton and Charles G. D. Roberts both began experimenting with a new way to write about animals. Their innovation was to attempt to write about wild animals *as animals*. It was a sincere attempt to imagine the world from the animal's own perspective. Their animal characters were not allegories or metaphors; they were the protagonists of their *own* stories. This new form of writing revealed an animal existence with its own inherent value. It was a world in which animals interacted through networks of meaningful interaction, which could include communication, companionship, social learning, exchange, cooperation, conflict, and rivalry. I identify this as the beginning of the wild animal story, as well as the *fantasy of knowing* the animal in Canadian literature.

It is worth noting that Seton and Roberts arrived at the wild animal story from different directions. Seton's stories grew out of his nature writing and natural history essays, whilst Roberts's sprang from poetry and short stories. Though the two men worked separately, they did have some contact and undoubtedly influenced each other's work. I suggest that Seton made the original innovation, but Roberts defined and refined the wild animal story. On the whole, Seton remained more experimental in his writing, which led to some inconsistencies in style. Roberts, on the other hand, wrote with such consistency that his stories became almost formulaic. Nonetheless, their different approaches enabled them to develop a common set of shared characteristics. Between them, Seton and Roberts wrote hundreds of stories. As Alec Lucas (1977) notes, wild animal stories "have not been especially numerous," but the history of the genre is almost entirely the record of Seton's and Roberts's work within it (398).

Undoubtedly, the differences between the approaches to animal representation discussed here have much to do with political, environmental, and scientific contexts in which they were written. Early English-Canadian nature writers may express a profoundly anthropocentric view of nature because colonization's ravages to wild populations had not yet been recognized. Similarly, they tend to disregard the suffering of animals because they lacked the appropriate language that would be supplied by the humane movement.

After the rise of these organizations, we find more compassionate representations of animals, such as Anna Sewell's *Black Beauty* (1877) in England or Margaret Marshall Saunders's *Beautiful Joe* (1893) in Canada. Inevitably, these texts focused on domesticated species because concern for these animals arose earlier than it did for their wild counterparts. However, I would suggest that they express an *indifference to knowing* the animal overall. Whilst they are advocacy-orientated, they are less concerned with imagining animal minds. They relate events in the lives of their characters but tend not to prioritize the animal's own perspective. This makes sense given that these books were written in the gap between the growth of animal protection movements and widespread acceptance of animal psychology as a scientific discipline.

As Lucas (1977) observes, the animal biography began by focusing on domesticated animals (396). By contrast, the biography of the wild animal tends to have a "greater scientific bent" (397). To some extent, we can argue that the *indifference to knowing* can be found in texts that do not engage with science. Naturally, such narratives would be less preoccupied with questions of animal learning, communication, and sensory experiences. The crucial point about the *fantasy of knowing* is its commitment to imagining animal perspectives. The wild animal story is both scientifically informed and advocacy-orientated due to the context in which it was written. Seton and Roberts engaged with conservation, animal rights, and animal psychology because they were writing just as these three topics were entering public discourse. No doubt this is also the reason that both men appeared to begin experimenting with the form at the same time.

By the beginning of the twentieth century, the wild animal story's engagement with animal psychology brought unexpected consequences. The increasing professionalization of the sciences meant that Seton and Roberts were soon deemed to be 'overstepping' their roles as authors. Seton (1898) claimed that his stories were "true," which implied that the animal behaviours depicted were real (9). Although Roberts (1907) was more cautious in his claims, he still hoped that his stories would be "contributing some of value" to the "question of animal psychology" (vi). In 1903, the American naturalist, John Burroughs, initiated the Nature Fakers controversy with an article published in the *Atlantic Monthly*, titled "Real and Sham Natural History."

The debate lasted four years until the President of the United States, Theodore Roosevelt, publicly took Burroughs's side. In June 1907, Edward B. Clark published an interview with Roosevelt about the controversy in *Everybody's Magazine*. A few months later, Roosevelt followed up with his own article titled "Nature Fakers" in September 1907. Even though Roosevelt's remarks were similar to those made by Burroughs and others, the weight of his authority brought the debate to an end (even though nothing had been resolved). Although Seton and Roberts continued writing for at least another decade, the controversy left a stain upon the wild animal story's reputation that has remained ever since. As we will see in subsequent chapters of this book, Seton, Roberts, and the Nature Fakers debate changed the way we write about animals forever.

It is important to note that Seton and Roberts were not the only targets of the controversy. Burroughs's (1903) original article identified several authors, though his focus was on Seton and his "awkward imitator" (300). This imitator was not Roberts, but an American author, Reverend William J. Long. Indeed, Burroughs wrote that "it is Mr. Long's book, more than any of the others, that justifies the phrase, 'Sham Natural History'" (298). Although Long's stories might seem to resemble Seton's, it is important to recognize that they were written from an opposing perspective. Seton wrote to popularize science, but Long wrote to resist it. Moreover, he actively fought against his detractors, but Seton and Roberts did not. Indeed, Long may have inadvertently exacerbated the controversy through his responses.

The problem is that Long has been largely forgotten. This means that there is often some confusion between the stories of Seton, Roberts, and Long. Indeed, Roberts received significantly less attention during the controversy than Seton or Long. Yet, the stigma of 'nature faker' remained attached to his work, as well as to Seton's. Jack London was also targeted during the controversy, but his reputation was unaffected. Two American and two Canadian authors were criticized in the debates. Yet, only Seton and Roberts are remembered as nature fakers. Almost seventy years after the controversy, James Polk (1972) branded their work as an "outdated, scarcely respectable branch of our literature" (51). Today, the wild animal story is still considered something of an embarrassment to the Canadian literary canon.

Conclusion

The debates established in this chapter were never fully resolved. These same issues will re-emerge in every chapter of this book. Questions about the existence of animal minds or who holds the authority to speak on behalf of other animals will remain perennial concerns throughout the twentieth century. With the publication of Darwin's *On the Origin of Species* (1859), stable Western beliefs in human uniqueness had been undermined. This narrowing of the gulf between humans and other animals seemed to generate two responses: enthusiasm or resistance. Where some might see a thrilling expansion in our ideas about animal intelligence, others saw the dangers of anthropomorphism. Those who embraced this expansion may have felt a deepening in our kinship with other species, but those who resisted saw a mere fashion for sentimentality. As scientific developments across the decades would seem to narrow or widen the gap between *Homo sapiens* and other animals, we will find that these two opposing responses remain a consistent thread throughout this book.

REFERENCES

An Act Further to Amend the Criminal Code, 1892, Statutes of Canada 1895, c. 40.

An Act Respecting Cruelty to Animals, Statutes of Canada 1869, c. 27.

Boakes, Robert. 1984. *From Darwin to Behaviourism: Psychology and the Minds of Animals*. Cambridge: Cambridge University Press.

Burroughs, John. 1903. Real and Sham Natural History. *Atlantic Monthly*. 91 (545, March): 298–309.

Chapple, J.A.V. 1986. *Science and Literature in the Nineteenth Century*. London: Macmillan.

Criminal Code, SC 1892, c C.29.

Crist, Eileen. 1999. *Images of Animals: Anthropomorphism and Animal Mind*. Philadelphia: Temple University Press.

Foster, Janet. 1998. *Working for Wildlife: The Beginnings of Preservation in Canada*. Toronto: University of Toronto Press.

Ingram, Darcy. 2013. Beastly Measures: Animal Welfare, Civil Society, and State Policy in Victorian Canada. *Journal of Canadian Studies*. 41 (1): 221–252. https://doi.org/10.3138/jcs.47.1.221.

Irmscher, Christoph. 2009. Writing by Victorian Naturalists. In *The Cambridge History of Canadian Literature*, ed. Coral Ann Howells and Eva Marie Kröller, 144–165. Cambridge: Cambridge University Press.

Jamieson, Dale, and Marc Bekoff. 1992. On Aims and Methods of Cognitive Ethology. *PSA* 1992: 110–124. https://www.jstor.org/stable/192828.

Lightman, Bernard. 2007. *Victorian Popularizers of Science: Designing Nature for New Audiences*. Chicago: University of Chicago Press.

Loo, Tina. 2006. *States of Nature: Conserving Canada's Wildlife in the Twentieth Century*. Vancouver: UBC Press.

Lucas, Alec. 1977. Nature Writers and the Animal Story. In *Literary History of Canada: Canadian Literature in English*, ed. Carl. F. Klink. 380-404. 2nd ed. Vol. 1. Toronto: University of Toronto Press.

Morell, Virginia. 2013. *Animal Wise: The Thoughts and Emotions of Our Fellow Creatures*. Brecon: Old Street.

Morgan, Conwy Lloyd. 1894. *An Introduction to Comparative Psychology*. London: Walter Scott.

Otis, Laura. 2002. Introduction. In *Literature and Science in the Nineteenth Century: An Anthology*, ed. Laura Otis, xvii–xxviii. Oxford: Oxford University Press.

Polk, James. 1972. Lives of the Hunted. *Canadian Literature*. 53: 51–59.

Roberts, Charles G.D. 1907. *The Haunters of the Silences*. Boston: L. C. Page & Co.

Rollin, Bernard E. 2007. Animal Mind: Science, Philosophy, and Ethics. *The Journal of Ethics*. 11 (3): 253–274.

Romanes, George. 1882. *Animal Intelligence*. London: Keegan Paul, Trench, & Co.

———. (1883) 1884. *Mental Evolution in Animals*. New York: D. Appleton & Co.

Salt, Henry S. (1892) 1980. *Animals' Rights: Considered in Relation to Social Progress*. London: Centaur.

Scholtmeijer, Marian. 1993. *Animal Victims in Modern Fiction: From Sanctity to Sacrifice*. Toronto: University of Toronto Press.

Seton, Ernest Thompson. 1898. *Wild Animals I Have Known*. New York: Charles Scriber's Sons.

Singer, Peter. 1980. Preface. In *Animals' Rights: Considered in Relation to Social Progress*, ed. Henry S. Salt, v–x. London: Centaur.

Washburn, Margaret Floy. 1908. *The Animal Mind: A Textbook of Comparative Psychology*. New York: Macmillan Company.

Wasserman, Edward A. 1981. Comparative Psychology Returns. *Journal of the Experimental Analysis of Behaviour* 35 (2, March): 242–257.

CHAPTER 3

1860s–1900s Texts

This chapter explores the wild animal stories of Ernest Thompson Seton and Charles G. D. Roberts. Although these stories hold a much-debated position in the Canadian literary canon, they were enormously popular at the turn of the twentieth century. Seton and Roberts created a shift from settler-colonial narratives in which animals only served human ends to stories in which animals existed for their *own* sake. Through a blend of fact and fiction, the wild animal story strove to capture the experiences of non-human beings as realistically as possible. This chapter examines a selection of Seton's and Roberts's stories in relation to contemporary comparative psychology and animal rights discourses, as well as the Nature Fakers controversy. This approach illuminates their various attempts to contribute to both science and animal advocacy at the time. Although the wild animal story attracts little respect today, it was a true innovation in animal representation at the time. Its legacy casts a long shadow that shaped subsequent English-Canadian animal fiction for decades.

Co-created by Seton and Roberts, I classify the wild animal story as a *fantasy of knowing* the animal. By which I mean that it expresses a sincere curiosity about the experiences of other animals. Until this point, English-Canadian literature had demonstrated an *indifference to knowing* the animal. Animals had been written about as anthropomorphic stand-ins for humanity or as mechanomorphic objects. Margaret Atwood (1972)

© The Author(s), under exclusive license to Springer Nature Switzerland AG 2023

C. Allmark-Kent, *Literature, Science, and Animal Advocacy in Canada*, Palgrave Studies in Animals and Literature, https://doi.org/10.1007/978-3-031-40556-3_3

argued that the creation of the wild animal story revealed an "important facet of the Canadian psyche" (73). Yet, it was also a focus of intense criticism during the Nature Fakers controversy between 1903 and 1907. Although the debate lasted only a few years, its consequences would be felt for decades. Even in the 1970s, James Polk described the wild animal story as "scarcely respectable" (1972, 51).

More recently, however, literary historians have begun to rethink Seton's and Roberts's roles in shaping the development of nature writing and animal fiction in Canada. For instance, Alec Lucas (1997) argued that the wild animal story was "one of the most important developments of nature writing in the late nineteenth century" (789). John Sandlos (2000) observes that Seton's and Roberts's work made a profound departure from previous traditions of "purely imaginative nature that emphasizes picturesque or sublime qualities" or "one that emphasizes the creative experience of the human observer" (78–9). Their "unique innovation" was a "realistic depiction of nature as a living terrain that contains many living, breathing, and interacting objects" (78). For John Wadland (2008), the wild animal story was "ultimately responsible for launching Canada's version of ecocriticism" (262). Indeed, I will be referencing Seton's and Roberts's stories throughout the rest of this book. In this chapter, I draw out their most significant contributions. Of course, such analysis can only scratch the surface of the plentiful stories penned by each man.

Ernest Thompson Seton: Selected Stories

Ernest Thompson Seton (1860–1946) was an artist, naturalist, hunter, and animal advocate. He was born in England, raised in Canada, and died in the United States as an American citizen. Despite this transnational identity, he is still seen as "chiefly responsible" for establishing a "distinctively Canadian" style of writing (Roberts 1913, 147; Atwood 1972, 73). Surprisingly enough, though, Seton did not think of himself as a writer. In interviews, he said that he did not write fiction at all and had "never even attempted it" (Whitelock 1901, 322). He opened his first collection of stories, *Wild Animals I Have Known*, with the now infamous words: "These stories are true" (Seton 1898, 9). To some, this was simply a literary device; the "truth-claiming preface" that makes a perverse "avowal of fictionality" (Walsh 2015, 12). Yet, for others, they were the claims of a charlatan.

There is something uncomfortable, even faintly embarrassing, about Seton's unwavering commitment to the idea that his stories were true. It is common practice to treat these claims with scepticism. Historians point out that they were heavily "disputed" during the Nature Fakers controversy (Lutts 1998, 2). Others apply quotation marks to Seton's efforts, such as: "the 'realistic' animal story" (Atwood 1972, 3). Indeed, most scholars of literary animal studies take it for granted that Seton was a fiction writer. Even in other fields, such as environmental history, he is referred to as a novelist and children's writer (Forkey 2012, 30–1). All too often, we forget that Seton thought of himself not as a writer, but as a science communicator.

When interviewed, he stated that all his work was done with the idea of "popularizing science" and "inducing people to take an interest in the animal world" (Whitelock 1901, 322). His "only object" in writing the wild animal story was to "attract a class of readers who would not otherwise care to read about [animals]" (322). This is a significant distinction. Of course, the sceptical would take these assertions with the same pinch of salt as his claims that he "never even attempted" fiction; in other words, the careful constructions of a skilled self-promoter (322). This is fair. Yet, Seton's claims make more sense when we look at his wider body of work.

The earliest records of Seton's published writing are from the 1880s. These begin with reports for the Manitoba Department of Agriculture in 1883. The following year, he published multiple times in the *Transactions of the Manitoba Historical and Scientific Society*, *The Auk* (an ornithology journal), and *Canadian Science Monthly*. Two years later, he was regularly contributing natural history articles to newspapers and popular magazines, such as *Forest and Stream*. Gradually, this led to pieces in the children's magazine, *St. Nicholas*. The first of these, "The Drummer on Snow-shoes" (1887), blended fact and fiction by conveying information about the ruffled grouse through a conversation between a boy and his uncle. His next piece for the magazine was about how to track animals in the snow. Others included "The Western Meadow Lark" and "The Screech Owl."

One of the first recognizable precursors to the wild animal story was "The True Story of a Little Grey Rabbit" published in 1890. It recounts Seton's observations of a rabbit's innovative strategy to evade a dog. Alongside the story, Seton included a diagram of both animals' movements.[1] Throughout these forays into popular nature writing, Seton not

---

[1] Seton continued this practice in his published collections of wild animal stories. His experience as an artist meant that he illustrated his own books. He also included maps, diagrams, outlines of animal tracks, and small line drawings in the margins of pages. This strategy helped create an impression of authenticity, as though each book was his own field journal.

only continued regularly producing scientific articles, but he was also working on a two-hundred-page monograph, *The Birds of Manitoba*. It was published by the United States National Museum in 1891.

Seton's science writing provides a crucial context for understanding his wild animal stories. Even though he is best known for his short stories, they constitute only a portion of his creative and intellectual output. The majority were published between the 1890s and 1910s. Yet, Seton was producing scientific work before, during, and after this period. Some of his most significant contributions include *The Mammals of Mantioba* (1886), the two-volume *Life Histories of Northern Animals* (1909) and the four-volume *Lives of Game Animals* (1925–1927). Ralph Lutts (1990) records that, rather ironically, the *Lives of Game Animals* won the John Burroughs Medal for outstanding nature writing (178). Despite these achievements, however, Seton could not receive the full scientific recognition he craved. He had attended art school but received little other formal education. Fundamentally, Seton lacked the university training required to become a scientist. As a result, he tried to seek recognition through writing, rather than conventional academic research.

To some degree, Seton did manage to establish himself as a "natural scientist," although his books never quite created the "springboard for an academic career" that he desired (Anderson 1986, 36–7). In the early 1890s, he was made the Official Naturalist to the Government of Manitoba, but this was an unpaid, largely honorary, title (44). Seton had grown up in an era of disciplinary fluidity. Yet, by the time that he was striving for recognition, the professionalization of the sciences was complete. It was already too late. When he had been born, the word scientist had existed for less than thirty years. Now, the title was inaccessible to anyone outside of academia. Seton could not become a scientist through writing alone. When we explore his work, we must bear in mind that his goal was science communication, not literary merit. Thus, we make a mistake when we only identify him as a fiction writer.

Another significant context that we often overlook is the relationship between Seton's stories and the work of early comparative psychologists. In essence, Seton was working from the same material as Charles Darwin and George Romanes: first- and second-hand observations of individual animals. The difference was that Romanes held enough scientific authority to meld that anecdotal evidence into the burgeoning field of comparative psychology. Lacking such credentials, Seton turned his observations into stories that might help to popularize science and advocate for animals.

Interestingly, both men's work was immensely popular with the public, yet drew criticisms from some of their peers. As a result, Seton and Romanes remain associated with the stigma of anthropomorphism, even today.

Whilst Romanes used his materials to make statements regarding the species at large, Seton restricted himself to the psychological study of individuals. This is a crucial distinction. At the beginning of *Wild Animals I Have Known*, he explains that he is focused on the "real personality of the individual, and his view of life," rather than "the ways of the race in general" (Seton 1898, 10). He comments that "natural history" has "lost much" through "vague and general treatment" (9). As indicated by the book's title, Seton is attempting to explore the psychology of real individuals he has known. Its frontispiece reinforces this idea, describing the book as "Being the Personal Histories of Lobo, Silverspot, Raggylug, Bingo, The Springfield Fox, The Pacing Mustang, Wully, and Redruff" (1). It is also worth noting that Seton's famous words, "These stories are true," are rarely quoted in context. In full, he writes:

> These stories are true. Although I have left the strict line of historical truth in many places, the animals in this book were all real characters. They lived the lives I have depicted, and showed the stamp of heroism and personality more strongly by far than it has been in the power of my pen to tell. (9)

Clearly, Seton is not claiming that his stories are true in their entirety. Instead, he asserts that they are based on some element of truth, some foundation of fact, established through his observations. He distinguishes between the fact and fiction by offering details such as names and dates, as well as noting the stories that were more "pieced together" due to the "fragmentary nature of the records" (10). The point here is not about the factuality of the story itself, but the 'realness' of the animals. By supplementing observation with imagination, Seton attempts to create biographies of animals he has encountered. Through the added element of storytelling, he presents compelling glimpses into the unseen, otherwise inaccessible, lives of wild animals.

Seton's approach bears a striking similarity to that of the best-known Canadian comparative psychologist of the nineteenth century, Thomas Wesley Mills. In 1885, he founded the nation's first scientific society for animal psychology. The Association for the Study of Comparative Psychology was established through the Faculty of Comparative Medicine and Veterinary Science at McGill University. The group gave lectures, published the proceedings of each meeting in the Montreal Gazette, and offered copies of research papers to the CSPCA (Canadian Society for the Prevention of Cruelty to Animals) to circulate amongst the public. In the same year that *Wild Animals I Have Known* went into print, Mills (1898) published *The Nature and Development of Animal Intelligence*. It was a collection of his own articles, lectures, and observations of young animals.

Throughout the book, Mills (1898) argues for a biographical approach to animal psychology. He writes that we must know the life history of the individual to understand them, particularly if we are to distinguish between instinct and learning (6). How can we identify the root of an individual's behaviour without knowing their personal history? Moreover, how can we tell what is typical of the species or unique to the individual? Mills argues that "the more perfectly the history of each step in the development of mind is traced, the better will the final product, the mature, or relatively fully-developed mind, be understood" (113). In the final chapters of the book, he includes extracts from his diaries of young dogs, cats, rabbits, guinea pigs, and chickens. Of course, a limitation of Mills's biographical approach is that it is best suited to animals kept in captivity. The same level of detail would be extremely difficult to achieve in studies of wild animals.

From this perspective, we can see that Seton's stories offer 'perfect' life histories of wild animals. By combining observation with speculation—imagining what cannot be seen or studied—they present psychological investigations that would be impossible under real conditions. In other words, they are truly a *fantasy* of *knowing* an animal. We can see how Seton developed this approach in writing "The King of Currumpaw," later known as "Lobo." It was first published in *Scribner's Magazine* in 1894. Upon publication, the story received worldwide attention (Anderson 1986, 56). Years later, Seton reflected that this time "proved one of the turning points" of his life (Witt 2010, 36). This is no exaggeration. It was not only the moment that Seton became a popular writer, but the moment he transformed from a hunter into an animal advocate. The "King of Currumpaw" was a semi-autobiographical account of his experiences hunting wolves in New Mexico. These wolves defied his expectations, challenged his thinking, and sparked his curiosity. After meeting them, Seton never killed another wolf. I would suggest that he wrote "The King of Currumpaw" and other stories so that he could get to know these wolves better.

In October 1893, Seton had arrived in New Mexico planning to kill about fifteen wolves. By early February, he was ready to leave after catching only five. In his journal, he records these experiences. According to Seton, the wolves of the Currumpaw Valley seemed particularly assertive. They escaped traps, detected poisons, and avoided being seen by humans. He describes wolves who found his baits and "urinated on them" and others who ate the meat but "carefully avoided the poisoned parts" (reprinted in Witt 2010, 29). A wolf he identifies as mammal specimen #653 had one leg held in an iron trap yet managed to drag the attached 40lb log over 450 yards of rough terrain before it became stuck (30). Following the tracks, Seton discovered that the wolf's companion had remained with them for almost the whole journey.

A white wolf, identified as #672, surprised Seton with the ferocity of her resistance. He managed to take two photographs before she "cut off both our ropes with her teeth;" even with "two traps weighed 52 lbs," she could "outrun a man" on level ground (33). That night, after they finally managed to kill the white wolf, "her mate came howling on the mesa—his calls repeated at intervals were most melancholy" (33). While looking for #672, her mate was caught in a trap, but managed to escape. Together, these wolves impressed Seton with their stamina, determination, intelligence, loyalty, and autonomy. They were not just objects with skins to be taken or scalps to be collected for bounties. They were, each of them, the unique *subject of a life* with richer feelings, experiences, and relationships than he could have imagined. All of them wanted to live.

The last wolf Seton would ever catch was #667, who seemed different to the others. His journal entry for 31st January 1894 reads:

> He was caught in 3 [traps] and had been in 4—he was unable to move at all—when I came near—he barked like a dog then broke into a prolonged howl […] we tied his mouth shut & carried him home—we staked him out for a decoy but he died in the evening. Why? (Reprinted in Witt 2010, 35)

Seton seems to have been unsettled by the question of the wolf's death. Witt (2010) observes that the "Why" in his journal must have been important because it appears in "large letters" with "dark ink, hard-pressed by his hand" (36). It was only a few days after the death of #667, who is thought to be the real 'Lobo,' that Seton cut his trip short to return home and write the story.

Seton's experience with the Currumpaw wolves had not only reshaped his thinking; it stirred his imagination. The unexpected behaviours of these wolves raised many questions. How did they avoid the traps laid for them? Did they learn from each other? What was the extent of their loyalty? Why did wolf #667 die? Writing "The King of Currumpaw" required an important shift in perception for Seton, a leap of empathy in which the wolves he had treated as objects were transformed into *subjects of lives.* This is the story Seton (1901) describes as the "earliest important example" of his "more scientific method" of animal representation (10–11).[2]

"The King of Currumpaw" mirrors Seton's (1951) accounts of his time in New Mexico as described in his journals and autobiography, *Trail of an Artist-Naturalist.* Much of the story revolves around his largely unsuccessful attempts to catch the wolves. Witt (2010) notes that Seton added the names "Blanca" and "Lobo" to his journal entries describing the white wolf #672, her unidentified mate, and wolf #667 (33–5). It is unclear whether Seton believed #672's mate and #667 were the same wolf, but they both became Lobo in the story.

Here, we can see how Seton built stories upon his experiences. He gives "The King of Currumpaw" a tragic end by blending the experiences of wolf #672, her mate, and wolf #667—no doubt also adding some of the loyalty demonstrated by wolf #653's companion as well. This means that when Blanca (#672) is killed and her mate Lobo comes looking for her, he does not escape the trap; instead, he dies suddenly and without explanation, just like #667. Interestingly, Seton illustrated the story with accurate reproductions of photographs he had taken of the Currumpaw wolves (see Witt 2010). Particularly distressing are the illustrations of Lobo and Blanca caught in traps. Presumably, the wolves in the photos are #672 and #667.

As one of Seton's (1894) more autobiographical stories, "The King of Currumpaw" is told through human eyes. Hence, it is a little more anthropocentric than the rest. Perhaps Seton was dissatisfied with this. Later he wrote two similar stories told from the perspectives of coyotes and wolves. "Tito: The Story of the Coyote That Learned How" was first published in *Scribner's Magazine* in 1900 and then reproduced in *Lives of the Hunted* (1901). "Badlands Billy: The Wolf That Won" was initially published in two parts as "Billy: The Big Wolf" in the *Ladies' Home Journal* in 1905. In the same year, it was also reprinted in *Animal Heroes* (1905).

---

[2] Seton (1901) differentiates "Lobo" from his earlier stories written in the 1880s and 1890s, such as those for *St. Nicholas,* which used the "archaic method" of "making the animals talk" (10).

We can read both "Tito" (1901) and "Badlands Billy" (1905) as more zoocentric retellings of "The King of Currumpaw." They share similar events with that story, as well as Seton's experiences in New Mexico more generally. Unusually, however, both protagonists survive. Seton is well-known for remarking in the preface to *Wild Animals I Have Known* that the "life of the wild animal always has a tragic end" (1898, 12). In both "Tito" and "Badlands Billy," however, Seton seems to have focused more closely on the spirit of resistance demonstrated by the Currumpaw wolves.

In "Badlands Billy," Seton (1905) explores how wolves might detect his traps and poisons. The protagonist's representation is far more intimate than Lobo's. Not only does Seton imagine what it might be like to be a wolf, he imagines what it might be like to be *this* specific wolf. The Yellow Wolf, as Seton calls her, knows about traps and poisons. So, when she detects the scent of a dead calf, she does not approach directly: "A Dog would have trotted right up to the carcass, an old-time Wolf might have done so, but constant war had developed constant vigilance in the Yellow Wolf" (126–7). From a distance, she stops and swings her nose, "submitting the wind to the closest possible chemical analysis" (127). Seton breaks down the results:

> First, rich and racy smell of Calf, seventy per cent.; smell of grass, bugs, wood, flowers, trees, sand, and other uninteresting negations, fifteen per cent.; smell of her Cub and herself, positive but ignorable, ten per cent.; smell of human tracks, two per cent.; smell of smoke, one per cent.; of sweaty leather smell, one per cent.; of human body-scent (not discernible in some samples), one-half per cent.; smell of iron, a trace. (127)

Her experience is identifiable but presented in a way that evokes a sensory world far beyond our own. It also suggests something of her unique perspective and life history.

Seton describes her as "a Wolf of modern ideas" (118). She knew the "old tricks" of wolf survival partly from "instinct" and partly from "the example of her more experienced relatives," but it had also become "necessary nowadays" to learn how to avoid hunters (121). She knew that "all men carry guns," she had "a fair comprehension of traps," and had come to associate a "sense of fear and hate" with the smell of strychnine (121–3). With this knowledge, the Yellow Wolf predicts the danger represented by human odours, particularly that of the iron trap. She backs away from the body and gives a low whine to encourage her cub to do the same. When she catches an even stronger human scent on the wind, she becomes fully alarmed; she communicates this to her cub through a "rigid pose" and "slightly bristling mane" (128). Here, we can see the ways in which Seton is speculating about the inner lives of the Currumpaw wolves. Not only does he imagine their individual perspectives, but he also considers how they might learn from experience and share that knowledge with others.

Explorations of learning and teaching feature heavily in Seton's stories. In "Tito," Seton (1901) outlines his theory of animal intelligence, which shares similarities with Romanes's definitions. He identifies "three sources of wisdom" for wild animals:

> First, the experiences of its ancestors, in the form of instinct, which is inborn learning, hammered into the race by ages of selection and tribulation. This is the most important to begin with, because it guards him from the moment he is born.
>
> Second, the experience of his parents and comrades, learned chiefly by example. This becomes most important as soon as the young can run.
>
> Third, the personal experience of the animal itself. This grows in importance as the animal ages. (284–5)

Similar to Mills's diaries, Seton's animal biographies enable him to explore a range of learning scenarios. Orphaned, abandoned, captured, or semi-domesticated animals offer a contrast to stories in which the protagonist learns from a parent or group.

In "Tito," a young coyote's family is killed. She is captured by humans who plan to make her a pet but mistreat her instead. Tito experiences the "mortal terror of traps," the "burning, stinging" sensation of being fired at with "bird-shot," and the "fearful pains" and "cramps" of rat poison (247–6). This abuse means that she has an unusual perspective: "Perhaps never before had a Coyote faced life with unusual advantages in the third kind of knowledge, none at all in the second, and with the first dormant" (285). When Tito escapes and hunts for herself for the first time, Seton speculates about the role of instinct: "Her mother had not taught her to hunt, but her instinct did, and the accident that she had an unusual brain made her profit very quickly by experience" (285). In such stories, Seton offers thought experiments about animal minds. They create 'what if' scenarios that explore the relationship between instinct and learning in ways that would be difficult to replicate through real-world experiments or observations.

Despite the speculative nature of his stories, Seton still seems to have built them upon a foundation of his own experiences. According to his autobiography, *Trail of an Artist-Naturalist*, while he was wolf-hunting in New Mexico in 1893, he also hunted coyotes. These experiences also seem to have contributed to a change in this thinking. In particular, he recalls watching a coyote ingest poisoned bait:

> He went on two hundred yards, then fell in the first horrible convulsion of strychnine poisoning. I galloped up, and drew my gun to end his suffering. [...] He staggered to his feet, vomited all he had in his stomach, then sought to escape. He dragged his paralyzed hind legs on the ground, but worked desperately with fore-feet, snapping at his own flank and legs with frenzied jaws. (Seton 1951, 242)

Eventually, the coyote manages to run and escape. Seton speculates that the coyote would "ever after know and fear the smell of strychnine, and would teach other coyotes to the same" (242). He reflects:

> I had often found my poison victims with gashes on loins and on limbs; I knew now that these were self-inflicted in their agony. [...] What right, I asked, has man to inflict such horrible agony on fellow beings, merely because they do a little damage to his material interests? It is not right; it is horrible—horrible—hellish! And I put out no more poison baits. (242–3)

In "Tito," Seton (1901) recreates this experience from the coyote's perspective. Tito finds a piece of meat with "a peculiar odor [sic]," but she is desperately hungry and eats it anyway (289). Within minutes she experiences "a terrific pain" and memories of the "poisoned meat the boy had given her" (289). With "trembling, foaming jaws she seized some blades of grass and her stomach threw off the meat; but she fell in convulsions on the ground" (289). Seton recreates himself in the form of a character called Wolver Jake. He describes a distressing scene, identical to the one in his autobiography, in which the coyote desperately tries to run with semi-paralyzed legs to avoid the shots of the hunter. Tito survives and learns that the "curious smell on the meat stands for mortal agony [...] she never forgot it; thenceforth she knew strychnine" (291).

Here, Seton takes his speculation about a real coyote and dramatizes it from the animal's perspective. Just as he imagined that the coyote in New Mexico might teach others of the poison, he describes Tito doing the same. When she forms companionships with other coyotes, she shares her knowledge through "the aid of a few signs and a great deal of example" (295). Similarly, her offspring learn not only "the ancient learning of the plains," but also "the later wisdom the ranchers' war had forced upon them" (350). In turn, they teach it to their children. The story concludes with this knowledge spreading to the wider coyote population of the area: "They have learned the deadly secrets of traps and poisons [...] and it was Tito that taught them how" (351).

Along similar lines, Seton (1905) explores this process in "Badlands Billy." The Yellow Wolf teaches her cub and he grows up to share this knowledge with others, as well as what he has learned from his own experiences. Seton describes wolves with "new cunning that were defying the methods of the ranchmen, and increasing steadily in numbers;" they were aided by "the big Wolf, [who] with exasperating persistence, continued to live on the finest stock [...] and each year was teaching more Wolves how to do the same" (143–4). In both stories we find explorations of how knowledge might spread through animal groups. After learning by experience, individuals instruct their young, who then share this information with others and may even improve upon it. The knowledge and tactics Seton explores in his stories are often novel and specific to those local populations. This is important because it means that they are not explained by instinct alone. They are what we might now describe as examples of animal *culture*.[3]

Evidently, in the stories of "Tito" and "Badlands Billy," Seton is exploring how the wolves and coyotes in New Mexico had adapted to avoid hunters. Significantly, he also considers what it might *feel* like to be hunted. This is a significant departure from "The King of Currumpaw," in which the events were described from Seton's (1894) own perspective. When Blanca and Lobo are caught in traps, he gives no indication that they would feel any pain. Indeed, rather than end their suffering immediately, he extends it. Seton chooses to ride home to get his camera to take pictures while the wolves are still alive. He even carries Lobo back to the

---

[3] We can think of animal 'cultures' as behaviours or strategies that are unique to specific populations. This process might begin when one individual develops a novel behaviour, which then spreads to others through social learning. As these activities are learned, rather than innate, they would not be found throughout the rest of the species. For instance, a group of captive animals might develop a set of behaviours that are not shared with their wild counterparts. It is worth noting, however, that the question of animal culture remains contentious in the scientific community. Some scientists prefer the term "animal traditions" to help create a distinction from "human cultures" (Galef 2012, 587).

camp while his legs are still caught in the same four steel traps in which they had been pinned for two days and nights. Perhaps Seton had not given the wolves' own experiences much thought.

By contrast, when the Yellow Wolf of "Badlands Billy" is caught in a trap, he prioritizes her perspective and describes the experience in distressing detail:

> Fear and fury filled the old Wolf's heart; she tugged and strained, she chewed the chains, she snarled and foamed. [...] Struggle as she might, it only worked those relentless jaws more deeply into her feet. [...] She bit at the traps, at her cub, at herself. She tore her legs that were held; she gnawed in frenzy at her flank, she chopped off her tail in her madness; she splintered her teeth on the steel, and filled her bleeding, foaming jaws with clay and sand. (Seton 1905, 138)

Interestingly, Seton does not state outright that the wolf is in pain, although the intensity of her response would seem to indicate it. The lengthy passage gives a powerful condemnation of steel jaw traps, just as the description of strychnine poisoning had done in "Tito." Evidently Seton's priorities—and perhaps even his thinking—had changed between the publications of "The King of Currumpaw," "Tito," and "Badlands Billy."

To increase dramatic tension in "The King of Currumpaw," Seton (1894) had inadvertently reinforced the same species stereotypes that legitimized the predator bounty system. He had emphasized the wolves' ravages on sheep and cattle through anecdotes from ranchers and cowboys. Yet, in doing so, he also naturalized prejudices against wolves. From an anthropocentric perspective, one could argue that Lobo and Bianca 'deserved' the retaliation. Joan Dunayer (2001) explains that when humans categorize a species as 'vermin' it "blames the victim" (57). It means that they can be "legally killed in any number at any time, including when they have dependent young" (57). The word transforms "speciesist genocide" into a "public service;" a legitimate "punishment" for those animals (57).

In "Tito" and "Badlands Billy," Seton redresses his use of speciesist stereotypes. Interestingly, he seems to come to the same conclusion as Dunayer. He demonstrates that 'vermin' call be killed even when they have dependent young, but also that those young can be killed themselves. Lobo and his pack were responsible for the deaths of many sheep and cows. Yet, the infant animals killed in "Tito" and "Badlands Billy" are too young to hunt. By focusing on their deaths, Seton demonstrates the indiscriminate violence of speciesism. To reinforce his point, he constructs sympathetic scenes of coyote and wolf families interacting prior to their attacks.

In these passages, it is also worth noting the negative representations of the bounty-hunters (a role Seton had performed himself). Whilst he makes no overt statements condemning them, it is clear who the 'villains' of both stories are. The way that Seton (1894) had mirrored traditional hunting narratives in "The King of Currumpaw," almost made it seem a battle of equals. In that story Seton had remained a sympathetic character, albeit one who later regretted his actions. The hunters of "Tito" and "Badlands Billy" are remorseless, entirely unaffected by their murder of infant animals. In some places, he uses their perspective to reinforce the all-encompassing prejudice of speciesism. These men are simply unable to see the animals as anything other than *objects of utility*.

The description of Tito and her family focuses on cuteness: "there poured a procession of little Coyotes, merrily tumbling over one another [...] barking little barks and growling little puppy growls" (Seton 1901, 267). For Wolver Jake, however, the "only appeal the scene had" lay in "the fact that the county had set a price on every one of these Coyotes' lives" (267). As he kills the family, Seton elicits our sympathy and contrasts it with Jake's indifference: "Their innocent puppy faces and ways were not noticed by the huge enemy. One by one they were seized. A sharp blow, and each quivering, limp form was thrown into a sack" (268–9). Importantly, however, he identifies that even at this age, there was "a certain individuality of character" amongst the infant coyotes; some "squealed," some "growled," and one or two "tried to bite" (269). Seton shows that they are already autonomous, individual, *subjects of lives*, even as they are being seen and treated as objects. When the hunter chooses to keep Tito as a pet, he throws her into the bag with the bodies of her dead and dying family. Again, Seton prioritizes her subjective experiences while she is treated as an object: "bruised and frightened, [she] lay there very still, understanding nothing" (270).

In "Badlands Billy," Seton (1905) uses similar techniques to point out further consequences of the bounty system. Wolves were already commodified for their fur, but the hunting was seasonal. Bounties, however, could be collected year-round: "Pelts were not good in May, but the bounties were high, five dollars a head, and double for She-wolves" (114). Not only does this system unfairly target females, it means that killing nursing wolves can be particularly profitable if the hunter can find her cubs as well. Evidently, the killing of infants is built into the arrangement. We can see how profitable this can be from the hunter's determination in "Badlands Billy." He makes a prolonged search to find the cubs of a female wolf he kills. Eventually, he is successful.

Seton uses a new strategy when the hunter finds the wolf cubs. This time, he allows the reader to catch a glimpse of their individual life stories:

> Now he dug into the den and found the litter, a most surprising one indeed, for it consisted not of the usual five or six Wolf-pubs, but of eleven, and these, strange to say, were of two sizes, five of them larger and older than the other six. Here were two distinct families with one mother, and as he added their scalps to his string of trophies the truth dawned on the hunter. (114)

He realizes that one group is the "family of the She-wolf he had killed two weeks before," adopted by a second wolf who "cared for the orphans, carried them to her own den, and was providing for the double family when the rifleman had cut the gentle chapter short" (114). This discovery offers a powerful challenge to speciesist prejudices. Presumably, an altruistic wolf is neither an insatiable beast nor an insentient automaton. It is the type of surprise Seton encountered with the Currumpaw wolves. This is an act of imaginative investigation, using traces of evidence to speculate about the lives of the already dead wolves. Seton's small insights into the Currumpaw wolves revealed an existence far richer than he expected. In "Badlands Billy," he re-enacts this moment of defamiliarization in which the *object of utility* becomes a *subject of a life*.[4] Crucially, Seton indicates that this altruism may not be unique to one wolf. When a single cub manages to survive and find a new "foster mother," it implies that the first adoption was not an isolated incident (118).

Seton's final technique is to historicize contemporary relationships between humans and predators. In "Tito," he points out that the unchecked violence of the bounty system had almost eradicated the local coyote population: "Fierce war had for a long time been waged against Coyote kind [...] Traps, guns, poison, and Hounds had reduced their number nearly to zero" (Seton 1901, 266). In "Badlands Billy," he historicizes wolf predation and begins to suggest that the wolves may, indeed, be victims:

---

[4] Defamiliarization is a concept developed by the literary theorist Viktor Shklovsky in 1917. It occurs when something disrupts our automatic, habitualized perceptions. As a result, the familiar becomes the unfamiliar. Animal fiction offers considerable scope for defamiliarization.

> In pristine days the Buffalo herds were followed by bands of Wolves that preyed on the sick, the weak, and the wounded. When the Buffalo were exterminated the Wolves were hard put for support, but the Cattle came and solved the question for them by taking the Buffaloes' place. This caused the wolf-war. (Seton 1905, 112)

Here, we can see Seton beginning to introduce a more ecological angle into his message. Rather than being insatiable, naturally violent creatures who kill for fun, Seton reveals that wolves are important members of the ecosystem who have simply been left with no other choice. This situation is not natural, it has been created by humans. Even in 1905, we can see an emerging recognition that humans have disrupted nature and created some form of 'imbalance.' Yet, the scientific field of ecology would not develop for another two decades.

Although Seton claims he only wrote to "popularize science" and encourage public "interest in the animal world," it is clear that animal advocacy was also central to his purpose (Whitelock 1901, 322). In the preface to his first book, *Wild Animals I Have Known*, Seton (1898) combined science and animal advocacy to state the "common thought" or "moral" running throughout his stories:

> [W]e and the beasts are kin. Man has nothing that the animals have not at least a vestige of, the animals have nothing that man does not in some degree share. Surely, then, the animals are creatures with wants and feelings differing in degree only from our own, they surely have their rights. (12)

Evidently, he echoes Darwin's and Romanes's characterization of the divide between humans and other animals as only a matter of 'degrees.' Perhaps less obvious is that he also mirrors Henry Salt (1892) in *Animals' Rights*, who uses the same language of degrees (113). Most unusually, both Seton and Salt apply the idea of *rights* to wild animals. At the end of *Wild Animals I Have Known*, Seton (1898) reinforces the message of his book: "Have the wild things no moral or legal rights?" (357). From across the Atlantic, Salt (1892) almost seems to provide the answer: "wild animals, no less than domestic animals, have their rights" (45).

What is unusual here is that wild animals are rarely discussed in terms of 'rights.' Ideas about rights, ethics, welfare, and individual suffering are more often applied to domesticated animals. Their wild counterparts are usually only described collectively, as a *species* or *population*. As such, they are protected in those terms through conservation, rather than the animal rights movement. In Canadian law, animals are protected as property, which means that anti-cruelty legislation was not designed to protect wildlife from suffering. Thus, it would have been particularly unusual for Seton to speak of wild animal rights in nineteenth-century Canada, where the humane movement was considerably more conservative than its British or American counterparts. Perhaps it was his more transnational perspective that enabled Seton to engage with these 'radical' forms of animal advocacy.

It is worth noting, however, that Seton's message of animal protection was not consistent. After his statements about animal rights in his first book, he dedicated his second, *Lives of the Hunted*, to the "Preservation of Our Wild Creatures" (Seton 1901, 3). Yet, in the book's preface, his stance becomes less clear. Salt (1892) had stated boldly that to take advantage of animal suffering, "whether wild or tame," for sport, food, or fashion was "quite incompatible with any possible assertion of animals' rights" (37–8). In his preface to *Lives of the Hunted*, however, Seton (1901) seems to distance himself from such thinking: "I do not champion any theory of diet. I do not intend primarily to denounce certain field sports, or even cruelty to animals" (12). He writes that his "chief motive" is to "stop the extermination of harmless wild creatures; not for their sakes, but for ours" (12). In a strangely objectifying stance, he argues that we must preserve "most animals" for the same reason that we must preserve "good pictures," that is: the "pure pleasure" of "those who see them" (13). In his following book, *Animal Heroes*, Seton (1905) made no overt statements of animal advocacy in the preface or dedication.

Strangely enough, it seems that while his stories became increasingly focused on advocacy, the prefaces of his books became considerably less so. The reason for this is unclear. Perhaps it was to distance himself from the stigma of anthropomorphism and sentimentality associated with concern for animals. It could be that he wished to create a greater sense of dispassionate objectivity as a would-be scientist, particularly during the Nature Fakers controversy. Whatever it may have been, Seton's contradictory statements reveal the complex tensions between literature, science, and animal advocacy at the time.

For a man who thought of himself as a naturalist and artist, but not a writer, Seton has had an astounding literary presence. In the first collection of Canadian literary animal studies essays, *Other Selves: Animals in the Canadian Literary Imagination* (2007), Seton is ubiquitous. John Wadland's (2008) review of the book notes that his name and work appear throughout: in multiple chapters, in all three sections, and in "numerous conflicting guises" (259). Some scholars "defer to his authority," some "attack his credibility," and others "claim him as a seminal influence" (262). This summary is representative of Seton's role in literary animal studies. Wadland continues: "See how often his name appears [...] and recognize, in the flawed work of Ernest Thompson Seton (an immigrant to Canada with no formal education beyond art school), ideas that simply will not go away" (262).

There are many ideas about Seton that will not go away, such as his associations with nature faking and anthropomorphism. We have seen, however, that these accusations have more to do with the professionalization of the sciences and changes in the study of comparative psychology than inherent deceptions on Seton's part. He attempted to make himself a scientist when it was no longer possible to do so without proper training. Likewise, the wild animal story attempted to engage with animal psychology at the very time that it became closed to amateurs. More than that, Seton was using anecdotal evidence and introspective methods just as these were being rejected by science. It is no wonder that his credibility was damaged.

Yet, we must not forget that he pioneered a new way to write about animals. His early stories were simply a way to popularize science, but they were transformed when he met the Currumpaw wolves. These animals changed Seton's thinking. Over the years, he built upon his new format and refined its message. His experiences as a bounty hunter informed his advocacy for predator species, but he also began to place greater emphasis on encouraging compassion and challenging speciesism in general. Nevertheless, his core commitment to imagining the complex lives of wild animals remained consistent throughout. He continued to explore animal psychology, especially the questions of animal learning, cooperation, and social relationships. His new approach to animal representation changed the way that we write about animals forever. As the rest of this book will demonstrate, a significant portion of Canadian animal literature has been written in response to Seton's work.

CHARLES G. D. ROBERTS: SELECTED STORIES

Charles G. D. Roberts (1860–1943) tends to be remembered not for his wild animal stories, but as the 'father' of Canadian poetry. He was given this title for both his early successes as a poet and for his work inspiring and encouraging his contemporaries, Bliss Carmen, Archibald Lampman, and Duncan Campbell Scott. All born during the 1860s, these four men were dubbed the Confederation Poets. Together, their work has been regarded as a core foundation of the English-Canadian literary canon. This solid reputation means that Roberts's involvement in the Nature Fakers controversy tends to be forgotten. However, it also means that his innovations in animal representation are also overlooked. Readers and scholars alike can be surprised to learn that the father of Canadian poetry wrote stories about salmons, ants, and dragonflies.[5] It seems contradictory that a figure of such importance to the literary canon also co-created a "scarcely respectable" branch of Canadian literature (Polk 1972, 51).

Whilst Roberts may have emerged from the Nature Fakers controversy relatively unscathed, it means that his significant contributions to the wild animal story rarely gain attention. Yet, without Roberts's influence, the form might not have developed at all. Seton may have made the original innovation of blending science with animal-centred storytelling, but his style was inconsistent. Even "The King of Currumpaw" is not quite representative of what the wild animal story would become. By contrast, Roberts brought together the varied stories written by Seton and himself, identified the common features, and forged them into a unique literary form. Most importantly, Roberts then wrote his subsequent stories within these parameters. Thus, whilst his stories can feel formulaic, his consistency strengthened the wild animal story's characteristics considerably. Crucial to this process were the prefaces Roberts wrote to each book. Whereas Seton used the opening pages of his books to discuss only his own work, Roberts used them to define the wild animal story, describe its features, and articulate its aims. I would suggest that the two men's different life experiences enabled these roles to develop.

Roberts studied at the University of New Brunswick, taught English and French literatures, and edited literary magazines and journals. During the same period, Seton was working inconsistently as a hunter, wildlife artist, naturalist, and occasional writer. When Seton and Roberts first met in New York in 1896, both men had already published their first wild animal stories: Roberts's (1892) "Do Seek Their Meat from God" in *Harper's Monthly* and Seton's (1894) "The King of Currumpaw" in *Scribner's Magazine*. Roberts had resigned from his teaching post and moved to New York where Seton was living already. There, they met, became friends,

---

[5] In this book, I pluralize nouns, such as fish or salmon, to reflect the heterogeneity of these individuals.

and even discussed collaborating on a collection of stories (Cappon 1923, 26; Adams 1986, 83). The idea did not come to fruition, but it was clearly an important moment of exchange. In fact, Roberts (1904) dedicated his second collection, *Watchers of the Trails*, to "My Fellow of the Wild, Ernest Thompson Seton" (v).

Initially, Roberts had struggled to get his animal stories published. When "Do Seek Their Meat from God" was finally accepted by *Harper's* in 1892, they paid him half of what they usually did for a story of that length (Adams 1986, 82). Indeed, he had all but abandoned the wild animal story when Seton published "The King of Currumpaw" in 1894. Seton's story was so successful that it created a new market for animal stories. As a result, the same editors who had rejected Roberts's work now asked him for new submissions (83). It seems that, were it not for Seton's popularity, Roberts might have stopped writing animal stories altogether. However, it is worth noting that Roberts's literary and academic experience may have enabled him to appreciate the wider significance of what was happening. Given his self-conscious statements about the wild animal story, Roberts seemed to have recognized that, together, they could develop their differing styles into something new and unique.

It was Roberts's (1902) preface to his first collection of stories, *Kindred of the Wild*, that created the idea of the wild animal story as a specific form of writing. He defines it as a "psychological romance built on a framework of natural science" (24). "Whether avowedly or not," he writes, "it is with the psychology of animal life that the representative animal stories of today are first of all concerned" (23). Interestingly, Roberts does not use the term 'wild animal story' or label it as a separate genre. Instead, he constructs it as merely the "animal story at its highest point of development;" essentially, the latest stage in the evolution of animal representation (24). The problem is that the precise characteristics he describes only applied to his and Seton's work at the time. It may be that Roberts expected future generations of writers to adhere to it as well. Whilst the Nature Fakers controversy may have prevented this from happening, we will see in subsequent chapters of this book that *some* future writers did keep core elements of the wild animal story alive.

Roberts's (1902) preface to *Kindred of the Wild* is a crucial document in the history of the wild animal story. We can use it as a milestone in the development of the genre, a concrete point at which separate stories— "[a]like in matter and in method"—became a new literary form with explicit aims and characteristics (15). But, more than this, we can also identify how its pseudo-scientific aspirations became explicit. This is because Roberts went beyond merely stating the wild animal story's interest in animal minds. He constructs it as a cousin to comparative psychology itself. Whilst he ostensibly presents a history of animal stories—from the fireside tales of "primitive man" to the "'Mowgli' stories of Kipling"—he actually gives a much broader genealogy of knowing animals throughout both science and storytelling (15, 27). Along the way, he carefully entwines science and literature together. Perhaps most striking is his identification of the shared origins between the wild animal story and comparative psychology.

As surprising as it may seem, there is some legitimacy to Roberts's claims. He observes that both the wild animal story and comparative psychology grew out of the "anecdote of observation" (21). His account chimes with Romanes's (1882) description of comparative psychology's origins in *Animal Intelligence*, as well as later histories, such as Robert Boakes's (1984) *From Darwin to Behaviourism*. Similar to Boakes, Roberts (1902) identifies the growing curiosity for animal minds that rose after the publication of Darwin's *On the Origin of Species* (1859). In particular, he notes that people who "loved their animal comrades" were beginning to observe the "astonishing fashion" in which the supposed "mere instincts" of animals were "able to simulate the operations of reason" (22). According to Roberts, the results of such observations were "written down" until "'anecdotes of animals' came to form a not inconsiderable body of literature" (22). This may have been what Romanes (1882) was describing when he lamented that the study of animal minds had been the work of "unscientific authors" and "anecdote-mongers" for too long (vi–viii).

In relaying the shared origins of comparative psychology and the wild animal story, Roberts (1902) often mirrors the language of both Darwin and Romanes, though he does not mention them by name:

> The mental processes of animals observed were seen to be far more complex than the observers had supposed [...] men were forced to accept the proposition that, within their varying limitations, animals can and do reason [...] the gulf dividing the lowest of the human species from the highest of the animals has in these latter days been reduced to a very narrow psychological fissure. (22–3)

Significantly, it is at this point that he switches, almost seamlessly, from describing the origins to animal psychology to establishing the characteristics of the wild animal story. Rather ambiguously referring to 'we' and 'they,' it is often unclear whether he is describing researchers or writers. To demonstrate this deft language, I quote him at length:

> We have come face to face with personality, where we were blindly wont to predicate mere instinct and automatism. It is as if one should step carelessly out of one's back door, and marvel to see unrolling before his new-awakened eyes the peaks and seas and misty valleys of an unknown world. Our chief writers of animal stories at the present day may be regarded as explorers of this unknown world, absorbed in charting its topography. They work, indeed, upon a substantial foundation of known facts. They are minutely scrupulous as to their natural history, and [are] assiduous contributors to that science. But above all they are diligent in their search for the motive beneath the action. (24)

Having identified a shared lineage between the wild animal story and comparative psychology, Roberts makes a claim to speak about animal minds. His vague language enables a blurring between the methods of introspective animal psychology and the writing of animal stories. Yet, despite the detached tone, Roberts is clearly referring to Seton and himself. Most unusually, he suggests that "writers of animal stories" are "assiduous contributors" to "science" (24). This striking idea may not have been appreciated at the time and, indeed, could well have exacerbated the Nature Fakers controversy. However, we must bear in mind, that Roberts's proposition—as unusual as it might seem coming from a fiction writer— would be rearticulated by the sciences a century later, albeit in a softened form. Biologists, Marc Bekoff (2007) and Hal Whitehead (2003), both called for greater collaboration between writers of animal stories and researchers of animal behaviour.[6]

To justify his extraordinary claims, Roberts (1902) makes two subtle moves. Firstly, he gently undermines the scientific credibility of comparative psychology. He notes that we have had to "grope our way toward" the "real psychology of the animals" by "deduction and induction combined"

---

[6] In "Animal Emotions: Exploring Passionate Natures," Bekoff (2000) postulates that a truly "rigorous study" of "animal emotions" may require input from diverse sources, including "nonacademics who observe animals and tell stories" (869). Similarly, in *Sperm Whales: Social Evolution in the Ocean*, Hal Whitehead (2003) argues that "communication" between scientists and writers should be "reciprocal" (371). Where writers can draw on the detailed work of science, scientists can use the "constructions" of fiction as "hypotheses to guide our work" (371).

(24–7). This mirrors the language of analogy and interference used by Romanes, while also weaking the authority of a newly established field of research. Secondly, Roberts distinguishes the writer of wild animal stories from other writers of animal fiction. In particular, he identifies his contemporaries, Anna Sewell, Margaret Marshall Saunders, and Rudyard Kipling as examples.

Roberts (1902) writes that the "psychology" of their animal characters is "human;" they "think and feel as human beings would think and feel under like conditions" (27). To reinforce this point, he references one of Seton's stories, "Krag," in which the "field of animal psychology so admirably opened is an inexhaustible world of wonder" (28). Clearly, Roberts is distinguishing the writer of wild animal stories as a new type of writer; one who straddles the realms of science and literature. Throughout the preface, he introduces the idea that such a writer might have the ability not only to present science, but also, perhaps, to produce it. Indeed, in his third collection of stories, *Haunters of the Silences*, Roberts (1907) wrote: "I have dared to hope I might be contributing something of value to the final disputed question of animal psychology" (vi).

Turning now to Roberts's wild animal stories, it is worth noting the differences in their construction compared to those of Seton. Although Roberts encountered plenty of animals in the woods of New Brunswick, he was not a naturalist. As he remarks in the preface to *Haunters of the Silences* (1907), some stories drew on "personal, intimate, sympathetic observation," but others were constructed through a combination of "the observations of others" and "the latest scientific information" (vi). Consequently, this meant that Roberts was able to write about a wide variety of species. Where Seton focused on the birds and mammals he could observe in North America, Roberts wrote about insects, amphibians, and fishes, in addition to birds and mammals. By writing sympathetically about underrepresented species, Roberts offers rare explorations of the inner lives of animals whose sentience or ability to feel pain remains controversial today.

As unusual as they might seem, Roberts's representations of curious ants and cautious salmons were all in line with the work of early comparative psychologists. According to Romanes's table of intellectual and emotional development, printed in *Mental Evolution in Animals* (1883), insects (other than hymenoptera) are capable of pain, pleasure, memories, association by contiguity, and recognition of offspring. They can feel surprise, fear, sexual emotions, parental affection, social feelings, pugnacity, industry, and curiosity. Romanes places fishes one step above insects, which means he views them as possessing these same capacities, as well as association by similarity, jealousy, anger, and play. Hymenoptera sit one level below birds, which means they are higher than reptiles, crustaceans, and cephalopods. Consequently, they are listed as capable of all the above, as well as reason, recognition of persons, communication of ideas, affection, and sympathy. It is worth noting here that Romanes does not recognize 'reason' in insects (other than hymenoptera) or fishes.[7]

In *Kindred of the Wild* (1902), Roberts had followed Seton's suit by restricting himself to depictions of birds and mammals. However, by his second and third books—*Watchers of the Trails* (1904) and *Haunters of the Silences* (1907)—Roberts expanded his sympathies to include more species. In these two volumes he offered rich explorations of the inner lives of underrepresented animals, particularly those we tend to consider 'alien' or 'uncharismatic,' such as a fishes and insects. Here, I focus on these depictions to offer a counterbalance to the marginalization of non-mammalian species in animal fiction.

Apart from Roderick Haig-Brown's *Return to the River* (1941) and Frederick Philip Grove's *Consider Her Ways* (1947)—both covered in Chap. 5—most of the texts addressed in this book focus on birds and mammals. Although these might be some of Roberts's lesser-known stories, they offer some of his richest challenges to speciesist thinking. It is almost inevitable that, by empathizing with the perspectives of insects and fishes, he provides a crucial alternative to our tendency towards mechanomorphism. In doing so, Roberts also ends up depicting aspects of their cognitive, emotional, or social complexity that would continue to divide the scientific community for the next century.

In "Master of the Golden Pool," from *Watchers of the Trails*, Roberts (1904) speculates about the inner life of an old male trout. This was his first exploration of a fish's point of view. He opens the story by distinguishing the trout's perspective from those of other creatures. It was "only to the outside world"—to the "dragonfly," "bird," and "red squirrel"—that the "deep water" of the pond "looked black" (27). To the trout, "looking upward to toward the sunlight," the whole pool had a "golden glow" (27). The "sky" of his "world" was the "flat surface" of the water, through which he could not see out "unobstructedly" (27). Instead,

---

[7] In *Animal Intelligence* (1882), Romanes defined reason as the "intentional adaptation of means to ends" (17).

from the "unknown place beyond that sky" came "moving shadows, arrangements of light and dark" (27). Most of these "moving shadows he understood very well" (27–8). When "broad and vague" they did not "greatly interest him;" but "when they got small and sharply black, he knew they might at any instant break through and splash and become real, coloured things, probably good to eat" (28).

This is what Shapiro and Copeland (2005) might describe as "empath[y] with the world-as-experienced by that animal" (345). In a similar way to Seton (1905) in "Badlands Billy," Roberts attempts to construct a unique nonhuman perspective by focusing on sensory experiences. He speculates about the trout's vision and imagines that, perhaps, the pool looks more beautiful underwater. By contrast, the outside world—appealing as it might be to human eyes—becomes a largely irrelevant set of shadows. Even this small speculation helps to show that an animal we might think of as an unfeeling object could have their own unique, individual experiences. Indeed, the trout even knows what is "good to eat" (Roberts 1904, 28). This suggests not only that he has subjective experiences but that he remembers and learns from them too. It means that he makes choices, forms opinions, and has preferences. It indicates that he prefers to eat some things more than others and that they may even taste 'good' too.

Roberts's trout has a memory, sensations of pain and pleasure, preferences, emotions, and feelings of play. The trout also has a "favourite position" in the pond (27). Certain shadows on the water are "always of interest to him," even if he isn't hungry, because "[e]xperience had taught him" that they would be mayflies, "which he liked" (28). Larger, slower shadows were moths, butterflies, beetles, bees, and wasps, which were also "good for food" (28). He would "dart from his lair" at the sight of a frog because they were "much to his taste" as well (29). Sometimes, "when he was not at all hungry, but merely playful, he would rise with a rush at anything [...] seize it between his hard lips and carry it down with him, only to drop it a moment later" (28).

The trout also recognized the shapes of fishermen's lures and "knew the significance" of a "fine thread" in the water (35). The sight of these would stir "an association of pain and fear" in his memory (36). After being caught on a fisherman's hook, the trout always "scrutinized" all unfamiliar shapes to "see if they carried any threadlike attachment" (37). It is by learning from his own experiences that the trout continues "defying every lure of the crafty fisherman" for several years (26). Unfortunately, however, he is finally caught by a novel threat, an unknown "stranger" in his pond: an otter (40). At first, he tries to hide by lying still against a stone, but then becomes "[f]rantic" with "terror" as he attempts to flee (39–40). Sadly, with no experience of otters, the old trout does not escape. Here, we can see that Roberts's fish representation aligns with Romanes's theory of animal intelligence: the trout experiences pain, pleasure, long-term memories, association by similarity and contiguity, surprise, fear, curiosity, and play.

In "The Last Barrier" from *Haunters of the Silences*, Roberts (1907) takes his fish representation further by presenting the biography of an Atlantic salmon. Where "Master of the Golden Pool" explored the product of an older trout's years of experience, Roberts uses the biographical structure of "The Last Barrier" to explore this learning process in depth. Interestingly, in the preface to *Haunters of the Silences*, Roberts (1907) reaffirms his "belief" that the "actions of animals are governed not only by instinct, but also, in varying degree, by processes essentially akin to those of human reason" (vii). In "The Ringwaak Buck" from the same volume, Roberts outlines his theory of animal intelligence. He identifies three sources of "varied knowledge which the wild creatures must carry in their brains" to survive: "inherited instinct," "experience," and "parental teaching" (174–5). It seems likely that Roberts may have drawn inspiration from Seton's (1905) "three sources of wisdom" outlined in the story "Tito" from *Animal Heroes*. One source of learning that Roberts neglects to mention here is observation of others, although he demonstrates its operation in "The Last Barrier."

Roberts's (1907) biography of a salmon demonstrates that instinct, individual experience, and learning through observation are all crucial for survival. As a juvenile, the protagonist experiences "a severe but invaluable lesson" when he is partially caught on a fishing hook (42). Already "somewhat more wary and alert than his fellows," the salmon remembers "ever afterward" to view "floating flies with suspicion" and to inspect them "cautiously" (44). At sea, he encounters new dangers. He watches his companions "stop abruptly and engage in what seemed to him a meaningless struggle" and eventually he detects "a mesh of fine, brown lines, which seemed to surround and grapple with the unfortunate fish" (53). He retreats with "a nervous flurry of speed," not returning to the "dangerous surface" until he is "nearly a mile beyond the throttling peril of the drift-net" (53). He remains "wary enough" to detect other nets but observes their "cruel toll" on his companions (54).

As a mature adult, the salmon returns to the river to spawn. There, he is attracted by the "bright, yellow body of a struggling wasp," before suddenly recalling "a memory, vague but terrifying" of a "sharp point piercing his jaw" and leaves it to be "gobbled up by one of his less wary companions" (54–5). After the "revival" of that "memory," he inspects every fly "to see if any slender, almost invisible lines were attached to it" (55). Here, we can see that the salmon has combined individual experience with social learning. He has experienced the pain of a hook and has watched others being caught in a net. Now, he is cautious of both flies and nets.

It is important to note the ways in which emotion drives these learning experiences. Even from his earliest days, instinctual fear guides the young salmon to avoid danger: "Terrified [...] by the sudden shadow, they hid in the gravel and for some time made no further trial of the dangerous world" (33). Whether acting on instinct, social observation, or experience, the salmon's learning is inherently shaped by emotion. However, Roberts does not describe instances of learning through positive emotions explicitly, even though both fishes do experience them. The trout feels "playful" and finds "enjoyment" in "taste;" the salmon is described as "happy" and is depicted "playing" with his companions (Roberts 1904, 28–9; 1907, 40, 44).

Emotional responses to pain and pleasure remain controversial tropics in fish cognition research. We might think of pain and its associated negative emotions as a survival advantage. Yet, as Jonathan Balcombe (2009) argues, the same is true of pleasure. Pleasure encourages beneficial activities, such as feeding or bonding. Pleasure teaches the trout what is "good to eat" (Roberts 1904, 28). Meanwhile, "playing in the cheerful, shallow 'run' beneath the cedar" helps the young salmon learn how to move through different bodies of water (Roberts 1907, 44). Interestingly, Romanes (1883) identifies both pleasure and pain in fishes, but also recognizes them as the 'lowest' species capable of play. Whilst intense debate still surrounds these topics, both "The Master of the Golden Pool" and "The Last Barrier" offer plausible depictions of fish emotions that offer survival advantages.

As we have seen, a consequence of Roberts's interest in a wide range of species is that we find depictions of intelligence and emotions in animals who are often objectified as 'automatons,' such as insects and fishes. In "The Prisoners of the Pitcher-Plant," printed in *Haunters of the Silences*, Roberts (1907) explores the perspective of an ant. According to Romanes's

(1883) table of emotions, hymenoptera are capable of the same emotions as fishes, as well as sympathy and affection. Unlike fishes, he also finds them able to reason, communicate ideas, and recognize persons. Accordingly, Roberts's (1907) ant experiences "curiosity," "amazement," "bewilder[ment]," "indignation," "panic," and "satisfaction;" she also feels "appalled" and "astonished" (85–91).

Another consequence of Roberts's interest in these more 'alien' species is the opportunity for defamiliarization. When the ant is inadvertently rescued from the pitcher plant, she experiences an "overwhelming cataclysm" descending upon her "tiny world" (90). A "bounding monster" crashes amongst the "clustered pitchers, crushing several to bits and scattering wide the contents of the rest" (90–1). What the ant perceives as a "monster" is a "furry" creature we might think of as traditionally charismatic: "rabbit, fox, or wildcat" (90–1). Likewise, Roberts's (1904) trout from "Master of the Golden Pool" encounters an "appalling," "horrifying phenomenon;" a "creature" with a "long, whitish body," swimming with "wide-sprawling limbs" while making "strange sounds" (31–2). This is the trout's perception of a man swimming in the lake.

The young salmon of "The Last Barrier" encounters "gigantic creatures dashing hither and thither" among the salmon, "snapping them up by twos and threes" (Roberts 1907, 34). Yet, these dangerous "monsters" are actually "young redfins, a couple of inches in length" (34). In these instances, we can see how Roberts extends his imaginative process further than Seton. Both writers imagine nonhuman perspectives that are specific to both the individual and species. Yet, Roberts goes deeper by considering how these perspectives might shape an animal's view of other species.

In two connected stories from *Watchers of the Trails*—"The Little Wolf of the Pool" and "The Little Wolf of the Air"—Roberts (1904) narrates the life of a female dragonfly: first as a naiad (the aquatic larval stage) and then as an adult. In the first story, the dragonfly is introduced from the perspective of a male tadpole. He watches the "fantastic-looking creature" swim into view, its head covered by a "smooth, cleft, shield-like mask," giving "the creature an expression both mysterious and terrible" (66–7). Roberts's language of monstrosity is an extension of these species-specific perspectives. The tadpole's "terror" at this "monster" is appropriate because, moments later, she eats him (68).

In the next story, "The Little Wolf of the Air," the dragonfly has matured into a "slender," "spritelike" being (74). She hunts amongst other dragonflies who are described as "winged and flashing gems" or "daring iridescences" (74). Here, Roberts focuses on the features that make dragonflies appealing to humans. This may be due to the introduction of a human observer into the story. This was an unusual choice for Roberts, as we usually only find human characters in Seton's stories. The man watches as the dragonfly lays her eggs. He reflects that he "liked all dragon-flies," but had "developed a personal interest" in "this one in particular" (79–80). "Suddenly and violently," however, the man jumps to his feet, "hoping to chase her away from" an "approaching doom," but is too late (80). As he jumped, "the big frog sprang, and a long, darting, cleft tongue clutched the busy fly, dragging her down" (80).

Through these two stories, Roberts explores our subjective relationships with other species. By narrating the end through human eyes, he emphasizes the contradictions in our concern for animal. His empathy with the dragonfly mimics our own as we, too, have been observing her for some time. Yet, the ending of her biography is ambivalent. Roberts's narration observes that, in killing the dragonfly, the frog had "avenged" the "lives of a thousand tadpoles," though he does not know it (80). Of course, we can read this as a lesson in Darwinian ecology. However, Roberts seems to be making a larger point. Along with his use of 'wolf' in both titles, he makes a connection with wolf predation and conservation. To do so, he draws an unusual comparison between dragonflies and wolves:

> With appetites insatiable, ferocity implacable, strength and courage prodigious for their stature, to call them little wolves of the air is perhaps to wrong the ravening grey pack whose howlings strike terror down the corridors of the winter forest. (74)

In other words, the predator-prey relationships that cause us moral concern are often motivated by anthropocentric priorities—whether it is the preservation of a species as a 'game' animal or as an 'attractive' curiosity. Afterall, the man from the story "liked all dragon-flies" (80).

Overall, Roberts's engagement with animal advocacy is more ambiguous than Seton's. Both men use the language of compassion and kinship, but only Seton mentions animal rights. Roberts seems more hesitant to make such declarations. Instead, he restricts himself to a language of kinship, which we can find in both the title of and preface to *Kindred of the Wild*. He argues that the wild animal story can lead us "back to the old kinship of the earth" and an "intimacy" between humans and animals that would encourage in all of us a more "humane" heart and a greater "spiritual" understanding (Roberts 1902, 29). Roberts gestures towards a less exploitative relationship with animals but seems uncertain how to proceed. Some stories argue against the captivity of wild animals and others include humans who attempt to protect animals.[8] On the whole, however, Roberts resists advocating for anything specific in favour of presenting a generally sympathetic view of a wide range of species. He also attempts to unpack certain aspects of speciesism, anthropocentricism, and the hypocrisies in our attitudes towards animals.

I would suggest that the two men's experiences could account for their different relationships with animal advocacy. Perhaps Roberts's approach is less well articulated than Seton's because he had less experience with animals. On the other hand, his stories do manage to inhabit a nonhuman perspective to a greater degree. It could be that Roberts's literary and academic experiences gave access to a wider range of techniques. For instance, Roberts utilizes defamiliarization much more than Seton who tends to maintain the perspective of the observer (often a fictionalized version of himself). This is an important technique that we will see used to great effect in later twentieth-century texts, such as *Consider Her Ways* (1947) and *The White Bone* (1998).

It is worth noting, however, that like Seton, Roberts exposes the limits of his own sympathy for animals when criticized. I suspect that Seton's unusual moments of anthropocentrism may have resulted, in part, from the accusations that arose during the Nature Fakers controversy. In Roberts's case, this is certainly the cause. In his preface to *Watchers of the Trails*, the volume that he dedicated to Seton, Roberts (1904) mentions a "very distinguished author" who has "gently called me to account" for "ascribing to my animals human motives and the mental processes of man" (ix). This is one of Roberts's few direct responses to the Nature Fakers controversy. The author he describes is, of course, John Burroughs. To defend himself, Roberts (1904) writes:

[8] In "The Moonlight Trails," the first story in *Kindred of the Wild*, a young boy reflects that he "loved" animals and was "fiercely intolerant" of "all cruelty toward them;" indeed it "hurt him to see them hurt" (Roberts 1902, 40). This is a rare declaration from Roberts, however. It is much more common for him to depict the distress caused to wild animals in captivity. Almost all his books feature at least one story with this message. In "The Homesickness of Kehonka" from *Kindred of the Wild*, Roberts depicts a captive goose's intense desire to migrate, even though his wings have been clipped. The story "Return to the Trails," printed in *Watchers of the Trails* (1904), explores the experiences of a bear who escapes from a circus. "The Summons of the North" from *Haunters of the Silences* (1907) features a miserable polar bear who dies in a zoo.

The psychological processes of the animals are so simple, so obvious, in comparison with those of man, their actions flow so directly from their springs of impulse, that it is, as a rule, an easy matter to infer the motives which are at any one moment impelling them. (ix)

It is interesting that both Seton and Roberts resort to objectification of animals in the face of criticism. Evidently, mechanomorphism is the remedy to anthropomorphism. This is something we will encounter in subsequent chapters of this book. In both Seton and Roberts, we can see the emerging discrepancy between their rich zoocentric representations of animals (including those commonly considered insentient automatons) and some strikingly anthropocentric statements made in the prefaces of their books. This may be the beginning of an increasing concern with the stigma of concern for animals. Certainly, it is a precursor to what we find in the next generation of animal fiction writers. In Chap. 4, we will find that authors writing in the aftermath of the Nature Fakers controversy tend to make oddly reductive statements about animal intelligence in otherwise vividly zoocentric texts.

Conclusion

We can better understand both the wild animal story and Nature Fakers controversy through the history of comparative psychology. At heart, Seton's and Roberts's writing mirrored the 'introspective' methods of Romanes or Mills. When seen through this lens, the Nature Fakers controversy becomes less about the credibility of Seton or Roberts. Rather, it expresses contemporary concerns about scientific authority. We can see how the transition from 'introspection' to experimentation in comparative psychology impacted interpretation of their stories. Descriptions of animal intelligence and emotions, which would have been accepted a decade earlier, were now deemed anthropomorphic and unrealistic. If nothing else, the Nature Fakers controversy should remind us that what is considered 'anthropomorphic' is not fixed or universal; it is culturally and historically determined. Over the next two chapters, we will see how efforts to combat anthropomorphism produced a reductive (and similarly inaccurate) mechanomorphism instead. Not until the cognitive revolution in 1970s, will we find confident discussions of animal minds, intelligence, or emotions in science or animal fiction.

REFERENCES

Adams, John Coldewell. (1986) 2014. *Sir Charles God Damn*. Toronto: University of Toronto Press.

Anderson, H. Allen. 1986. *The Chief: Ernest Thompson Seton and the Changing West*. College Station: Texas A&M University Press.

Atwood, Margaret. 1972. *Survival: A Thematic Guide to Canadian Literature*. Toronto: Anansi.

Balcombe, Jonathan. 2009. Animal Pleasure and Its Moral Significance. *Applied Animal Behaviour Science*. 118: 208–216. https://doi.org/10.1016/j.applanim.2009.02.012.

Bekoff, Marc. 2000. Animal Emotions: Exploring Passionate Natures. *BioScience*. 50 (10, October): 861–870. https://doi.org/10.1641/0006-3568(2000)05 0[0861:AEEPN]2.0.CO;2.

———. 2007. *The Emotional Lives of Animals: A Leading Scientist Explores Animal Joy, Sorrow, and Empathy – And Why They Matter*. Novato: New World Library.

Boakes, Robert. 1984. *From Darwin to Behaviourism: Psychology and the Minds of Animals*. Cambridge: Cambridge University Press.

Cappon, James. 1923. *Charles G.D. Roberts*. Toronto: Ryerson Press.

Dunayer, Joan. 2001. *Animal Equality: Language and Liberation*. Derwood: Ryce.

Forkey, Neil S. 2012. *Canadians and the Natural Environment to the Twenty-First Century*. Toronto: University of Toronto Press.

Galef, Bennett G. 2012. Social Learning and Traditions in Animals: Evidence, Definitions, and Relationship to Human Culture. *WIREs Cognitive Science*. 3 (6, November/December): 581–592. https://doi.org/10.1002/wcs.1196.

Lucas, Alec. 1997. Nature Writing in English. In *The Oxford Companion to Canadian Literature*, ed. William Toye and Eugene Benson, 786–792. Oxford: Oxford University Press.

Lutts, Ralph H. 1990. *Nature Fakers: Wildlife, Science & Sentiment*. Colorado: Fulcrum Publishing.

———. 1998. *The Wild Animal Story*. Philadelphia: Temple University Press.

Mills, Wesley. 1898. *The Nature and Development of Animal Intelligence*. New York: Macmillan.

Polk, James. 1972. Lives of the Hunted. *Canadian Literature*. 53: 51–59.

Roberts, Charles G.D. 1892. Do Seek Their Meat from God. *Harper's Monthly*. 86 (511, December): 120–123.

———. 1902. *Kindred of the Wild*. Boston: L. C. Page & Co.

———. 1904. *The Watchers of the Trails*. Toronto: The Copp, Clark Company.

———. 1907. *The Haunters of the Silences*. Boston: L. C. Page & Co.

———. 1913. Ernest Thompson Seton. *The Bookman*, December: 147–149.

Romanes, George. 1882. *Animal Intelligence*. London: Keegan Paul, Trench, & Co.

———. (1883) 1884. *Mental Evolution in Animals.* New York: D. Appleton & Co.

Salt, Henry S. (1892) 1980. *Animals' Rights: Considered in Relation to Social Progress.* London: Centaur.

Sandlos, John. 2000. From Within Fur and Feathers: Animals in Canadian Literature. *TOPIA: Canadian Journal of Cultural Studies.* 4: 73–91. https://doi.org/10.3138/topia.4.73.

Seton, Ernest Thompson. 1894. The King of Currumpaw: A Wolf Story. *Scribner's Magazine.* 16 (5, November): 618–628.

———. 1898. *Wild Animals I Have Known.* New York: Charles Scriber's Sons.

———. 1901. *Lives of the Hunted.* London: David Nutt.

———. 1905. *Animal Heroes.* London: Constable & Company.

———. 1951. *Trail of an Artist-Naturalist.* London: Hodder and Stoughton.

Shapiro, Kenneth J., and Marion W. Copeland. 2005. Toward a Critical Theory of Animal Issues in Fiction. *Society and Animals.* 13 (4): 343–346. https://doi.org/10.1163/156853005774653636.

Wadland, John. 2008. Review: *Other Selves. American Review of Canadian Studies.* 38 (2): 259–262. https://doi.org/10.1080/02722010809481714.

Walsh, Sue. 2015. Nature Faking and the Problem of the 'Real'. *ISLE.* 22 (1, Winter): 132–153. https://doi.org/10.1093/isle/ist032.

Whitehead, Hal. 2003. *Sperm Whales: Social Evolution in the Ocean.* Chicago: University of Chicago Press.

Whitelock, William Wallace. 1901. Ernest Seton-Thompson. *The Critic.* 39 (July–December): 320–325.

Witt, David L. 2010. *Ernest Thompson Seton: The Life and Legacy of an Artist and Conservationist.* Layton: Gibbs Smith.

PART II

Adaptation

CHAPTER 4

1900s–1950s Contexts

This chapter charts a growing fear of anthropomorphism in the early twentieth century. As a result, we find a shift towards mechanomorphic perceptions of animals in science, as well as wildlife conservation. In response to the 'introspective' methods of comparative psychology, the new fields of behaviourism and ethology emphasized objectivity, experimentation, and external observation. To avoid speculations about consciousness or emotions, these approaches established the idea that animal minds were 'unknowable' to humans. By strengthening the divide between humans and other animals, however, these developments also sent ripples of mechanomorphic thinking into other areas. The language of machinery and productivity entered ecology and wildlife management. Within this atmosphere, humane societies made little significant progress and discussions of animal rights were absent. As a result, there were no meaningful improvements to federal anti-cruelty laws during the opening decades of the twentieth century.

NATURE FAKING

When the heat of the Nature Fakers controversy died down, not much had changed. The fierce terms in which it was conducted had achieved little, apart from providing a new insult within the scientific community. Undoubtedly, the concept of a 'nature faker' grew beyond the specific

© The Author(s), under exclusive license to Springer Nature
Switzerland AG 2023
C. Allmark-Kent, *Literature, Science, and Animal Advocacy in Canada*, Palgrave Studies in Animals and Literature,
https://doi.org/10.1007/978-3-031-40556-3_4

issues of the wild animal story. Many people using the phrase would have been unaware of the Nature Fakers controversy itself. Scientific books and journals from the early twentieth century are littered with references to the problem of 'nature faking.' We find vague comments about the "perversities" of the nature fakers and their "fanciful" interpretations of animal behaviour (Wheeler 1910, 507; Philips 1903, 118). Book reviews might criticize an author's "tendency" towards nature faking or, alternatively, reassure readers that "there is no flagrant nature-faking" to be found (Taylor 1908, 143; Bates 1954, 318). Other articles, such as those by S. F. Aaron (1926), expressed fears that the numbers of nature fakers were still "growing" (322). Indeed, Aaron (1935) wrote a second article about the problem nine years later.

By the 1930s, the phrase 'nature faker' had also spread into the National Parks Service. It was used as a derogatory term for rangers who "taught natural history to park visitors" (Lutts 1990, 189). Other insults included "pansy pickers," "bug sniffers," "posy pickers," "tree huggers," and "butterfly chasers" (189, 283). Evidently, the associations between heteronormative masculinity and scientific authority that had informed the controversy remained attached to the idea of being a 'nature faker' over the subsequent decades.[1]

The key players of the Nature Fakers debate did not amend their positions and so, in time, each returned to their own work. Yet, the controversy left a clear impression on both Ernest Thompson Seton and Charles G. D. Roberts. Seton seemed to lose his zeal for the wild animal story. He continued to write animal stories, but only a few. For the next twenty years, Seton returned his focus to scientific writing. His most significant achievements during this period were two monumental works, the two-volume *Life Histories of Northern Animals* (1909) and the four-volume *Lives of Game Animals* (1925–1927). The latter sprawled over 3115 pages with 1500 of Seton's own illustrations, fifty range maps covering over a hundred species, and numerous wildlife photographs (Witt 2010, 90). Whilst Seton might be remembered for nature faking, his science writing did offer solid contributions to the fields of natural history, ecology, animal psychology, and North American mammalogy.

By contrast, Roberts's reputation was relatively untarnished. His stories had drawn less attention during the debates and, for the most part, he had

---

[1] Even in the 1960s, books and articles were still accusing the National Parks Service of "emotionalism and nature-faking" (Major 1961, 456).

not engaged with his detractors directly. His position within the Canadian literary canon remained strong and he returned to the poetry, fiction, and nonfiction for which he was otherwise known. He was still the 'father' of Canadian poetry and was even knighted by King George in 1935. Nonetheless, Roberts still wrote wild animal stories and kept at it longer than Seton. Yet it seems that the public's enthusiasm for animal stories was waning. Despite Roberts's reputation, editors who could have easily afforded to publish his new stories were no longer interested (Adams 1986, 160). In 1930, Roberts's New York agent, Paul Reynolds, told him that his latest story about a cat, "Tabitha Blue," was not as desirable as his older work. He wrote to Roberts: "it is well written but [...] the stories of yours in the past [...] were about wilder animals and were more dramatic" (160). Roberts's final book of animal stories, *Eyes of the Wilderness*, was published in 1933. The reviews were mixed.

It is important to note that neither the controversy nor the label 'nature fakers' prevented Seton's or Roberts's subsequent involvement with wildlife conservation. Whatever damage had been done to their reputations, both were still public figures who held considerable influence. The enormous popularity of their wild animal stories had created a mass of readers concerned about wildlife. In the early decades of the twentieth century, Seton and Roberts were two of the most influential participants in a surge of popular support for conservation. Whilst Seton was the more active lobbyist, both men contributed to the signing of the Migratory Birds Convention in 1916. They were spokesmen for an unofficial, but powerful, coalition of naturalists, writers, hunters, and scientists from both Canada and the United States (Burnett 2003, 29). This was a period in which dedicated groups and committed individuals were integral to preventing species loss when the actions of government were insufficient.

Wildlife Management

At the turn of the twentieth century, the government's approach to wildlife conservation was focused on restricting who was allowed to kill certain animals. Bounties were set on the heads of predators, meanwhile rural subsistence hunters—both Indigenous and non-Indigenous—were severely restricted. These measures motivated by a new attitude towards wildlife: an "ethic of exploitation that endorsed non-commercial and non-consumptive use" (Loo 2006, 16). The operative idea was that "Canada had reached a stage in its development where it was no longer necessary to consume wild meat" (26). Rather conveniently, these new policies preserved wildlife for the recreational hunting of white upper- and middle-class tourists.

The 'sportsman's creed' asserted that wild animals were too important to be eaten. Instead, they were required to elevate the human condition by "providing sport and diversion for modern men" (Loo 2006, 27). These ideas were the product of anti-modernism, a belief that modern life was empty, sterile, and lacking meaning (29). Urban, middle-class, white men seem to have been particularly affected by the "over-civilizing" consequences of modernity (30). Interestingly, we can see early elements of such thinking in Roberts's (1902) preface to *Kindred of the Wild*. He describes the wild animal story as a "potent emancipator" from the "shop-worn utilities" of which we "grow weary" (29). It helps us "return to nature," back to the "old kinship of earth," with the promise of "refreshment and renewal" (29). Alongside such revitalizing nature writing, many sought a cure through 'authentic' experiences in the great Canadian 'wilderness.' Thankfully, national parks provided a carefully managed version of nature.

As discussed in Chap. 2, the first national parks were established for the benefit of wealthy white tourists. Not only did they not serve the needs of animals—or even local peoples—they required the removal of Indigenous communities from their traditional territories. The lure of economic development, tourism, and traffic for Canadian railways drove the creation of many parks (Burnett 2003, 6). Ironically, these changes threatened the very wild animals that tourists wanted to see. Indeed, tourism itself was a threat to wildlife: from the eradication of unwanted 'vermin' to the violence of hunter-tourists themselves. In order to create an 'authentic' experience with a wild animal in its 'natural habitat,' nature needed to be managed. This required killing certain species while actively increasing the numbers of others. In 1911, the Commissioner of Parks, Howard Douglas, purchased 703 Plains Bison and shipped them from Montana to Wainwright, Alberta (Burnett 2006, 7). He even established a new national park for them: Buffalo National Park. Thus, it was the interests of tourists—not the animals themselves—determining which species belonged where.

Despite the notional aim of preventing species loss, there can be little doubt that these conservation efforts were self-serving. Canada's wild animals were a natural *resource*. At a 1919 conference for the Conservation of Game, Fur-Bearing Animals, and Other Wild Life, Arthur Meighen, the Minister of the Interior, declared: "We have only realized very late the importance of great truths—that the conservation of our game is a vital subject for consideration and attention as is the conservation of any other of our natural resources" (quoted in Foster 1998, 3). The contradiction in Meighen's words encapsulates the attitude of the time. As with "any other of our natural resources," wild animals were to be both protected and exploited (3). Moreover, it is also significant that he specifies the preservation of 'game.'

Conservation ensured that wild animals were commodities, preserved so that they be killed by the right person at the right time. There was no question of preventing their exploitation altogether. This attitude was shaped by American Progressivist thinking. Rather than prohibit exploitation, it promoted efficiency and the "wise use" of natural resources (Loo 2006, 19). These ideas would continue to shape the government's approach to conservation for several decades.

Canadian conservation had been undergoing a long process of bureaucratization for decades. The government consolidated provincial game laws, centralized enforcement, and created new offices, such as that of the game warden (Loo 2006, 18). Of course, the rising influence of science was integral to this process. Previously, the government had shown strikingly little knowledge about wildlife. Policies had been dictated by the whims of recreational hunters, rather than the needs of wild animals or rural peoples. However, the professionalization of the sciences during the nineteenth century had now been fully realized. Scientific authority was absolute.

In 1927, Charles Elton, a zoologist from the University of Oxford (with connections to Canada, coincidentally), published a landmark book, *Animal Ecology*. This established the new field of ecology and it would have a profound influence on conservation. Combined with the emerging discipline of wildlife management, Canadian conservation became a numbers game. As Loo (2006) remarks, towards the middle of the century, the "gap between Progressivist rhetoric and conservation practice closed" (122). Government wildlife work became a coordinated "research-based enterprise directed by scientists and formally trained personnel" (122).

By the mid-twentieth century, a 'New Ecology' was describing the natural world in economic terms. Donald Worster (1994) labels it as "mechanistic, energy-based bioeconomics" (314). This new approach studied the transfer of energy through ecosystems from plants to herbivores to carnivores and scavengers. From this perspective, plants and animals became producers, manufacturers, traders, and consumers. With increasing abstraction, scientists would describe the "field-mouse production of an acre of grassland" or the "'energy budget' of a lizard on a tree trunk" (311). This meant that ecologists could now predict the 'yield' of a habitat and, perhaps, increase its 'productivity.'

New Ecology took the aspirations of Canadian conservation from mere preservation and 'wise use' to an active intervention that ensured ecosystems produced the 'correct' numbers of the desired species. For a government viewing wildlife as a natural resource, this was a useful way of thinking. As Worster (1994) observes, New Ecology held a built-in bias towards a "controlled environment" that served the "best interests of man's economy" (314). By the 1950s, this mechanistic view of nature was fully in place. Now, the natural world had become a well-running machine which, if properly managed, could be used to maximize profits.

It is worth noting that this utilitarian view of nature came at the same time as the science of animal behaviour was also describing animals in increasingly mechanistic terms. During the early-to-mid twentieth century, we find the alignment of three key factors: the rising influence of science in Canadian wildlife conservation, the emergence of New Ecology's mechanistic view of nature, and the growth of mechanomorphism in the study of animal behaviour. In other words, New Ecology's mechanomorphic approach to conservation coincided with the height of North American behaviourism in the 1950s. For John B. Watson, the founder of behaviourism, animals were little different to machines; indeed, neither were humans.

ETHOLOGY AND BEHAVIOURISM

In the early years of the twentieth century, comparative psychology was split between introspection and experimentation. Introspection became associated with anecdotes, anthropomorphism, and amateurs. It seemed an unscientific remnant of the previous century. Even in 1898, Edward Thorndike had argued that such work would be described better as eulogy than psychology. He wrote: "How can scientists who write like lawyers, defending animals against the charge of having no power of rationality, be at the same time impartial judges on the bench?" (4).

For Thorndike (1898), anecdotal evidence was the central issue. Given the "well-nigh universal" human tendency to "find the marvellous wherever it can," anecdotes tended to showcase the unusual or exceptional, which gave rise to an "*abnormal* or *super-normal*" psychology of animals (3–5, emphasis original). Even the work of reliable observers was unscientific due to inescapable issues with the anecdotal method. These were: that observations could only describe single cases, they could not be repeated, the conditions could not be regulated, and the previous history of the animal could not be known (5). According to Thorndike, the only remedy would be to replace observations and anecdotes with experiments.

In her textbook, *The Animal Mind*, Margaret Floy Washburn (1908) described Thorndike's work as the "first definite effect" of the experimental movement "upon the study of the animal mind" (11). Experimentation bestowed comparative psychology with the objectivity necessary for it to become a credible scientific field. These changing attitudes then set the stage for the emergence of behaviourism. In *Behaviour: An Introduction to Comparative Psychology*, Watson (1914) described behaviourism as a "purely objective experimental branch of natural science" with the "theoretical goal" of the "prediction and control of behaviour" (1). He justified this aim through the argument that all behaviour could be explained through a simple relationship between stimulus and response. Indeed, he conceptualized the activities of all organisms in this way, including humans.

Watson (1925) argued that a stimulus could be "an object in the general environment" or changes in the "physiological condition of the animal" (6–7). A response could be anything the animal does, from "turning toward or away from a light" or "jumping at a sound" to "building a skyscraper" or "writing books" (7). Even speech and thought fell into this category: "Speaking overtly or to ourselves (thinking) is just as objective a type of behaviour as baseball" (6). Integral to this approach was Watson's insistence that the "real field of psychology" must be "what we can *observe*" (6). By reframing every activity as a 'response,' behaviourism made obsolete all the questions about animal reasoning that had previously preoccupied introspective psychology. Indeed, by the 1930s, behaviourism had completely dominated North American comparative psychology.

One of the most significant and far-reaching consequences of behaviourism was that the animal mind became suddenly 'unknowable.' From the beginnings of comparative psychology, it had been taken for granted that nonhuman animals had minds and that those minds could be studied and eventually understood by humans. The introspective method was built on this assumption. As part of the backlash against its perceived tendency towards anthropomorphism, the question of whether we can ever know the minds of animals was raised. Washburn (1908) summarized the fundamental "dissimilarity between animal minds and ours" by focusing on physiological differences (3). She argued that if "my neighbour's mind is a mystery to me, how great is the mystery which looks out of the eyes of a dog, and how insoluble the problem presented by the mind of an invertebrate animal, an ant or spider!" (2).

These concerns were taken a stage further by behaviourism. Not only had Watson insisted that animal psychology should only concern itself with the observable, but behaviourism had also taken Morgan's Canon as its central tenet. In *An Introduction to Comparative Psychology*, Conwy Lloyd Morgan (1894) had proposed a remedy to anthropomorphism:

> In no case may we interpret an action as the outcome of the exercise of a higher psychical faculty, if it can be interpreted as the outcome of the exercise of one which stands lower on the psychological scale. (53)

It is worth noting, however, that Morgan had not intended his rule to be used so dogmatically to argue against the existence of animal intelligence.[2] Nevertheless, these ideas combined to have a powerful effect. For the rest of the century, most scientists of animal behaviour would insist that questions of animal minds or consciousness were fundamentally unanswerable.

Across the Atlantic, European researchers had been drawing parallel conclusions about animal minds. In a similar way to behaviourism, ethology had developed in reaction to the introspective methods of comparative psychology in the nineteenth century. The field had a long history, but it was fairly undeveloped until the work of Konrad Lorenz and Niko Tinbergen between the 1930s and 1950s. At the same time as behaviourism was developing within psychology, ethology was emerging from zoology and natural history. As a biological approach to animal behaviour, early ethology emphasized the observation and description of innate, naturally occurring behaviours in a wide range of species. This meant a focus on inherited, instinctual responses, observed in the wild. These methods developed in reaction to behaviourism's reliance on controlled, laboratory testing of a few species. Ethology held that behaviourism's value was limited to the study of arbitrary, learned actions in an artificial, human-controlled environment.

---

[2] As George A. Miller (1962) puts it, Morgan understood that it was almost impossible to describe the activities of other animals without projecting *any* mental characteristics or using at least *some* anthropomorphic language. Instead, all that "Morgan had hoped for were a few reasonable rules for playing the anthropomorphic game" (215).

Whilst ethology and behaviourism opposed each other on most points, both rejected any discussion of inner subjective states in animals. In *The Study of Instinct* Tinbergen (1951) reasoned that, because we cannot observe these states, it is idle to even debate their existence and any effort to study them would just impede ethology's progress. However, ethology's emphasis on observation and description still posed a dilemma for the researcher. How to write about animals without inferring the individual's experience or intent? In response, ethologists found a solution similar to that of the behaviourists. Rather than the basic descriptive language of introspective comparative psychology, both ethology and behaviourism developed technical terms aimed at greater objectivity. Despite their opposing approaches and methods, both fields adopted a similar model of description that focused solely on the relationship between stimulus and response (whether learned or innate). As Eileen Crist (1999) observes, an inevitable consequence of such language was a mechanomorphic depiction of animals (89).

Of course, the irony is that mechanomorphism is no more accurate than anthropomorphism. Nonetheless, it is important to recognize that the scientific study of animals was guided by mechanomorphic language on both sides of the Atlantic for much of the twentieth century. Decades before, descriptions of animal activities had taken the individual's mentation (internal mental processes, such as awareness or intentionality) as a given. Now, a language without mentation was required in both behaviourism and ethology. This shift in perception had widespread consequences. Crist (1999) notes that the change in language produced an "objectification" (8). Animals' behaviours "emerge as involuntary," as if they are being "compulsively steered by" stimuli "beyond their control and comprehension" (8). Regardless of their different methods, both behaviourism and ethology both produced reductive or objectifying explanations of animal activities. Thus, it is not difficult to see how these developments would lead to public perceptions of animals as 'mechanistic.'

Animal Protection

Between the 1900s and 1950s, there were few significant changes to Canadian anti-cruelty legislation. In 1905, section 512 of the Canadian Criminal Code, "Cruelty to Animals," was renumbered as section 542. In 1925, *An Act to Amend the Criminal Code* expanded the definition of animal cruelty offenses to include: "abandons in distress" and "fails to provide and supply food, water and shelter" (*An Act to Amend the Criminal Code*, SC 1925, c.38, s.12). In 1930, the words "proper and sufficient food, water, bedding, care and shelter" were added (*An Act to Amend the Criminal Code*, SC 1930, c.11 s.11). In 1938, section 542 (a) was repealed. It was reintroduced but without reference to food, water, bedding, care, or shelter (*An Act to Amend the Criminal Code*, SC 1938, c.44 s.35). In 1953, the Criminal Code was revised for clarity and consistency. Animal laws were reorganized into sections 385–389 but remained under "Part IX: Wilful and Forbidden Acts in Respect of Certain Property" (*Criminal Code*, SC 1953–4, c.51, s.385–389). Other than some rewording and minor amendments, the substance of the laws was largely unchanged.

The laws of the 1953–4 Criminal Code were clearly built on the framework established in 1892. They introduced some subtle changes to wording, which meant that "wantonly" became "wilfully" and "proper and sufficient" became "suitable and adequate" (*Criminal Code*, SC 1953–4, c.51, s.385–389). Rather than "beats, binds, ill-treats, abuses, or overdrives or tortures" from the original code of 1892, the new offences became more specific. Sections 385–6 address "Cattle and Other Animals" and describes "wilfully" killing, maiming, wounding, poisoning, or injuring any "cattle," "dogs, birds, or animals [...] kept for a lawful purpose" (s.385–6).

Section 387 is titled "Cruelty to Animals" and specifies "unnecessary pain, suffering or injury," and "wilful neglect" (*Criminal Code*, SC 1953–4, c.51, s.387). Section 388 prohibits the keeping of cock fighting pits and section 389 establishes regulations for the transportation of cattle (s.388–389). As with the previous iterations of the Criminal Code, protections for wild animals only applied when in captivity. Thus, the law against "wilfully" and "without reasonable excuse," poisoning "an animal or bird wild by nature" only dealt with those "kept in captivity" and did not interfere with the poisoning of feral or non-captive wild animals (s.385–387). Hence, the predator bounty system, integral to twentieth-century Canadian 'wildlife management' could continue undisturbed.

Given the turbulent context of the early twentieth century—two world wars and economic depression—it is no surprise that little progress was made in Canadian animal protection. Mechanistic perceptions of animals in the sciences made the identification of 'suffering' less clear. Meanwhile, as we have seen, the government's approach to conservation was driven largely by economic need: more 'game' meant more tourists. Elaine Hughes and Christine Meyer (2000) observe that, until the First World War, humane societies had been focused on "working animals and blood sports" (27). However, early twentieth-century urbanization meant that animal exploitation moved out of the city. Horses were replaced with cars and the cruelty of animal agriculture became less visible. Thus, public sentiment moved to the plight of companion animals (27–8). Again, the urban upper- and middle-class supporters of humane societies steered Canadian advocacy away from more radical iterations of animal protection (just as they had done in the previous century). By focusing on cats and dogs, they ensured that the exploitation of farm animals remained "out of sight, out of mind" (28).

However, we can see the beginnings of change in the late 1950s. By 1957, animal protection organizations across the country had coalesced into the Canadian Federation of Humane Societies, the first national group of its kind. Their increased influence is clear in the parliamentary 'humane slaughter' debates of 1957–1959. Hansards from both the Senate and House of Commons contain repeated references to the "great deal of attention" that humane slaughter had received in recent years, including multiple appeals from "humane societies," efforts from "many thousands of citizens across this country," and "hundreds of letters from constituents" (Canada 1959a, 1059; 1959b, 6076, 6077). In a House of Commons Debate from 15th July 1959, Margaret Aitken uses the example of the Toronto Humane Society to demonstrate changing public attitudes. She explains that when they began campaigning for humane slaughter in 1948, the "main obstacle was apathy, indifference and even hostility of the general public," but that "apathy has now disappeared" (1959b, 6077). Evidently, the first stirrings of the twentieth-century animal rights movement were beginning to emerge.[3]

---

[3] The Humane Slaughter of Animals Act was passed in 1960. Yet, it is worth noting that, even such a limited attempt at animal protection did not last long. Any emphasis on the animals themselves would be undermined in 1985 when the act was repealed and incorporated into the Meat Inspection Act. Just as anti-cruelty laws only protected animals as property, so too were animals intended for slaughter only protected as objects under meat trade regulations.

CONCLUSION

To some extent, we can read the events of this chapter as a reaction to the changes described in Chap. 2. Evolutionary theory, early comparative psychology, animal rights discourses, and popular wild animal stories had seemed to bring the gap between humans and other animals closer together. By the early twentieth century, however, the burgeoning fields of ethology and behaviourism had reinforced the fundamental impossibility of knowing the minds of other animals. Rejecting the study of animal minds meant that any discussion of animals having subjective inner states, such as emotions, would be seen as unscientific for decades. This led to mechanomorphic descriptions of animals in which they seemed to act without intention or awareness. Because this type of language seemed objective and unsentimental, it encouraged the spread of reductive attitudes towards animals for much of the twentieth century. Even writers of animal fiction were affected. As we will discover in the next chapter, authors writing in the wake of the Nature Fakers controversy became considerably more cautious around the topics of animal intelligence or emotions compared to Seton or Roberts.

REFERENCES

Aaron, S.F. 1926. Nature Faking. *Scientific American*. 134 (5, May): 322–323.
———. 1935. Nature Faking Again. *Scientific American*. 153 (4, October): 186–187.
Adams, John Coldewell. (1986) 2014. *Sir Charles God Damn*. Toronto: University of Toronto Press.
An Act to Amend the Criminal Code, SC, 1925, c.38, s.12.
An Act to Amend the Criminal Code, SC, 1930, c.11, s.11.
An Act to Amend the Criminal Code, SC, 1938, c.44., s.35.
Bates, Marston. 1954. Publications Received. *The American Naturalist*. 88. (841, July–August: 318–319.
Burnett, J. Alexander. 2003. *A Passion for Wildlife: The History of the Canadian Wildlife Service*. Vancouver: UBC Press.
Canada, Parliament. *Debates of the Senate*, 24th Parl, 2nd Sess, (15 Jan–18 Jul 1959a).
———. *House of Commons Debates*, 24th Parl, 2nd Sess, Vol 5 (25 Jun–18 Jul 1959b).
Criminal Code, SC 1953-4, c C.51.
Crist, Eileen. 1999. *Images of Animals: Anthropomorphism and Animal Mind*. Philadelphia: Temple University Press.

Foster, Janet. 1998. *Working for Wildlife: The Beginnings of Preservation in Canada*. Toronto: University of Toronto Press.

Hughes, Elaine L., and Christiane Meyer. 2000. Animal Welfare Law in Canada and Europe. *Animal Law*. 6 (23): 23–76.

Loo, Tina. 2006. *States of Nature: Conserving Canada's Wildlife in the Twentieth Century*. Vancouver: UBC Press.

Lutts, Ralph H. 1990. *Nature Fakers: Wildlife, Science & Sentiment*. Colorado: Fulcrum Publishing.

Major, Jack. 1961. Ecology and Wilderness. *Ecology*. 42 (2, April): 455–457.

Miller, George A. 1962. *Psychology: The Science of Mental Life*. New York: Harper & Row.

Morgan, Conwy Lloyd. 1894. *An Introduction to Comparative Psychology*. London: Walter Scott.

Philips, E.F. 1903. Social Order of the Honeybee. *Social Science*. 5 (2, February–April): 186–191.

Roberts, Charles G.D. 1902. *Kindred of the Wild*. Boston: L. C. Page & Co.

Taylor, Norman. 1908. Review: *The Guide to Nature and to Nature Literature*. *Torreya*. 8 (6, June): 141–143.

Thorndike, Edward L. 1898. Animal Intelligence: An Experimental Study of the Associative Processed in Animals. *Psychological Review Monograph Supplement*. 2 (8, June): 1–109.

Tinbergen, Niko. (1951) 1989. *The Study of Instinct*. Oxford: Clarendon Press.

Washburn, Margaret Floy. 1908. *The Animal Mind: A Textbook of Comparative Psychology*. New York: Macmillan Company.

Watson, John B. 1914. *Behavior: An Introduction to Comparative Psychology*. New York: Henry Holt and Company.

———. 1925. *Behaviorism*. New York: W.W. Norton & Co.

Wheeler, William Morton. 1910. *Ants: Their Structure, Development and Behavior*. New York: Columbia University Press.

Witt, David L. 2010. *Ernest Thompson Seton: The Life and Legacy of an Artist and Conservationist*. Layton, UT: Gibbs Smith.

Worster, Donald. 1994. *Nature's Economy: A Historical of Ecological Ideas*. 2nd ed. Cambridge: Cambridge University Press.

CHAPTER 5

1900s–1950s Texts

This chapter identifies the ways in which three authors adapted the wild animal story in the aftermath of the Nature Fakers controversy. These texts share core characteristics with Ernest Thompson Seton's and Charles G. D. Roberts's stories, as well as their interests in science and animal advocacy. Yet they also include self-conscious attempts to avoid accusations of anthropomorphism or 'nature faking.' Each one reflects the use of mechanomorphic language in ethology and behaviourism at the time. As part of this engagement with contemporary scientific discourses, each author also gives their perspective on the role of instinct in animal behaviour. Comparing these texts, we can identify a new development in the *fantasy of knowing* the animal. This a divide between 'realistic' and 'speculative' styles. Roderick Haig-Brown's *Return to the River* (1941) and Fred Bodsworth's *Last of the Curlew* (1955) reflect the 'realistic' method. Whereas Frederick Philip Grove's *Consider Her Ways* (1947) introduces a new approach that blends accurate scientific information with speculations about complex animal societies and the inclusion of pseudo-magical or fantastical elements.

© The Author(s), under exclusive license to Springer Nature Switzerland AG 2023
C. Allmark-Kent, *Literature, Science, and Animal Advocacy in Canada*, Palgrave Studies in Animals and Literature, https://doi.org/10.1007/978-3-031-40556-3_5

RODERICK HAIG-BROWN: *RETURN TO THE RIVER* (1941)

Understanding the Nature Fakers controversy is crucial to reading the work of Roderick Haig-Brown (1908–1976). Over thirty years after the debates had ended, their lasting effects profoundly shaped both the writing and reception of his biography of a pacific salmon, *Return to the River* (1941). Born at the end of the controversy, Haig-Brown seems to have been acutely aware of the criticisms levelled against Seton and Roberts. Determined to prevent similar accusations, he made careful adaptations to the wild animal story's format whilst also maintaining its core elements. For instance, Haig-Brown (1941) engages with both science and animal advocacy in *Return to the River*, yet avoids making any specific claims on behalf of salmons. He also demonstrates the curious tension common to animal fiction from this period, in which the author is caught between attempting a zoocentric representation and adhering to the more mechanomorphic language favoured by the sciences at the time. Understandably, this produces some contradictions.

In March 1942, the journal of the American Society of Ichthyologists and Herpetologists, *Copeia*, published a review of *Return to the River*.[1] The reviewer, Willis H. Rich, describes Haig-Brown as writing "too biologically for the layman" and yet "too much in the grand manner of the nature faker for the biologist" (1942, 59). Evidently, even decades later, the controversy remained an inescapable context for realistic animal fiction. Yet the reviewer does not reference Seton, Roberts, or the controversy itself. By this point, the phrase 'nature faker' needed no further explanation. Although Rich's review of *Return to the River* is a favourable one, it seems that the fundamental issue of a non-scientist writing scientifically engaged animal fiction was still of concern. Unfortunately, this was precisely what Haig-Brown had tried to avoid.

In an interview with Ernest Schwiebert (1984), Haig-Brown references his own concerns about nature faking. He explains: "I wanted to write about animals without faking anything—without any of the anthropomorphic tricks that portray animals made to think and feel like people" (xi). Indeed, he comments that "there's been plenty of nature faking" and cites "Ernest Thompson Seton" as an example (xi). Haig-Brown's words are quite revealing. Not only do they further demonstrate the long-lasting

---

[1] Ichthyology is the scientific study of fishes and herpetology is the study of amphibians and reptiles.

repercussions of the controversy, but they also indicate that Seton's name had already become synonymous with nature faking and anthropomorphism. Meanwhile, Roberts's association with the controversy seems to have been forgotten. We can also sense the growing embarrassment associated with the genre. As Haig-Brown indicates, it is clear that, whilst an author may write in the style of the wild animal story, they do not necessarily do so in support of Seton or Roberts. This is something we see in many twentieth-century zoocentric texts.

Even the writing of *Return to the River* was shaped by Haig-Brown's efforts to distance himself from the 'nature fakers.' In 1931, he published his first salmon book, *Silver: The Life of an Atlantic Salmon*. It bears a strong resemblance to Seton's and Roberts's early (arguably less zoocentric) wild animal stories. Haig-Brown (1931) uses playful anthropomorphic metaphors, such as "Silver, King of the River" and describes the salmon's mate as his "wife" (87, 75). Seton (1901) employed similar techniques in his stories for the children's magazine, *St. Nicholas*, which he later described as using the "archaic" method of animal representation (10). Certainly, *Silver* seems aimed at a younger audience. It is dedicated to "Master Dickie P." and the author's note states that it originated as a bedtime story (Haig-Brown 1931, 5). In 1976, Haig-Brown remarked: "I wasn't too happy with my story of the Atlantic salmon" (Schwiebert 1984, xi).

Between the publications of *Silver* (1931) and *Return to the River* (1941), he wrote another work of animal fiction, *Panther* (1934), and two nonfiction books: *Pool and Rapid* (1932) and *The Western Angler* (1939). The latter was written with the conscious aim of bolstering Haig-Brown's name as an authority on the fishes of the Pacific Northwest. Indeed, he had already begun writing *Return to the River* (1941) when he stopped to write *The Western Angler* instead. In their interview, Schwiebert (1984) asked: "You mean it was written [...] just to make future book critics accept your story about salmon?" (xii). In response, Haig-Brown laughed: "That's about right" (xii). His sensitivity to the issues raised by the Nature Fakers controversy is clear. Given that Haig-Brown did not trigger another controversy, we could argue that he was successful. Although, as indicated by Rich's (1942) review, he could not escape the label 'nature faker' entirely.

In spite of these efforts to establish his credentials to write about salmons, Haig-Brown still adopted a range of strategies within the text to prevent accusations of nature faking and anthropomorphism. One issue at the core of the controversy had been the authors' claims that their stories were 'true' or that the behaviours depicted were real. In *Return to the River*, Haig-Brown (1941) sidesteps this issue entirely by making no explicit statements on behalf of salmons. Instead, he engages with debates about salmon behaviour by staging conversations between two human characters: Senator Evans, an angler and amateur ichthyologist, and Don Gunner, a field biologist. The characterization of these figures is quite telling.

Gunner is the embodiment of what Theodore Roosevelt described in his article, "Nature Fakers," as the "scientist worthy of the name," as well as the "real outdoor naturalist" (Roosevelt 1907, 427–8). By contrast, Evans condemns himself as an "[i]ncorrigible old sentimentalist" (Haig-Brown 1941, 7). He defers to the biologist's authority and asks to be "save[d]" from his "romantic self" (7). Even as an amateur observer, he is preoccupied with the 'threat' of anthropomorphism: "He was afraid of his love of the fish, afraid of reading things that were not really there" (7). This association between shame and anthropomorphism became increasingly common throughout the twentieth century.[2] Meanwhile, mechanomorphism continued to be favoured as 'rational' and 'objective,' despite being equally inaccurate.

At the beginning of the book, Evans notices that a dying female salmon remains with her eggs, even after she has finished spawning. He wonders whether it might be "nearly a maternal urge to protect" (Haig-Brown 1941, 6–7). When speaking to Gunner, Evans asks "almost timidly," whether there could be "anything of maternal instinct" in a salmon (8). As we might expect, Gunner's reply uses the mechanistic language of behaviourism and ethology. He warns that we "have to be very cautious" and call it "evidence of post-spawning parental care" (8). Overlooking any intentionality in the salmon, Gunner frames her actions through a relationship between stimulus and response: "a persistence of whatever stimulation it is that produces the egg-laying and redd-making activities" (8). However, he also adds: "Nothing about fish is easy to prove" (9). Here, we can see Haig-Brown's strategic deferral of his own authority within the text. By staging conversations between characters, he raises questions without making any overt statements himself.

Through these cautious approaches, Haig-Brown also attempts to contribute to other contemporary scientific discussions. In the

[2] For instance, the embarrassment of anthropomorphism can often be found in *failure of knowing* narratives, such as Yann Martel's *Life of Pi* (2001).

early-to-mid twentieth century, 'home stream theory' was a contentious issue. The hypothesis that salmons returned to the waters of their birth to spawn had widespread ramifications for conservation, aquaculture, and the building of hydroelectric dams. However, Rich (1937) outlines the difficulties of establishing "rigid observational proof" of home stream theory, which would involve "marking young fish" in their "natal river," capturing them at sea, marking them again, and finally recapturing them again back in their original stream (478). "Needless to say," he concludes, "it will be some time before such proof will be accumulated" (478). Rather remarkably, Haig-Brown's (1941) aptly named *Return to the River* contributes to this conversation by offering a kind of home stream theory thought experiment. The book's biographical structure enables us to follow the protagonist, Spring, from birth to death and throughout her entire migration.

To reinforce this engagement with home stream theory, Senator Evans creates his own experiment and uses the same methodology outlined by Rich. At the beginning of the book, he captures Spring in her birth stream. Evans 'marks' her for the experiment by clipping her adipose fin. Coincidentally, when she is out at sea, she is captured by other researchers and tagged again. Then, at the end of her life, she returns to her home stream to lay eggs. Evans sees her, noticing the tag from the sea and the clipped fin, but he cannot catch her to confirm. Although the thought experiment is complete, Evans does not obtain the "rigid observational proof" that Rich (1937) describes (478).

With humour, Rich (1942) concludes his review by lamenting Haig-Brown's inconclusive experiment: "Never shall I forgive him because I fear that never again will that crucial experiment be so close to consummation" (59). Despite his tone, Rich makes a good point. Of course, Haig-Brown's thought experiment does not constitute scientific evidence. However, we can see the potential for exchange between the sciences and animal fiction. This is the same potential articulated by Roberts (1902) and again by scientists, Marc Bekoff (2000) and Hal Whitehead (2003). I would suggest that the author's ability to imagine what cannot be *observed* allows for speculation. These speculations may encourage greater empathy with the species in question, while also stimulating future research. They may even influence the design of future experiments. Given that, as Rich (1937) remarks, it would "be some time" before "rigid observational proof" of home stream theory could be "accumulated," I would suggest that Haig-Brown's thought experiment offers plausible speculations (478).

It is worth noting, however, that the mechanisms by which Spring returns to her home stream are unclear. Haig-Brown (1941) does not offer explicit answers, though Gunner remarks: "'Homing instinct' doesn't mean a thing [...] you simply mean that something you can't explain or name brings a salmon back to its home stream" (11). Instead, he suggests that external factors may be at play, such as "currents and temperatures and perhaps chemical differences in the water, and that their response to these things will be conditioned by factors inside themselves—such as increasing maturity" (11).

Rather than a single guiding influence, Spring's migration seems to be shaped by a range of internal and external factors. Haig-Brown (1941) tends to use a vague language of 'urges' or 'restlessness' to describe her subjective experiences of these changing conditions. Sometimes her journey is driven by practical concerns, which may include simply following other fishes or seeking out new food. Yet, one rather unexpected, but frequent, influence is that of pleasure. Whether emerging into new waters or returning to familiar ones, Spring's experiences are usually described as pleasurable. Perhaps pleasure may be that thing that we "can't explain or name" (11).

Return to the River (1941) includes many rich descriptions of fish pleasure. Spring gains pleasure from the movement of her body in water, the pursuit of prey, the feeling of a full stomach, playing with other fishes, and responding to the urge to migrate or mate. In a particularly detailed passage, Haig-Brown compares these different experiences. He remarks that, "all through her life," there had been "strong physical satisfactions" (89). There was the "strong pleasure in feeding to repletion" early in her life, the "stronger pleasure of feeding" on larger prey as she neared the ocean, and a "vibrant ecstasy in driving time after time upon the schools of silver herrings" (89).

There was "pleasure in the drive of her muscles through the water," in "free curved leaping" to ease the irritation of sea lice, and perhaps even a "pleasure of speed and strength in the terror for flight from enemies" (89). The "closeness of other salmon about her" gave "pleasure" and an "ease of security" (89). There was also pleasure in responding to "conditions within her and around her that led her down the rivers to the sea" (89). But "none of these had been as strong as the thing that ruled her now" (89). In "responding" to this urge to complete her migration, which "stirred her," "drove her," and "drew her in a sudden change of current or light," there was a deeper "pleasure" (89). It was the "pleasure of release" and "pleasure in the gradual shifting of pressures and changing of shapes within her body cavity" (89).

These passages are particularly striking, given the controversial nature of fish pleasure. The capacity for pleasure in fishes—or, indeed, any animal—remains a contentious issue. Yet, as Jonathan Balcombe (2009) argues, pleasure is "a product of evolution" (209). Just as the "capacity for pain is adaptive" by ensuring that an individual will "move away from aversive things," so too is "pleasure beneficial" (209–210). In essence, it rewards individuals for pursuing activities that benefit survival. Balcombe explains that "pleasure encourages animals to behave in 'good' ways, such as feeding, mating, and—depending on climactic conditions—staying warm or cool" (210). Clearly, then, we can see the survival advantages in Spring's sources of pleasure: food, movement, companionship, migration, and reproduction.

Even though Haig-Brown (1941) uses mechanistic language at times, he also presents some of the most vivid, detailed explorations of animal pleasure in any work of fiction. These seem at odds with some of his more reductive statements, however. Given his careful strategies to avoid making specific claims regarding other aspects of fish behaviour, it seems unusual that he would place such emphasis on the role of pleasure in Spring's life. I suggest that this may be because it forms a crucial part of his conservation message. By inviting readers to imagine the pleasurable, joyous elements of salmon existence, Haig-Brown makes the case for them having a certain quality of life. As Balcombe (2009) points out, an animal's ability to feel pleasure carries a moral significance. It suggests that we owe them more than the mere avoidance of suffering.

In the foreword to the 1984 edition of *Return to the River* (written in 1974, two years before his death), Haig-Brown outlines the book's historical context. He reflects:

> The lives and deaths of Spring and the other chinook salmon described in this book occurred more than thirty years ago, in the early stages of the orgy of dam-building that transformed the Columbia from a magnificent river to a series of freshwater impoundments. [...] The Columbia system was at the very heart of the salmon's range and so favourable to the species that chinooks ran to it every month of the year and in three major waves—spring, summer, and fall. [...] Dams have blocked off more than 60 percent of the Columbia's spawning areas; pathetic remnants of the runs still struggle up past some of the dams and into the distant headwaters. (Haig-Brown 1984, iv)

Rather than a general plea against hunting or abuse, Haig-Brown (1941) wrote *Return to the River* in response to a specific threat. Here, we find one of the first direct, specific conservation messages of twentieth-century English-Canadian animal fiction. This indicates both the changing focus of animal fiction and the steady public recognition of environmental degradation. Haig-Brown's adaptation of the wild animal story offers advocacy on behalf of both the suffering individual and the suffering species. Unusually, however, he is also critical of contemporary conservation practices.

Between the 1920s and 1950s, New Ecology brought an increasingly mechanistic perspective to species preservation. In *Return to the River*, Haig-Brown (1941) explores hatchery programmes and the practice of transporting salmons in trucks to bypass dams. Using Senator Evans as a mouthpiece, he attempts to express why these measures are insufficient. He explains: "they would come and gather the fish [...] take them up to the ponds, hold them to ripeness and strip the eggs from them" (105). He reflects that "[i]n a way it didn't really matter" and the "result probably wouldn't be much less good than natural spawning," yet he still felt "disturbed" by it (105–6). Evans continues:

> The salmon were the river, they were the country, of it and helping to make it. In words, he told himself, it becomes meaningless, merely sentimental. But you can feel it, know that this is right, the other wrong. The river is there for their use, they are its yield, growing from it, growing on it, giving themselves back to it in a cycle that no mere human farming has yet been able to match. (106)

Haig-Brown is advocating not only for the preservation of the species but the preservation of the river itself. The river is, in part, there for *their* use. Evans struggles to fully articulate the thought to himself but, looking at the fishes, he remarks "poor devils" (106). What lies at the heart of Haig-Brown's conservation message—and what Evans cannot quite express—is the idea that the salmons deserve a certain quality of life. This is where the role of pleasure comes into play.

Haig-Brown best illustrates the inherent value of a salmon's quality of life when comparing Spring's migration with that of previous generations. When Spring begins her journey, he sets up a historical juxtaposition that continues throughout the narrative. Haig-Brown (1941) writes: "the three-hundred-mile way they had to follow to the sea was not the clear, clean way of their ancestors. There were poisons in it and obstructions across it and false ways leading from it" (40). After travelling through polluted rivers, Spring's "belly [is] empty," her gills feel "clogged and hot," and "much of her fine energy [is] spent" (49). Haig-Brown comments that she barely survives a "journey that had been glad and easy for her ancestors, a joyous prelude to the fullness and strength of the sea" (49).

These qualitative comparisons emphasize the wellbeing and subjective experiences of the migrating salmons. By demonstrating the damage to Spring's quality of life, Haig-Brown makes a plea on behalf of all salmons in the Columbia River system who deserve the 'joy' of their ancestors. Yet he also makes it clear that this poor quality of life has profound implications for the species. Once, "the passage of the chinooks had made a mark that no one could miss, even in that wide, full-flowing river," but now there were "not one-fourth, perhaps not one-tenth of the numbers that ran just seventy years ago" (Haig-Brown 1941, 50).

Given the zoocentricism of Haig-Brown's approach to conservation, it is worth noting the limitations of his ethics. In contrast to his empathetic representation of fish pleasure, he seems more reticent when it comes to the topic of pain. Of course, the question of whether fishes feel pain is still controversial. Today, there is growing evidence for both pain reception and subjective experiences in fishes, though it has not yet been accepted fully by the scientific community.[3] Yet, I would suggest that early twentieth-century scepticism for fish pain is not necessarily the cause of Haig-Brown's hesitancy. For instance, when one salmon is bitten by a lamprey, his description of pain is clear. The salmon feels "agonized" and attempts to "shake the pain" from himself (Haig-Brown 1941, 63). However, this is not the case when humans harm fishes.

When Spring is 'marked' for Senator Evans's home stream experiment, Haig-Brown (1941) uses a human point of view: "Holding her firmly, but with a slow, almost an awed gentleness, he clipped off the little fatty fin above her tail, turned her in his hand, and clipped away the left ventral" (33). Haig-Brown emphasizes the care and caution with which Evans cuts the young fish, rather than exploring the possibility of her pain. Indeed, it

---

[3] Victoria Braithwaite's (2010) comprehensive study of the evidence for fish pain reception leads her to conclude: "'Do fish feel pain?' Yes they do" (183). Yet, others still dispute the validity of this evidence, such as J. D. Rose et al. in "Can Fish Really Feel Pain?" (2014).

is only when the encounter is over that the narration returns to Spring's perspective: "her panic returned and she swam off, a little queerly, towards the bottom. She found a place between two stones [...] and lay there, still as a stick, her head in the shade" (33). For two or three days afterwards, Spring's movements are "awkward and uncertain" and she scarcely feeds (33). The change in behaviour indicates her distress and emotional response to the pain. Nonetheless, Haig-Brown avoids describing her pain directly.

In considering Spring's loss of two fins, Haig-Brown is simultaneously reductive and empathetic. He remarks that the "loss of her adipose fin affected her not at all" (34). But Spring still must "readjust her whole body to the loss of the one ventral fin" and even "the short journey from the old Senator's hand to the shelter of the rocks" is enough to "destroy her easy confidence in her power of movement through the water" (34). Whilst unwilling to speculate about Spring's experiences of pain, Haig-Brown does imagine that she feels confidence. Likewise, although he refuses to enter her perspective while in the hands of a human, he is strikingly zoocentric when considering the impact on her movements and self-assurance in her environment.

I would suggest that Haig-Brown's inconsistencies are a product of his interest in angling. This is similar to Seton's (1898) appeal "Have the wild things no moral or legal rights?" juxtaposing his later (1901) assertion that he did not oppose hunting or even "cruelty to animals" (357; 12). Glen Love (1998) observes that Haig-Brown characterized himself as a "writer who happened to fish," rather than "a fisherman who happened to write" (2). Similar to Seton, his dependence on animal exploitation reveals the limits of his zoocentrism. Likewise, Haig-Brown advocates for *conservation*, not animal *welfare*. As such, he does not explore abuse or cruelty to the same extent as other animal fiction from the period. Of course, it is also worth remembering that in the 1930s and 1940s, Canada's humane movement was focused on the protection of companion animals. There was no campaign for fish welfare or the ethics of angling. Moreover, fishes were not protected by the nation's anti-cruelty laws (as is still the case today).

Although there are some limitations to Haig-Brown's (1941) approach, his overall portrait of salmon life is richly compelling. For a seemingly uncharismatic species whose sentience was still a matter of debate, he presents a vivid impression of an underwater existence that was valuable for its own sake. Spring and her fellow salmons are full of emotions. They have preferences and make choices. They make inferences based on each other's body language and react accordingly. They form companionships and feel comforted by each other's presence. They dislike polluted water and the irritations of parasites. They feel pain and emotional distress. They engage in play and seek out pleasurable experiences. They continue learning throughout their lives, adapting to novel situations, and observing each other's strategies. Whilst Spring is not an 'exceptional' salmon, she is undoubtedly a unique individual who has been shaped by a specific set of life experiences. In short, she is without question the *subject of a life*.

Although *Return to the River* is fiction, Haig-Brown evidently wrote with the serious intention of contributing to both science and animal advocacy, just as Seton and Roberts had done. He presents a persuasive home stream theory thought experiment, in which he speculates about how a salmon might *feel* during different stages of migration. Simultaneously, he also makes a plea on behalf of the salmon against dam-building, water pollution, and mechanistic approaches to wildlife conservation. To join both elements of his argument together, he focuses on the salmons' quality of life. He indicates that the salmon *deserve* clean water and an uninterrupted migration, though he does not state it outright.

Instead, Haig-Brown tempers his zoocentric representation through mechanomorphic language. He also uses human characters to negate salmon intentionality and mentation. Likewise, whilst he demonstrates that his salmon are capable of pain, he avoids describing it when inflicted by humans. Through these contradictions, we can see the tensions in writing realistic animal fiction, particularly for authors who rely on animal exploitation themselves. In the early decades of the twentieth century, these issues were compounded by the lingering shadow of the Nature Fakers controversy. Evidently, the unexpected repercussions of Seton's and Roberts's work would continue to ripple throughout English-Canadian literature for the next century.

FREDERICK PHILIP GROVE: *CONSIDER HER WAYS* (1947)

Typically, Frederick Philip Grove (1879–1948) is remembered as a writer of Canadian prairie fiction. Less well-known is that he spent decades working on his so-called Ant book, a novel written from the perspective of a South American leafcutter ant. *Consider Her Ways* (1947) was the final book Grove published, but the writing of it spanned his entire career.[4] It obsessed him, made other projects seem irrelevant, and was excruciatingly difficult to write.[5] It went through multiple revisions under a few different titles. The most significant differences are between his first manuscript completed in 1925, titled "MAN, His Habits, Social Organization, and Outlook," and a heavily rewritten draft from 1933 under the new name: "Go to the Ant." From the titles alone, we can see that these two versions reveal a shift in focus from human societies to ant societies. Indeed, we might think of it as a transition from an *anthropocentric* to an *ant-centric* perspective.

Grove's first manuscript, "MAN," was heavily influenced by Árpád Ferenczy's (1924) *The Ants of Timothy Thümmel,* which used a fictional history of ant societies as a lens to examine humanity. Whilst Ferenczy drew on myrmecology, I would suggest that he expressed an *indifference to knowing* the animal overall.[6] Fundamental inaccuracies, such as his ants being mostly male and ruled by 'kings,' were no doubt employed to serve as allegories for patriarchal human societies. Grove's first 1925 "MAN" manuscript also used ants as *objects of utility* to illuminate human concerns. In the story, the ants meet an amateur myrmecologist and communicate with him by using ink to dot letters in his notebook. They give him a report of their findings from an expedition to observe and judge humanity. The results are not good. As Margaret Stobie (1978) observes, however, the "ant world disappears entirely" after this point in the story (421). What remains is some rather "flat-footed preaching" about humans (421).

As Grove continued working on the book, the presence of the ants increased considerably. In "Go to the Ant," their purpose was no longer focused on humanity. Instead, the ants' mission was to study other *ant* societies. Whilst Stobie (1978) notes that there are "vestiges of the earlier version" in the manuscript, they are "properly subordinated to the new

---

[4] According to Grove, he had the original idea in "1892 or 1893" but only began work on it in the "fall or early winter of 1919" (Martens 2007, 549). He finished the first full draft in 1925 and another, extensively revised, draft in 1933 (Stobie 1978, 418). After further work, he sent a manuscript to the publisher Lorne Pierce in 1940 (418). It was rejected. In 1945, however, it was accepted by Ellen Elliot for Macmillans and in January 1947 *Consider Her Ways* finally appeared in print (431). Grove died in the summer of 1948. His revision of the book's introduction was his final piece of work.

[5] In 1923 Grove remarked that the "Ant-book" had "gripped" him (Martens 2007, 195). Elsewhere, he wrote: "apart from the 'Ant-book,' it all seems so irrelevant" (179).

[6] Myrmecology is the scientific study of ants.

purpose" (426). Through his years of rewrites, Grove's 'Ant book' transitioned from an *indifference to knowing* into a *fantasy of knowing* the animal. Consequently, his ants transformed from objects to *subjects of lives.*

The published version of *Consider Her Ways* (1947) retains elements from both "MAN" and "Go to the Ant." This means it can appear somewhat disjointed at times. Instances of satire can punctuate otherwise zoocentric depictions of ant societies. For instance, Grove (1947) describes honeypot ants in terms of "authors" and "critics" and makes references to an intoxicating pheromone called "money" (97, 160). In one striking scene, the ants learn to read English in the New York Public Library. This device would have been necessary in the first version of the story when the ants 'wrote' in the myrmecologist's book. However, one of Grove's final edits before he died was to change the book's beginning to remove any need for this. Instead, he opted for the more direct, albeit even less realistic, method of telepathy. Of course, we cannot know whether the library scene would have remained in subsequent rewrites. Nonetheless, as we proceed, it is worth keeping in mind the novel's unusually long and complex writing process, particularly when we counter some of its more awkward elements.

Consider Her Ways is written from the perspective of Wawa-quee, a leafcutter ant who leads a vast 'scientific' expedition from Venezuela to New York city. She is the book's 'author' who communicates her memories of the journey telepathically to an amateur myrmecologist who, in turn, writes it down and serves as the book's 'editor.' From Wawa-quee's point of view, the book is a "popular account" of a scientific survey to catalogue and classify "all forms of life to be found on the continent" (Grove 1947, 31). However, the 'editor' comments in an author's note that, whilst he "believes the picture of antdom given in these pages to be essentially true to fact," he can only "vouch for the veracity of the introduction" (8). Indeed, he suspects that Wawa-quee's account is simply "the product of an ant's imagination and, therefore, pure fiction" (8).

In this fantastical scenario, Grove almost seems to parody Seton's (1898) infamous claim in *Wild Animals I Have Known* that: "These stories are true" (9). Rather than an avowal of truth, Grove (1947) offers a declaration of fictionality. In the introduction to *Consider Her Ways*, the 'editor' reiterates this point. He asserts: "I cannot [...] claim that what follows is my work. It is the work of Wawa-quee, the ant; and it must be read in that sense" (25). To add to this complex layering of authorship, however, the editor identifies himself as "F.P.G.," which are, of course,

Grove's own initials (9). Moreover, F.P.G. encounters Wawa-quee on a "prolonged holiday" devoted to "hunting down one or two colonies of the leaf-cutter ant of intertropical America" (13). In Klaus Martens's (2007) *Over Canadian Trails: F.P. Grove in New Letters and Documents*, we can read a copy of a letter dated 30th April 1926 in which Grove references a "holiday trip" to South America "undertaken to see the ants of which I had read" (329). Evidently, there is a blending of writer and narrator here that goes beyond their shared initials.

Clearly, Grove's approach to animal representation is a departure from the methods we have encountered thus far. Yet, his first book *Over Prairie Trails* was much closer to Seton's and Roberts's works. Through a combination of autobiography and nature writing, Grove (1923) recounts various encounters with animals, all of which are shaped by a potent blend of curiosity and compassion. He identifies his fictionalized self as an "outdoor creature" who loved "Nature more than Man" (13–4). Indeed, most of his interactions are with animals.

The two most richly drawn characters are his two horses, Peter and Dan. By the end of the book, we know more about their personalities and habits than we do his own family (who barely step beyond the front door). On the trails, Grove (1923) references a feeling of "great tenderness" when coming upon "the home of frog and toad, of gartersnake and owl and whip-poor-will" (35). He mentions wanting to "shield and help them all and tell them not to be afraid of me," though he suspects that they "know it anyway" (36). Indeed, at one point, he even shares his sandwich with a wolf who had become a frequent presence on his trips: "he came to know me, as I knew him" (27–8).

It is difficult to tell whether Grove read Seton's or Roberts's work, but it is easy to see the common themes. Certainly, they were all engaged with similar ideas. Yet we can be confident that Grove knew about 'nature faking.' One of his main scientific sources for writing about ants was William Morton Wheeler's (1910) *Ants: Their Structure, Development and Behaviour*. Even at a surface level, we can see Wheeler's influence in the title of Grove's first manuscript, "MAN, His Habits, Social Organization, and Outlook." There are also several direct references to Wheeler in *Consider Her Ways*, including a human character known to the ants as "the Wheeler" (Grove 1947, 100).

In *Ants*, Wheeler (1910) identifies a division between "scientific" and "intuitional" approaches to studying ant behaviour (505). At the extremes, the former can tend towards oversimplification and reliance on reductive "reflex theories," whilst the latter can lead to the "humanizing of animals" with "all the perversities of the American 'nature-fakers'" (506–7).[7] Grove (1947) makes a similar point in the introduction to *Consider Her Ways* but does not mention nature faking directly (12, 18). Thus, it is plausible that Grove came to know about 'nature faking,' not through his involvement with Canada's literary scene, but through his *scientific* reading. This is another example of the surprising repercussions of the Nature Fakers controversy, as well as the complex interactions between science and literature at the time.

I suggest that Grove's innovative method of animal representation could be an adaptation in response to the idea of nature faking. In *Over Prairie Trails* (1923), his blend of fact and fiction had been similar to Seton's semi-autobiographical stories. Yet, for his 'Ant book,' he adopted a considerably more complex approach. There are no direct references to the controversy, yet *Consider Her Ways* (1947) holds similar indicators of post-Nature Fakers awareness as Haig-Brown's *Return to the River* (1941). Just as Haig-Brown used human characters to discuss salmon behaviour, Grove uses a complex layering of 'authorship' to bury his voice within the text. Even though each 'author' of *Consider Her Ways* (1947) claims that *their* part of the story is true, the context is absurd. Under such circumstances, any concerns about accuracy become irrelevant. As such, Grove frees himself to speculate about ant intelligence without accusations of anthropomorphism or nature faking.

We find similar layers of complexity in Grove's (1947) interactions with science. Despite his playfulness, he still seems to have been interested in conveying accurate details of myrmecology. Strangely enough, *Consider Her Ways* may hold more scientific information than any work of fiction addressed in this book, even those written by naturalists and biologists. In the novel, Grove references several real scientists by name and presents portraits of various ant societies based on their work.[8] In the introduction, he gives a detailed description of leafcutter ant behaviour and biology.

---

[7] Interestingly, as an American himself, Wheeler (1910) seems to identify 'nature faking' as an American problem. It could be that Wheeler did not realize that both Americans and Canadians were involved. Or perhaps the prominence of American figures—such as John Burroughs, Theodore Roosevelt, and Jack London—led to the assumption that the whole affair was between Americans.

[8] The naturalists and entomologists listed by Grove (1947) include: Pierre André Latrielle, Fritz Müller, Auguste Forel, François Huber, Carlo Emery, William Morton Wheeler, Henry Walter Bates, Thomas Belt, and François Sumichrast (12–16).

However, he also dedicates an appendix to a "Note on the Habit and Mode of Life of *Atta gigantea*" (207). The problem is that the species does not exist. This is a detail that can escape both readers and scholars alike. Yet, Grove builds his description of the species using information about real leafcutter ants. Only someone versed in myrmecology would get the joke. Even then, they might need to know every species of the genus *Atta* to realize that *Atta gigantea* were fictitious.

It is significant that Grove chose an imaginary species for his protagonists. In the introduction, F.P.G. remarks that the largest *Atta gigantea* possess "relatively enormous" heads with "brains of corresponding development" (16). He believes their brains to be the "largest single organ of any living being" relative to size (16). Playing on the myth that brain size equates with intelligence, Grove creates a fictional species with brains larger than those of any other ants. Thus, he sets himself up to speculate about the upper limits of ant intelligence. He also frees himself to explore an ant-centric perspective without making claims on behalf of any real species. At the same time, however, he builds this speculation upon accurate scientific information.

Grove's playful approach produces an innovative form of animal representation that I would call *speculative* animal fiction. It is a *fantasy of knowing* the animal that releases itself from issues of realism or accuracy to speculate about the outer limits of a zoocentric perspective. As we have seen, though, it still engages with science. Indeed, such work may even seek to contribute to contemporary scientific debates or to challenge accepted explanations of animal behaviour. In *Consider Her Ways*, Grove (1947) uses this speculative approach to challenge the concept of *instinct*. He outlined his perspective in a letter to his friend Watson Kirkconnell in 1927:

> Generally speaking, I'm not so sure about instinct. My own, very limited observations—the only ones I have made under scientific conditions were made on ants—lead me to the conclusion that you may just as well ascribe the building of the city wall at Winnipeg to instinct, as, for instance, the careful and scientific fungus-farming of the oecodoma ants of Central America and South America north of the Amazons. I have not found anything new, but I have seen observations of Bates, Belt, and others confirmed, and they seem to point to the fact that education, among ants, plays at least the same part as with us. (Quoted in Stobie 1978, 419)

It is worth noting here that Henry Walter Bates and Thomas Belt were nineteenth-century naturalists. Bates's *The Naturalist on the River Amazons* was published in 1863 and Belts's *The Naturalist in Nicaragua* in 1874. Thus, neither account would have been shaped by the mechano-morphic language of twentieth-century behaviourism or ethology. Indeed, both were written before the full development of comparative psychology. Bates and Belt would have been free to describe animal minds, emotions, reason, and learning.

By contrast, Grove's later scientific sources would have perceived things differently. For instance, Wheeler (1910) challenged observations of leaf-cutter ant behaviour that were previously used as evidence of reason. To do so, he broke them down into a series of simple actions that could be governed by instinct alone. When comparing these sources, it is easy to see how Grove might reject contemporary scientific explanations based on involuntary responses. Indeed, in *Consider Her Ways*, he remarks that a "good deal of controversial literature" has been written on the "seemingly automatic functioning of the ant-state;" on the whole, "instinct has been held to explain it all" (Grove 1947, 17–8). In almost an imitation of Roberts's (1907) preface to *Haunters of the Silences*, Grove declares: "The present book, I believe, will settle that question" (1947, 12).[9]

Grove's position on the concept of instinct is clear. Interestingly, his language is similar to Haig-Brown's (1941) statements about instinct in *Return to the River*. In both cases, they identify the use of instinct as an indicator of ignorance. Grove (1947) writes:

> Instinct is a convenient word without real meaning which, for that very reason, serves admirably to veil the ignorance of those who use it. There can be no doubt any longer that, as with us, not instinct, but tradition and edu-cation furnish the true explanation of the facts: that much this book settles beyond question. (18)

In this playful reversal of the wild animal story's scientific aspirations, he aims to 'settle' the question of instinct by writing about an imaginary spe-cies. Yet, for all the absurdity, there seems to be something sincere in Grove's argument that instinct alone is insufficient to explain the com-plexities of ant behaviour.

---

[9] In the preface, Roberts (1907) expresses his hope that his book would contribute "some-thing of value" to the "question of animal psychology" (vi).

In one playful—yet poignant—section, Grove (1947) aligns the concept of instinct with human supremacy. He remarks that, according to whether the "human-race conceit of the investigator was strongly or weakly developed," the behaviour of the ants has been "placed either in contrast or in comparison with the behaviour of man" (12). Whilst an obvious oversimplification, there is an element of truth here. Arguably speciesism and ideas about human supremacy *have* shaped the interpretation of animal behaviour. Wheeler (1910), for instance, makes frequent comparisons between human and ant societies, often using anthropocentric metaphors to aid his descriptions. Even the notion of ant 'soldiers,' 'workers,' and 'queens' carries a host of human assumptions. Returning to his humorous tone, Grove (1947) comments: "It is interesting to see, in the pages that follow, how much of man's activities ants ascribe to instinct" (18).

Alongside his rejection of instinct, Grove presents an idealized version of the introspective or intuitive methods of comparative psychology. When F.P.G. meets Wawa-quee, he experiences a fantastical act of knowing. In the introduction to *Consider Her Ways* (1947), F.P.G. recounts his trip to Venezuela to study leafcutter ants. He spends weeks patiently observing a colony of *Atta gigantea*. Over time, he begins to feel a "bond of sympathy" with them (20). One day, a single ant climbs a tree and begins watching him with glittering black eyes that seem "so human" (22). They sit watching each other, eye to eye, for over an hour. Later, F.P.G. reflects: "With all the intensity of which I was capable I wished to understand what this ant was about" (22).

A gradual process of telepathic exchange develops and F.P.G. experiences the ultimate act of empathy: "I walked and acted like a human being; but my mind was that of the ant" (25). Significantly, F.P.G. is not telepathically connected to *all* ants. Instead, he knows the mind, life history, and unique perspective of one specific ant, Wawa-quee: "I had lived her life; and her memory was mine" (25). Despite the supernatural plot device, these passages express a sincere desire to *know* animal minds. They also operate from the assumption that animal minds exist and are knowable in the first place; something that was at odds with the mechanomorphism of the sciences at the time. We can read these passages as a metaphor for the perfect knowledge of an individual animal's life history to which someone such as Seton, Roberts, or even Thomas Wesley Mills, might aspire. It is a magical vision of Grove's own observations of ants: a form of wish fulfilment for anyone curious about animal minds.

It is worth noting that F.P.G.'s encounters with the ants are the only nonviolent human-animal interactions of the book. All other humans pose a danger, whether intentionally or not. During his weeks of observation, F.P.G. does not capture, dissect, experiment upon, or otherwise interfere with the *Atta gigantea*. Indeed, he never even digs into the burrows of the colony: "I felt I had no right to destroy their elaborate works" (Grove 1947, 16). Grove's tone here almost echoes his reverence for wildlife in *Over Prairie Trails*. There is a sense that it is F.P.G.'s compassion which enables this act of knowing to take place. Indeed, he reflects that he may well have been "singled out for the mission" with which he was "entrusted" *because* he "never dug into the burrows of the colony" (16). F.P.G.'s benign, non-intrusive observations are in stark contrast to the fear and destruction posed by the Wheeler.

In a few sections of *Consider Her Ways* (1947), Grove borrows methods from Wheeler's *Ants* (1910) and describes them from an ant perspective. During their long expedition, Wawa-quee and her companions have several dangerous encounters with an entomologist. They name him "the Wheeler," due to his habit of travelling on a "curious machine consisting of two revolving wheels" (Grove 1947, 100). To their "horror," they witness the Wheeler digging into burrows and abducting the inhabitants (87). "Laughingly," he scoops up "frightened" ants who are "wildly" trying to "escape with their larvae and pupae" (137). The disparity between the ants' distress and the man's laughter reflects the strangely light-hearted tone used in Wheeler's writing. In *Ants*, he writes that there is "no form of entomological work more fascinating than collecting ants" (549). Moreover, there is "no more delightful avocation" for a man who "desires a not too strenuous employment" out in the "open air" (549). Where Wheeler uses the language of pleasure and relaxation, Grove describes the same scene as a terrible abduction.

Likewise, when a member of the expedition is captured, she witnesses "whole tribes of ants in captivity," confined in "artificial nests," in the Wheeler's office (Grove 1947, 106). The ant, Bissa-tee, watches as he drops her companions into "alien nest[s]" before they are "torn to pieces" by the ants within (106). Her "blood curdle[s]" at a large wooden case containing "innumerable ants of all descriptions, dead, and pierced by steel spears four ants long" (106). The Wheeler intends to preserve Bissa-tee as one of these specimens too. He places her under a jar with a "small wad of cotton" that had been "dipped into a liquid" from a "stoppered glass" (106–7). Bissa-tee feels a "poison" slowly entering her body and "spreading through her tissues" (107). She escapes the jar but is "soaked in poison" capable of "liquefying" an ant's body fat (105). The equipment and methods described resemble Wheeler's (1910) techniques for collecting and preserving ants in the wild. He mentions using "vials" of "commercial alcohol" and "[s]mall wads" of "cotton" to preserve the "specimens" (545–6). Presumably, the ants are alive when put in the vials of alcohol.

Consider Her Ways (1947) is the first text we have encountered so far to criticize animal exploitation in science. In *Return to the River* (1941), Haig-Brown carefully avoided describing the home stream theory experiments as painful. Yet, clearly each of the ants' encounters with the Wheeler are designed to show the destructive side of science. Elsewhere, Grove (1947) also exposes the use of ants in medicine. A doctor uses *Eciton hamatum* (army ants) to suture a wound quickly:

Twenty-five Ecitons had buried their jaws in the human flesh and were holding the edges of the wound together. And now comes the most amazing thing of all: a thing so horrible that I can barely bring myself to relate it. The master had risen and was bending over the bounded arm. In one fore-foot he held a new instrument, a pair of scissors [...] With this he severed the heads of the Eciton from their bodies, allowing the latter to fall to the ground. I nearly swooned. (48)

Wawa-quee's narration brings a different perspective to an otherwise well-known procedure. From an anthropocentric stance, this is a necessary emergency operation. Yet, Grove's *fantasy of knowing* transforms it into something monstrous. Here we can see how his first-person speculative representation can offer a more intimate defamiliarization of exploitative practices.

Perhaps most striking about Grove's depictions of human violence is that he also criticizes animal agriculture. Whilst there are many instances of cruelty in the book, the most harrowing scene involves a pig being slaughtered. At first, from Wawa-quee's perspective, the situation seems benign: "This man, I thought, realizes that he is dealing with a life like his own; he knows that even in a pig there lives happiness and joy; sorrow and pain, trust and anguish and dependency" (83). After establishing this idea, Grove goes on to expose the inevitable violence at the heart of even the most idealized image of farm life:

Then he brought [the axe] down with a tremendous, relentless swing, straight into the centre of the pig's head. The pig did not fall but stood stunned; blood rushed into its eyes; it was completely taken by surprise. An immense, bottomless abhorrence was mingled with the agony of pain; it tried to take a step; but it reeled; and then it seemed to awaken to its purpose and tried to escape. But the man had cooly raised his axe again and stood motionless, waiting for his chance; [...] he brought the powerful weapon down on that head a second time. The pig collapsed; its legs went rigid, though still atremble. (84–5)

Afterwards, the ants flee "in horror" and have no desire to "see any more of man's doings" (85). They conclude that humanity's "self-styled civilization is a mere film stretched over a horrible ground-mass of savagery" (85). Grove's stark depiction of animal agriculture (of which I have only included a small extract) is rare, particularly given the state of Canadian animal advocacy at the time. This is one of the few such criticisms made by any text addressed in this book.[10]

The strength of Grove's (1947) challenges to anthropocentrism lies in his use of defamiliarization. In turn, the efficacy of this defamiliarization relies on his creation of a zoocentric perspective. To create Wawa-quee's first-person narration, Grove employed a range of ant-centric terms and concepts. Using this sense of 'translation,' the ants measure distance using "common ant-lengths" and describe human clothes as their "integuments" (37, 136).[11] Grove also used what was known of ant behaviour to explore methods of communication relying on touch, scent, and body language. One ant greets another by touching first "antennae," then "thorax and head" (40). In conversation, she might use a slight "motion of her antennae" or a precise "scent" (40). An ant can use a "scent of horror" to communicate her distress and then be comforted by a companion "strok[ing] her antennae affectionately" (108). Grove's ants also use "scent-trees" to communicate large amounts of information; indeed, Wawa-quee records her journey "in detail on 813 scent-trees" (31).

For the most part, Grove is successful in his speculative representation of ant life. Yet, due to the legacy of "MAN," his zoocentrism is

---

[10] Coincidentally, the Toronto Humane Society began campaigning for humane slaughter the year after *Consider Her Ways* (1947) was published. Whilst the timing may have been unrelated, both the campaign and Grove's criticisms of animal agriculture reflect a burgeoning concern for farm animals in the mid-twentieth century.

[11] Integument is a scientific term for an organism's skin or shell.

inconsistent. On occasion, he even appropriates certain species, such as honeypot ants, to serve as satire. The fundamental issue is that *Consider Her Ways* (1947) is two books merged as one. Whilst they share themes and concerns, their priorities pull in opposite directions. One urges us to study 'man' and the other to 'go to the ant.' It is interesting to note, though, that Grove's writing process led him more and more towards the ant. Over decades of rewrites, the ant presence increased considerably. Moreover, Grove undertook considerable research to represent a detailed, scientifically accurate portrait of ant life. Although the book's more fantastical or satirical elements cannot be denied, there is also a sustained attempt to imagine what complex ant societies might look like. Karla Armbruster (2013) observes that most, if not all, "talking animal stories" still express a "yearning to know the otherness of nonhuman animals" (19).

Whilst so much of Grove's 'Ant book' was reworked, the introduction remained relatively consistent. Throughout the fifty-five years of rewrites, the core idea of an amateur myrmecologist observing, knowing, and communicating with ants was consistent throughout each manuscript. Yet, one of the most important developments in his writing process was that Grove increasingly expressed a *fantasy of knowing* the animal. Unlike Ferenczy, his interest in the ants themselves seems to grow with each manuscript. Indeed, his final addition of telepathy to the introduction seems an explicit *fantasy of knowing* an animal: a creative exploration of the ultimate act of empathy. To assume that such a well-researched and vividly imagined depiction of ant societies would have no interest in ants themselves seems reductive. Even if we read parts of the story as allegory, we cannot overlook Grove's commitment to a sincere, seemingly exhaustive, effort to speculate about the inner lives of imaginary ants.

FRED BODSWORTH: *LAST OF THE CURLEWS* (1955)

Last of the Curlews (1955) was initially published in *Maclean's* magazine on 15th May 1954. It was the first novella of journalist, Fred Bodsworth (1918–2012), who wrote for *Maclean's*, the *St. Thomas Times-Journal,* and the *Toronto Star*. In a similar way to Seton, Bodsworth was an amateur naturalist who wrote both fiction and nonfiction. He was president of the Federation of Ontario Naturalists between 1964 and 1967 and published *The Pacific Coast: The Illustrated Natural History of Canada* in 1970.

Bodsworth (1959) wrote an article about Seton for *Maclean's* titled, "The Backwoods Genius with the Magic Pen." He attributed to Seton the creation of a "strikingly new literary form," which made a "monumental step toward realistic animal portrayal" (22). Moreover, he credits Seton with inspiring a new "respect and concern for wild animals" in Canada that gave "birth" to "conservation groups, humane societies, game laws and wildlife sanctuaries" (22, 32). According to Bodsworth, Seton had a "special significance" in Canada, both as a literary innovator and the stimulus behind the nation's animal protection movements (32).

As with many Canadian authors addressed in this book, Bodsworth's childhood had been profoundly affected by Seton's work. In the 1959 article, he "vividly" recalls being at school with "the classroom in tears" as they listened to the teacher read "Lobo" and other stories (32). However, some would grow up to reject Seton as a nature faker, as we found with Haig-Brown's Schwiebert (1984) interview. This is something we will encounter again in Chap. 7 in Marian Engel's *Bear* (1976). Indeed, it is much rarer to find twentieth-century authors who sing his praises. Yet Bodsworth (1959) defended Seton against what he called the "homegrown belittlers of Canadian art and culture" (32). In the article, he argues that those who "bemoan" that "Canada had originated nothing of artist merit" continue to "overlook Seton's wildlife fiction" (32). Indeed, Seton had created an "original Canadian literary form" that was "quickly imitated" by "literary greats throughout the world" (32).

Despite Seton's influence, however, Bodsworth seems to have been aware of the man's limitations. In his article, Bodsworth (1959) points out that "biologists today" claim Seton "fell short of depicting animals as they actually are" (22). Even with "his reputation as a scientist," there are "glaring scientific flaws" in his stories (32). Interestingly, Bodsworth does not discuss the Nature Fakers controversy. His long article makes no mention of John Burroughs or Theodore Roosevelt. Instead, he identifies the issue as Seton succumbing to a "fallacy common for his time—the error of anthropomorphism" (32). Thus, he frames the problem not as one of 'nature faking,' but simply of Seton being out of step with contemporary science: "Modern biologists contend that Seton's animal heroes are too liberally endowed with human emotions like love, grief, and hate. Some possess too much reasoning power to be accepted as animals today" (32).

In the 1950s, behaviourism was at the height of its influence and ethology was not far behind. This means that mechanomorphic language would have been widely accepted in the sciences on both sides of the Atlantic. As a result, the modern biologists Bodsworth describes would not have referred to animals as having minds or emotions at all. Even though mechanomorphism had been adopted as an antidote to anthropomorphism, it carried unintended consequences. Eileen Crist (1999) observes that mechanomorphic language presents animals as "puppetlike" (85). Individuals appear "mindless," steered by "theoretically explained forces that are beyond their control and understanding" (85). Rather than depicting animals as active agents in their own lives, mechanomorphism breaks down their complex activities into involuntary responses described in mechanical terms, such as: release, activate, or trigger (98).

Given his awareness of the issues in Seton's work, Bodsworth seems to have been determined that his own fiction would be in line with contemporary science. In his article, Bodsworth (1959) states that "Seton tried to show animal lives and personalities as they are in nature," but that "viewing Seton in the sharper light of modern biological knowledge" reveals that he "fell short" (22, 32). Here, Bodsworth entwines realistic animal representation with accurate scientific engagement. As a result, his first work of animal fiction, *Last of the Curlews* (1955), borrows the core characteristics of the wild animal story while also employing the language of mechanomorphism. This approach is similar to Haig-Brown's adaptation of the form in *Return to the River* (1941). However, whilst Haig-Brown tended to restrict his mechanomorphic language to conversations between human characters, Bodsworth does not do this. Instead, his mechanomorphic statements come from the omniscient narration itself. This creates something of a paradoxical representation.

Last of the Curlews is a vivid example of the tension between zoocentric representation and mechanomorphic language. In this case, it produces a discrepancy between the individual's actions and Bodsworth's (1955) descriptions of them. His protagonist is cognitively and emotionally complex, yet throughout the book, there are jarringly reductive statements about the bird's "instinct-dominated brain" (9). It is worth noting that, in contrast to the other texts addressed in this book so far, Bodsworth adopts an overtly instinct-based theory of animal behaviour.

Where other authors have perceived animals as acting through a combination of intelligence and instinct, Bodsworth relies almost entirely on instinct. As we have seen, the other two authors addressed in this chapter—Haig-Brown and Grove—both made direct statements rejecting the concept of instinct, particularly when used to explain complex behaviours. Perhaps Bodsworth's approach to animal representation indicates a shift in attitudes towards the concept of instinct, particularly after the increasing influence of ethology in the second half of the century.

To some extent, we can read *Last of the Curlews* as a thought experiment on the role of instinct in determining animal behaviour. Bodsworth (1955) applies the concept universally to almost all animal activities. This means that, unlike Seton, Roberts, or Haig-Brown, he does not explore any examples of animal learning. Indeed, his curlew protagonist does not seem to change at all. His behaviour is largely fixed. This suits Bodsworth's narrative, however. *Last of the Curlews* explores the life of the last Northern curlew, also known as the 'Eskimo' curlew.[12]

Bodsworth's protagonist is a five-year-old male who completes an annual migration from the Canadian arctic tundra to the southern tip of Patagonia and back again without knowing another member of his own species. Each year he secures a potential nesting site for his mate, despite not remembering the nest of his own birth, his parents, siblings, or any females of his kind. His only companions are members of other species, such as large Hudsonian curlews or small Golden plovers. Where Seton's animal biographies explored individual learning in a range of unusual contexts (such as orphaned animals or those who were raised by humans), Bodsworth resists making such speculations. Instead, his protagonist's behaviour is almost unaffected by being the last member of his species.

Of course, the tragedy of Bodsworth's book lies in this dramatic irony: the curlew's innate expectation of finding a mate versus our knowledge that he is ultimately alone. Instinctually, he pursues species-typical behaviours without understanding why there are no other curlews to join his migrations or to challenge his mating territory. Bodsworth (1955) elicits our sympathies through this discrepancy between what the curlew anticipates and the reality of his solitary existence. Throughout *Last of the Curlews*, even up to its final lines, he never stops looking for the "female his instinct told him soon would come" (122). In order to create this naive optimism, the curlew must be controlled by instinct. He must have these innate expectations for the dramatic irony to work. Otherwise, he might just adapt to an entirely different existence, perhaps amongst the Hudsonian curlews or Golden plovers. Bodsworth is caught in a bind between requiring the curlew to be almost entirely controlled by instinct and yet remain

---

[12] It should be noted that Bodsworth uses this name throughout the book. For the sake of historical accuracy, I have included some examples of the term, particularly in the sources he quotes. That this was the English name of the species for so long reveals yet further complexities in the deeply entwined relationship between science and colonization in North America, particularly for this species. Given the racist connotations of the word, however, I will be using the modern name, Northern curlew.

cognitively and emotionally complex enough to be a sympathetic protagonist. No doubt the story would be less effective if the curlew were an insentient automaton with no reaction to his isolation whatsoever.

Although Bodsworth (1955) claims that the curlew's brain was "so keenly keyed to instinctive responses that there was little capacity for conscious thought or memory," the bird *does* seem to live a vivid internal existence (14). He demonstrates a wide range of complex emotions, including ecstasy, excitement, torment, fury, hope, nostalgia, tenderness, and loneliness (9, 14–6, 33, 74–5, 86, 90, 115–9). The book opens in early June, just as the curlew has completed his migration to the Arctic. As soon as he recognized the "familiar S-twist of the ice-hemmed river," the curlew "knew" that "he was home" and felt the "ecstasy of homecoming" (8–9).

Each year, the curlew returned to the same territory, the borders of which he knew precisely, even though in the "harsh emptiness," there was nothing that "stood out" as a "landmark" (12). Nonetheless, he knew "every rock, gravel bar, puddle and bush of his territory" (12). He was drawn by an "instinctive urge he felt but didn't understand" to this place and the specific spot where "the nest would be" (18). In the intensity of his emotions, the curlew "hardly remembered" that he had been "mysteriously alone" each mating season when, "inexplicably, no female had come" (9).

Evidently, the curlew possesses a keen memory and a strong emotional attachment to his territory, which seems to be a highly specific location that he has chosen and avidly defends from other birds. Yet Bodsworth's narration asserts that the curlew is unaware, lacks intention, and does *not* understand his actions. "Instinctively," the curlew fought off "every other shorebird that ventured near," but as soon as the "annual rhythm of glandular activity" began to pass and the "belligerent drive of the mating time" died off, he was suddenly less concerned with defending his territory (Bodsworth 1955, 21–3). His behaviour is so determined by instinct that his actions seem out of his control. As his hormones change, his behaviour becomes erratic: "suddenly remembering that there were intruders on his territory" and then "just as suddenly forgetting them" (24). Here, we can see the consequences of mechanomorphism. This is what Crist (1999) describes as animals appearing "compulsively steered" by "stimuli beyond their control and comprehension" (9). In essence, animals seem "blind to the upshot of their behaviours," which apparently emerge as "involuntary" (9).

Throughout the book, Bodsworth (1955) frequently reiterates that the curlew's behaviour was "not controlled by mental decisions" but by an "instinctive behaviour code" planted "deep" in his brain by "the genes of countless generations" (27). These genes told him "what to do" but "without telling him why" (27). The problem is that sometimes instinct becomes an almost supernatural force giving the curlew access to information that he would not possess otherwise. For instance, he "didn't know" that the closely related Hudsonian curlew was a "slower flying-bird" (27). But when it is time to migrate, they fail to "release the flocking response in his inner brain" and thus he feels an "instinctive rejection" of them (27, 34).

Instead, it is the Golden plovers, "much smaller than the curlew," who do satisfy the his "urge to join a flock" (34). As it turns out, of the "thirty-odd shorebirds" migrating south each autumn, "only the golden plover is suited as a migration companion" for the curlew (35). Rather than the curlew coming to this knowledge by learning from his four previous migrations, he is unknowingly guided to the 'correct' answer by instinct alone.

By migrating with the plovers, the "curlew's flocking urge was satisfied," yet there was still a "vague, remote feeling of loneliness deep within him still" (34). On occasion, the curlew seems to become suddenly aware of his isolation. At the beginning of the book, Bodsworth asserts that the "curlew's instinct-dominated brain didn't know or ask why" there were no other members of his species (9). But, after spending yet another mating season without seeing any female curlews, "somewhere in his tiny, rudimentary brain the simple beginnings of a reasoning process" asks: "Why was he always alone?" (25). These moments of awareness are arresting. They evoke a little of the surprise Seton experienced with the Currumpaw wolves (Witt 2010). The curlew's acknowledgement of his isolation and related feelings of loneliness requires a degree of cognitive complexity that seems at odds with Bodsworth's reductive statements. I would suggest that, though these moments risk accusations of anthropomorphism, they are required for Bodsworth's message of advocacy.

Last of the Curlews is not only significant for the contradictory depiction of its protagonist. It is the earliest example we have of a text written in response to the extinction of a species. Where Haig-Brown's (1941) *Return to the River* attempted to advocate against the building of hydroelectric dams happening at the time, *Last of the Curlews* laments the loss of a species that was already extinct.[13] This produces a different form

---

[13] Note that the species was not *quite* extinct when Bodsworth was writing in the 1950s. The last confirmed sighting of the Northern curlew was in 1962. No doubt the species is extinct by now.

of animal advocacy. Rather than campaigning to prevent violence or cruelty, Bodsworth (1955) provides an account of how the destruction of the Northern curlew took place. He presents this alongside the novel's fictional narrative. The technique is similar to Seton's (1901, 1905) use of historical context in the stories "Tito" and "Badlands Billy". Where Seton demonstrated the violence perpetrated against wolves and coyotes after they became labelled as 'vermin,' Bodsworth explores the consequences of the curlew's status as a 'game bird.' In both cases, historicizing human-animal relations in North America reveals the enormous destruction wrought by European colonization.

Excerpts from historical materials intersect each chapter of *Last of the Curlews*. Under the heading, "The Gauntlet," these sections provide a record of the Northern curlew's decline from one of the most prolific birds of the Americas to extinction in less than two centuries. The sources used range from the "Philosophical Transactions of The Royal Society of London" to "The Proceedings of the Nebraska Ornithologists' Union" (Bodsworth 1955, 19, 73). Their publication dates span 1772 to 1955. Through these materials, Bodsworth traces the curlew's changing status from prolific new species to abundant game bird. As these extracts progress chronologically, we see a corresponding decline in population. Towards the end of the book, as these sources begin to describe the curlew as 'endangered' and eventually 'extinct,' the numbers of birds fall until a final reported sighting of only two curlews in 1945.

In Bodsworth's (1955) overtly colonial history, there can be no doubt about the cause of the Northern curlew's extinction. "The Gauntlet" begins with a report by the ornithologist, Johann Reinhold Forster, published by the Royal Society in 1772. He describes a "species of curlew" that was "not yet known to the Ornithologists," which he identifies as the "Eskimaux Curlew" (20). The birds had been sent to the "factory at Hudson's Bay" along with a "large collection of uncommon quadrupeds, birds, fishes, &c." (19). Throughout "The Gauntlet," we find many references to the Hudson's Bay Company. Initially a fur-trading business, the Company was instrumental in colonization and the exploitation of wildlife. Forster's account also demonstrates the relationship between science and colonial enterprise. In this instance, animals brought to a fur-trading post could be identified by naturalists who then sent their reports back to the Royal Society in London for both publication and prestige.

In Forster's account from 1772, he notes that the curlews migrated in "enormous flocks" (Bodsworth 1955, 20). The next "Gauntlet," from

1884, describes an "immense flock of several hundred individuals" (30). After this, the population diminishes rapidly. In the third "Gauntlet," a paper titled "Birds of Labrador" from the *Proceedings of the Boston Society of Natural History* for 1906–1907 describes the Northern curlew as a "very rare" visitor after being "persistently harassed" by the people of Labrador (40–1). According to the report, the community had not realized there was "any diminution" in the birds' numbers until "about 1880 to 1890" (41). Even by the 1900s, the curlew was "a vanishing race—on the way to extinction" (41). Yet, despite this evident population loss, "The Gauntlet" continues to record a rising death toll. A report from 1915 states: "In a day's shooting by 25 or 30 men as many as 2,000 curlews would be killed for the Hudson Bay Co.'s store at Cartwright, Labrador" (49).

Interestingly, as "The Gauntlet" continues, we begin to see the relationship between science and conservation developing in the early twentieth century. From previously describing the habits of the curlew or reporting the numbers of bids shot for the Hudson's Bay Company, the scientific publications Bodsworth includes become increasingly concerned with species loss. A paper from *The Proceedings of the Nebraska Ornithologists' Union* in 1915, titled "The Eskimo Curlew and Its Disappearance," describes the species as "at the verge of extinction" (Bodsworth 1955, 79). Likewise, the American Ornithologist's Union created the Committee on Bird Protection and its inquiries in 1939 found that the "most dangerously situated" species were "unquestionably" the "California condor, Eskimo curlew and ivory-billed woodpecker" (79). In a subsequent extract in "The Gauntlet," the Committee on Bird Protection lists the numbers of Californian condors and ivory-billed woodpeckers but identifies the Northern curlew population as "unknown;" it is "quite possible that the bird is extinct" (93).

In less than two centuries, the Northern curlew population is reduced from "enormous flocks" to "probably extinct" (20, 123). This timescale aligns with the colonization of North America. Indeed, as the dates of Bodsworth's historical sources progress chronologically, their locations move geographically. From the first published by "The Royal Society of London" in 1772 to the last published by "The University of Toronto Press" in cooperation with the "Royal Ontario Museum of Zoology and Palæontology" in 1955 (19, 123). Bodsworth's use of historical documents demonstrates the catastrophic impact of colonization on wildlife. Evidently, the Indigenous peoples of the Americas had hunted the Northern curlew for generations without such catastrophic species loss. As we observe the changing tone of "The Gauntlet," we can see how the colonial myth of superabundant wildlife was replaced by an abrupt recognition of looming extinction.

Several sources used in "The Gauntlet" make the cause of the Northern curlew's extinction clear. A bulletin from the United States National Museum asserts the issue outright: "there was only one cause, slaughter by human beings" (Bodsworth 1955, 69). Likewise, "The Eskimo Curlew and Its Disappearance" describes the "wholly unreasonable and uncontrolled slaughter of our North American bird life" during "the last half of the nineteenth century" (77). One unidentified source notes that the "greatest killings" occurred during the curlews' spring migration, "after the birds had crossed the Gulf of Mexico" and "the great flocks moved northwards up the North American plains" (102). Not only were there "numerous gunners who shot these birds for local consumption or simply for the love of killing," there also developed "a class of professional market hunters, who made it a business to follow the flights" (103).

In a short statement at the beginning of the book, Bodsworth (1955) writes that the Northern "curlew, originally one of the continent's most abundant game-birds, flew a gauntlet of shot each Spring and Autumn" (7). Labelling the curlew 'game' spelled their death, just as 'vermin' had done for Seton's (1901, 1905) coyotes and wolves. One extract in "The Gauntlet" mentions that gunners also called them dough-birds. This name came from the "thick layer of fat" around the curlew's breast— "so soft that it felt like a ball of dough"—required for the birds to endure such a vast migration (Bodsworth 1955, 57). Ironically, this survival mechanism, gradually honed by evolution, rapidly accelerated the curlew's extinction at the hands of European colonizers:

> two Massachusetts market gunners sold $300 worth from one flight ... boys offer the birds for sale at 6 cents apiece ... in 1882 two hunters in Nantucket shot 87 Eskimo curlew in one morning ... by 1894 there was only one dough-bird offered for sale on the Boston market. (58)

This correlation between the name dough-bird and the extreme scale of the species' slaughter demonstrates the direct link between speciesism and violence. As Joan Dunayer (2001) reminds us: the "way we speak about animals is inseparable from the way we treat them" (9).

Bodsworth's innovative technique of intersecting the lone curlew's story with these archive materials drives the force of his critique. The curlew's awareness of his isolation poses an unspoken question and "The Gauntlet" provides the answer. Towards the end of the novel, both the curlew's narrative and "The Gauntlet" are brought together in an unlikely encounter with a female curlew. Of course, "the instinct of generations past" ensures that the two curlews' recognition of each other is "sure and immediate" (Bodsworth 1955, 79). What is striking, however, is that their interactions mirror recording sightings presented in the final sections of "The Gauntlet."

An extract from *The Auk* describes "[t]wo Eskimo curlews which appeared to be a mated pair" spotted in "March at Galveston, Texas" (111). The birds are "amongst a huge assemblage of marsh and shore-birds" feeding along the "sand flat, shallow ponds and grassy patches on Galveston Island" (111). "A Summary of the Spring Migration" comments that the "most noteworthy record" of the season was an "observa-tion" of a pair of "curlews on Galveston Island, Texas" (112). The extract continues: "For twenty years only an occasional lone Eskimo curlew has been seen and the fact that these were probably a mated pair makes it a record of great significance" (112). These records appear at the same point in the book that Bodsworth's curlews visit a "long, narrow island of sand dunes and grasslands" in the "salt marshes of the Texas coast" and feed amongst "[h]osts of other shorebirds" (108). The pair spend "three weeks" on the island before leaving in "early April" (109–110). This would seem to suggest that Bodsworth's protagonists are the curlews observed on Galveston Island in March.

By interweaving his narrative with these pieces of evidence, Bodsworth subtly positions his book as a real animal biography. Whilst he is not so bold as Seton, who claimed that his stories were true, there are some simi-larities here. Bodsworth's investigations into the life of the last Northern curlew is reminiscent of Seton's speculations about the real animals he encountered.[14] In particular, Bodsworth's exploration of how the last member of a species might engage in migratory or nest-building behav-iours is similar to Seton's questioning of the activities of the Currumpaw Valley wolves. However, whereas Seton considered these processes in depth through speculations about animal social learning, Bodsworth bases his explanations of animal behaviour on instinct alone. Nonetheless, we

---

[14] This technique is clear in Seton's book, *Animal Heroes* (1905), particularly in the stories of "Arnaux" and "Warhorse," both of which employ evidence from newspaper articles and other archive materials.

can see that, in this guarded manner, Bodsworth does engage with one of Seton's more controversial techniques. He produces a 'factual' wild animal story without causing a controversy. All that is lacking, of course, is the assertion that the story is true.

The extract from "A Summary of the Spring Migration" remarks: "As long as one pair remains there is hope that the species may yet escape extinction" (Bodsworth 1955, 112). Inevitably, *Last of the Curlews* does not end on this optimistic note. Just as the two curlews are about to mate, the female is shot by a farmer. This ironic tragedy is reminiscent of Seton's and Roberts's wild animal stories, in which death would befall the animal or their family just as their survival seemed assured. As Seton (1898) remarked: the "life of the wild animal always has a tragic end" (12). Of course, in Bodsworth's (1955) book, the tragedy of the female's death is compounded because it is both the death of an individual and the species simultaneously. Without her, there is no more "hope that the species may yet escape extinction" (112).

In the death of the female curlew, we can see that any efforts to protect the species have been insufficient. Despite widespread recognition that the Northern curlew had been near extinction for decades, they were not protected sufficiently. Curlews were still being shot. As we have seen in other texts, the narrative demonstrates the ways in which anthropocentric perceptions of animals (often as 'useful' dead objects) exacerbates the precarious serendipity of survival in the wild. The female curlew's death is the tragic culmination of the male curlew's silent interrogation. Of course, the male never quite understands why he has been so mysteriously alone all his life. Instead, the answer is provided for the human readers.

The male curlew's solitary life is all the more distressing for his strong emotional responses, with loneliness dominating above all. On a grand scale, the extinction of a species is terrible but without the individual narrative the loss is reduced to statistics, dates, and the inconceivable mass of deaths. Again, as in Haig-Brown's (1941) *Return to the River*, we find an emphasis on the connection between the suffering individual and the suffering species. Bodsworth (1955) takes the general extinction of the Northern curlew and transforms it into a unique individual's story of isolation and grief.

Yet, for all the emotional intensity of *Last of the Curlews*, Bodsworth was not accused of anthropomorphism. Indeed, the book was well-received, particularly in reviews from scientific journals. A review for *The Murrelet* (a journal of ornithology and mammalogy) commented that Bodsworth clearly had "a scientifically acceptable understanding of bird behaviour" (Edwards 1955, 13). Whilst "[s]cience usually frowns on fiction in its field," *Last of the Curlews* is a "good example" of a "fictitious narrative, carefully told," that will "reach a wider audience" with a more powerful and "palatable message" than the "scraps of fact available ever do" (13). Likewise, a review in the *Journal of Field Ornithology* remarks: "We rarely use fiction to put the case of an endangered species before the public, yet this is exactly what Bodsworth has done" (Burtt 1988, 425). However, the reviewer adds: "Don't get the wrong idea. This is not a cute, anthropomorphic story" (425). Indeed, he goes on to praise Bodsworth's ability to convey scientific details "concisely and accurately" (425).

It seems that Bodsworth 'succeeded' in his realistic wild animal story where Seton and Roberts did not. Each reviewer praises the balance between fact and fiction, the accuracy of his scientific explanations, and the overall avoidance of anthropomorphism. By repeatedly and overtly undermining the cognitive complexity of his protagonist, Bodsworth avoided criticisms. Yet, at the same time, the curlew seems filled with emotions. Evidently, Bodsworth's somewhat paradoxical approach reveals the difficulty of writing texts that were both scientifically informed and advocacy-orientated at this time. For many of the authors addressed in this book, depictions of animals with cognitive and emotional complexity are integral to their messages of advocacy. This can be difficult to achieve if the author wishes to write a book that would be considered scientifically accurate by the standards of the time.

CONCLUSION

In this chapter we can see the direct influence of the Nature Fakers controversy. Perhaps more than in any other chapter of this book, these texts reveal the profound impact of science on the writing of animal fiction. As discussed in the two previous chapters, the controversy had more to do with the changing state of the sciences than with the accuracy of wild animal stories. By the early twentieth century, however, 'nature faker' had taken on its own meaning. No longer was the term restricted to writers of animal fiction. Now, it was used to disparage scientists whose work was seen to lack objectivity.

Haig-Brown, Grove, and Bodsworth all adapted the wild animal story to avoid accusations of nature faking or anthropomorphism. Where Seton and Roberts made confident statements regarding animal intelligence and emotions, Haig-Brown and Bodsworth avoided mention of animal minds altogether. Meanwhile, Grove gave accurate scientific information about an imaginary species of ant. These innovative measures demonstrate the difficulty of writing compelling animal protagonists whilst also adhering to the language of mechanomorphism.

REFERENCES

Armbruster, Karla. 2013. What Do We Want from Talking Animals? In *Speaking for Animals: Animal Autobiographical Writing*, ed. Margo DeMello, 18–33. New York: Routledge.

Balcombe, Jonathan. 2009. Animal Pleasure and Its Moral Significance. *Applied Animal Behaviour Science*. 118: 208–216. https://doi.org/10.1016/j.applanim.2009.02.012.

Bekoff, Marc. 2000. Animal Emotions: Exploring Passionate Natures. *BioScience*. 50 (10, October): 861–870. https://doi.org/10.1641/0006-3568(2000)05 0[0861:AEEPN]2.0.CO;2.

Bodsworth, Fred. (1955) 1956. *Last of the Curlews*. London: Museum Press.

———. 1959. The Backwoods Genius with the Magic Pen. *Maclean's*, June 6, pp. 22–40.

Braithwaite, Victoria. 2010. *Do Fish Feel Pain?* Oxford: Oxford University Press.

Burtt, Edward H., Jr. 1988. Review: *Last of the Curlews*. *Journal of Field Ornithology*. 59 (4, Autumn): 425–426.

Crist, Eileen. 1999. *Images of Animals: Anthropomorphism and Animal Mind*, 1999. Philadelphia: Temple University Press.

Dunayer, Joan. 2001. *Animal Equality: Language and Liberation*. Derwood: Ryce.

Edwards, R.Y. 1955. Review: *Last of the Curlews*. *The Murrelet*. 36 (1, January–April): 13.

Ferenczy, Árpád. 1924. *The Ants of Timothy Thümmel*. London: Jonathan Cape.

Grove, Frederick Philip. 1923. *Over Prairie Trails*. Toronto: McClelland and Stewart.

———. (1947) 2001. *Consider Her Ways*. Toronto: McClelland and Stewart.

Haig-Brown, Roderick. (1941) 1984. *Return to the River: A Story of the Chinook Run*. Oshkosh: Willow Creek.

———. (1931) 1946. *Silver: The Life Story of an Atlantic Salmon*. 2nd ed. London: A&C Black.

———. 1984. Foreword. In *Return to the River*, by Roderick Haig-Brown. Oshkosh: Willow Creek.

Love, Glen. 1998. Roderick Haig-Brown: Angling and the Craft of Nature Writing in North America. *ISLE*. 5 (1, Winter): 1–11. https://doi.org/10.1093/isle/5.1.1.

Rich, Willis H. 1937. Homing of the Pacific Salmon. *Science* 85: 476.

———. 1942. Return to the River: A Story of the Chinook Run. *Copeia*. 1 (March): 59.

———. 2007. *Over Canadian Trails: F.P. Grove in New Letters and Documents.* Würzburg: Königshausen & Neumann.

Roberts, Charles G.D. 1902. *Kindred of the Wild.* Boston: L. C. Page & Co.

———. 1907. *The Haunters of the Silences.* Boston: L. C. Page & Co.

Roosevelt, Theodore. 1907. Nature Fakers. *Everybody's Magazine.* 17 (3, September): 427–430.

Rose, J.D., et al. 2014. Can Fish Really Feel Pain? *Fish and Fisheries.* 15: 97–133. https://doi.org/10.1111/faf.12010.

Schwiebert, Ernest. 1984. Introduction. In *Return to the River*, by Roderick Haig-Brown. Oshkosh: Willow Creek.

Seton, Ernest Thompson. 1898. *Wild Animals I Have Known.* New York: Charles Scriber's Sons.

———. 1901. *Lives of the Hunted.* London: David Nutt.

———. 1905. *Animal Heroes.* London: Constable & Company.

Stobie, Margaret. 1978. Grove and the Ants. *Dalhousie Review.* 58 (3): 418–433.

Wheeler, William Morton. 1910. *Ants: Their Structure, Development and Behavior.* New York: Columbia University Press.

Whitehead, Hal. 2003. *Sperm Whales: Social Evolution in the Ocean.* Chicago: University of Chicago Press.

Witt, David L. 2010. *Ernest Thompson Seton: The Life and Legacy of an Artist and Conservationist.* Layton: Gibbs Smith.

PART III

Divergence

CHAPTER 6

1950s–1980s Contexts

This chapter describes a period of social, cultural, political, and scientific transformation. In the mid-twentieth century, the cognitive revolution swept through the sciences. By challenging the dominance of mechano-morphic language in behaviourism and ethology, it enabled the new field of cognitive ethology to develop in the 1970s. Explicitly concerned with the topic of consciousness, cognitive ethology reintroduced questions of animal minds and emotions back into the sciences. Meanwhile, increasing awareness of pollution, environmental destruction, and species loss coalesced into the environmental movement. This helped to transform wildlife conservation from 'management' into 'protection.' For the first time, this included the protection of predators. Growing animal advocacy movements began to receive wider public attention during this period. In this atmosphere, some advocates also reintroduced the question of animals having *rights* for the first time in eighty years.

Cognitive Revolution

During the height of behaviourism's influence in the 1950s, another scientific movement was beginning to rise. If behaviourism had removed 'the mind' from the study of psychology, the cognitivist movement would

© The Author(s), under exclusive license to Springer Nature Switzerland AG 2023

C. Allmark-Kent, *Literature, Science, and Animal Advocacy in Canada*, Palgrave Studies in Animals and Literature, https://doi.org/10.1007/978-3-031-40556-3_6

ultimately restore it. These changes were part of the cognitive revolution, a multidisciplinary transformation that spanned both the sciences and humanities. In fields as diverse as philosophy, linguistics, and computer science, questions about cognition were changing both theory and methodology. For decades, behaviourism had framed the activities of *all* living beings—including humans—through the relationship between stimulus and response. This all-encompassing approach was even applied to complex phenomena, such as language.

An early success for the cognitivist movement came in 1959 when the American linguist Noam Chomsky wrote a highly critical review of B. F. Skinner's book, *Verbal Behaviour* (1957). Unusually, Skinner chose not to respond. Some took this as the beginning of behaviourism's decline. As Howard Gardner (1987) puts it, Skinner's choice not to publicly defend his position, seemed to indicate its inherent "theoretical bankruptcy" (193). Of course, it would be an overstatement to suggest that behaviourism vanished from the study of psychology overnight. Still, the cognitive revolution represented a profound shift in attitudes towards mental states. Whilst this process was relatively quick in human psychology, it took a little longer to develop in animal psychology. It would be another decade until the cognitive revolution reached the scientific study of animal minds in the 1970s.

In Europe, ethology had been gaining traction for years. Yet, it lacked a clear definition and was generally misunderstood by the public. Recognizing this, Niko Tinbergen offered a remedy in his 1963 paper, "On Aims and Methods of Ethology." Lamenting that ethology was "still very far from being a unified science," he set out to establish definitions, approaches, aims, and methods (Tinbergen 1996, 114). Here, he sought to strengthen the field by establishing a concrete framework through which ethology could operate. Most famously, he built upon the work of British biologist Julian Huxley to contribute four core questions designed to shape all future ethological inquiry. These can be divided into two 'how' questions (causation and development) and two 'why' questions (function and evolution). In 1973, ethology finally gained recognition as a science when Tinbergen shared the Nobel Prize with Konrad Lorenz and Karl von Frisch. Ironically, however, ethology's influence was already beginning to wane by this time. The theory of instinct upon which the field had been built had lost credibility. After a series of attacks and heated debates about instinct in the 1950s, the foundations of traditional ethology had been considerably weakened.

On both sides of the Atlantic, significant changes were taking place for the scientific study of animal behaviour. After the steady rising prominence of both behaviourism and ethology in the early decades of the twentieth century, the period after the 1950s was one of upheaval and transition for both fields. We can characterize these final decades as a time of divergence, transition, exchange, debate, controversy, and innovation. As the grand old theories of behaviourism and ethology fell, a flurry of new methods and approaches rose up including sociobiology, behavioural ecology, neuroethology, and cognitive ecology. One development most relevant to this book was *cognitive ethology*.

In 1976, Donald Griffin published *The Question of Animal Awareness*, in which he made the case for the scientific study of animal thinking and feeling. He began by noting the discovery of "increasing complexities in animal behaviour" in both ethology and behaviourism over the "past few decades" (1976, 3). These activities spanned social organization, courtship, nest-building, navigation, and so on. Most significant for Griffin, though, were developments in the study of animal communication. In particular, he emphasized the complexities of the honeybee 'waggle dance' and the primate sign language experiments of the 1970s. This is because these forms of communication seemed to express *intent*. In other words, they could not be explained through automatic or unconscious processes.

For Griffin, the intentionality behind complex communication seemed to indicate the presence of *conscious thought*. Using the primate language experiments as a model, he proposed the "extension and refinement of two-way communication between ethologists and the animals they study" (105). Given recent insights into the "versatility of some animal communication systems," it seemed possible, at least in principle, to use these strategies to "detect and examine any mental experiences or conscious intentions that animals may have" (105). Whether through learning new communication systems—such as sign language—or utilizing the animal's own communication behaviours, Griffin identified this approach as the best prospect for developing a "truly experimental science of cognitive ethology" (105).

Although a tone of excitement pervades *The Question of Animal Awareness*, Griffin (1976) still stressed the need for caution. He observed that reductive approaches to animal behaviour had developed due to the widespread acceptance of "unsupported and highly implausible" anecdotes of animal intelligence towards the end of the nineteenth century (71). He described this as an "excellent reason" for caution (71). Nonetheless, he also pointed out that by ignoring the "possible existence of mental experiences and conscious intent in animals" for decades, we may have "held back our scientific progress" (74). Thus, Griffin called for the creation of a cautious "middle ground" between an uncritical acceptance of animal thinking and the reductive assumption that animals are incapable of *any* mental experiences whatsoever (72).

Cognitive ethology's commitment to questions about animal thoughts and subjective feelings marked a significant departure from earlier scientific attitudes towards animal minds. Whilst the cognitive revolution did not wipe out mechanomorphism from the sciences, it did enable a significant shift from the traditions of previous decades. With the question of inner states back on the table, a new science of animal welfare could emerge. In 1980, Marian Stamp Dawkins published *Animal Suffering: The Science of Animal Welfare*. It was a new convergence of science and animal advocacy, a consequence of both the cognitive revolution and the animal rights movement.

Dawkins (2006) points out that, unlike classical ethology or behaviourism, the science of animal welfare is "unashamedly about what animals feel" (347). Understanding both an animal's physical and *mental* health are integral to assessing their welfare. Of course, Dawkins is all too aware of the difficulties of judging an animal's mental or emotional state. Yet, the field is driven by more urgent concerns:

> Not for us the luxury of being able to put the problems of animal consciousness to one side [...] Animal consciousness is no intriguing philosophical hobby for us. It's the day job. (348)

Here, we can see the renewed potential for communication between scientists and animal advocates after the cognitive revolution. Indeed, Dawkins notes the importance of both Griffin's work and reputation in making animal consciousness a respectable topic of scientific inquiry once more. Just like the relationship between comparative psychology and the humane movements at the end of the nineteenth century, cognitive ethology offered crucial scientific support for the ethical treatment of animals.

Environmentalism and Wildlife Protection

In our contradictory impulse to simultaneously exploit and protect animals, exploitation usually wins out. We find abundant examples in the treatment of both wild and domesticated animals. At the same time as campaigners in Canada were fighting for the humane slaughter of farm animals at the end of the 1950s, the 'wild' animals in national parks were being slaughtered for their meat. By the 1960s, some parks had become "almost indistinguishable from the agricultural operations that surrounded them," complete with "corrals, chutes, squeezes, and abattoirs" (Loo 2006, 121). Ironically, this was a result of conservation practices.

Canada's perception of its wildlife as a natural resource had combined with a New Ecology that viewed animals as organic machines. From this perspective, the land in national parks could be managed to ensure 'correct' yields of the wildlife tourists wanted to see. It was perhaps inevitable that this idea would extend to extracting more profit from the animals themselves. However, this is not to say that all were in favour of this approach. Objections from scientists and wildlife workers combined with changing public attitudes to end the commercial slaughter. This was the beginning of a shift in wildlife conservation. Ecologists were making it clear that nature was best left alone and so began a new policy of non-intervention for the final decades of the twentieth century (Loo 2006, 148).

The hands-off approach did not always extend to predators, however. Even though ecologists had been arguing for the importance of predators since the 1920s and 1930s, they were often still seen as 'vermin.' As such, the informal predator control and local bounty systems had remained in place. Government wildlife workers needed little excuse beyond mere curiosity, fear, or greed to poison, shoot, and trap predators by the tens of thousands (Loo 2006, 152). Evidently, the speciesist stereotypes against which Ernest Thompson Seton had written in the nineteenth century were hard to shake. Yet, decades later, a new generation of Canadians were ready to challenge these ideas again.

During the 1950s, Disney's *True-Life Adventures* film series had made wildlife documentaries enormously popular. As Gregg Mitman (2009) puts it, they "succeeded in capturing and monopolizing a mass market for nature on the big screen" (110). This vision of nature—with jaunty music and comical sound effects—stood in contrast to the more subdued style of Canadian wildlife films. Most Canadians would have been familiar with the documentaries produced by the National Film board, which tended to reflect a "state way of seeing nature" as a "static object" to be "controlled and then exploited" (Clemens 2022, 96). From the 1960s, however, some Canadian filmmakers began to advocate for wildlife more directly. For instance, Andy Russell began filming grizzly bears to rehabilitate their public image (see Chap. 7). According to his son, Charlie Russell, and Maureen Enns (2003), he wanted to avoid the artificiality of Disney films by "depicting grizzly bears as they really were" in the wild (16). The result was an intimate, silent film that Russell narrated to live audiences (Loo 2006, 204–5).

Most successful were Bill Mason's films about wolves, *Death of a Legend* (1971) and *Cry of the Wild* (1972). Almost echoing Seton's stories, these documentaries presented wolves as unique individuals with emotions, personalities, and complex social relationships. Along similar lines, Farley Mowat's autobiographical account of his encounters with wolves *Never Cry Wolf* (1963) was adapted into a successful drama of the same name in 1983. Together, these films were part of a wider effort to transform attitudes towards predators. They encouraged audiences to sympathize with wolves and bears as *individuals*, while also spreading scientific information about their crucial role in the ecological balance. Emphatically, these writers and filmmakers argued that nature should be left alone.

Perhaps the most important shift towards non-intervention came from Rachel Carson's *Silent Spring* (1962). At the core, she thoroughly dismantled the idea that humans should—or even *could*—attempt to control nature. Not only were humans too reckless and short-sighted to be stewards of the earth, Carson argued that the idea of 'stewardship' itself was unnecessary. Over "hundreds of millions of years" of evolution, life on earth has "reached a state of adjustment and balance with its surroundings" (Carson 2018, 14). Given time, life always "adjusts" and finds "balance" again (14). The problem is that this process takes "not years" but "millennia" and "in the modern world there is no time" (14). Carson presented abundant evidence of the widespread destruction caused by contemporary Western lifestyles to animals, plants, land, air, and water. Moreover, as a striking counterbalance, she also revealed that human efforts to control nature were not only destructive, but utterly ineffectual. At a time when human-animal relations were starting to be re-examined from multiple angles, Carson's book demonstrated a dual failure in human relationships with other species: unintended destruction *and* ineffectual control.

Silent Spring (1962) was immensely popular throughout North America and Carson found a significant audience in Canada. After considerable expansion and urbanization during the years of post-war prosperity, Canadian citizens had become concerned about the environmental costs of modern consumer society. High-profile environmental disasters happening throughout the world were making the public increasingly aware about the various ways that human industries polluted land, water, and air. *Silent Spring* provided urban Euro-Canadians with a new ecological perspective: life was interconnected.

The mainstream environmental movement in Canada began with local groups who targeted a specific issue, such as Pollution Probe, organized by the students and professors at The University of Toronto, to address the pollution of Great Lakes (Forkey 2012, 96). Of course, the most famous environmental group to emerge from Canada was Greenpeace, founded in Vancouver in 1971. Unlike previous advocacy movements, environmentalism addressed both local and global issues. However, these concerns shifted over time: "from nuclear, water, and air pollution in the 1960s and 1970s to acid rain, the ozone layer, and forests and wildlife protection in the 1980s and 1990s" (MacDowell 2012, 246). The environmental movement revealed the ecological destruction and violence to animals upon which Western consumer society was built. Where the conservation and environmental movements overlapped, the public gained more awareness of species loss and threats to biodiversity.

ANIMAL RIGHTS

In the 1960s and 1970s, Canada's animal welfare issues suddenly became an international concern. Graphic footage of a seal hunt filmed in the Gulf of St. Lawrence in 1964 caught the attention of environmental and animal protection groups across Europe and North America. Brian Davies of the New Brunswick SPCA instigated an international media campaign to end seal hunting in Canada. He began taking media representatives to visit the "ice floes where the hunt took place," giving talks across "Canada, Western Europe, and United States," and soliciting support for the SPCA's "Save the Seals Fund" through newspaper advertisements (Barry 2005, 5). The plan was not just to raise awareness but to create pressure on the Canadian government by mobilizing public outrage on a global scale (20).

Davies's strategy of creating foreign opposition to the hunt worked. A core component was to discourage international markets from buying

Canadian seal skins. In 1972, the United States passed the Marine Mammal Protection Act, which included a ban on importing seal products into the country. In 1983, the European Economic Community adopted a similar ban. This closure of the "pivotal European market for seal pup skins and products" was a catastrophic loss for the seal-hunting industry (2). Further international pressure also came from boycotts of Canadian fish products in Britain and the United States (2). Finally, the Canadian government banned the hunting of infant harp seals and hooded seals in 1987.

As John Sorenson (2010) puts it, the international reaction to images of seal hunting in Canada "helped build a global animal protection movement" (79). Across the world, scientists, artists, and celebrities joined to voice their opposition (79). The campaign marked a historic precedent for international collaboration in animal protection. Given the dramatic image of a baby seal being clubbed to death, it is easy to see why the campaign gained mainstream support. As with the creation of most animal protection laws in Canada, its predominantly white middle-class proponents would be unaffected by the ban. Broad public support for the campaign was possible because seal hunting was not seen as a 'necessary' form of animal exploitation. Indeed, it was during this period that Margaret Atwood (1972) characterized Canada, "as a whole" nation, joining in "animal-salvation campaigns such as the protest over the slaughter of baby seals and the movement to protect the wolf" (79).

Of course, the destruction of the international market for seal skin products was disastrous for Inuit communities reliant on these sales. Whilst the laws attempted to protect Inuit interests by allowing for subsistence hunting, they did not safeguard economic security. Even though the campaign was focused on large-vessel commercial sealing, their efforts to undermine international markets for the products cut off a vital source of income for remote Inuit communities. Ongoing deprivations from the impact of Davies's campaign would be felt for decades.[1]

Here, we find another example of animal protection policies created at the expense of Indigenous sovereignty. Darren Chang (2020) observes that mainstream animal protection groups in Europe and North America tend to demonstrate greater "aggression and persistence" when targeting "culturally specific animal practices and industries" (32). By contrast, they "show relative moderation" when "confronting issues of animal exploitation with European or Western origins," such as "industrial animal

---

[1] See Alethea Arnaquq-Baril's (2016) documentary, *Angry Inuk*.

farming and slaughter" (32). Indeed, animal advocacy groups that *do* challenge these more 'acceptable' forms of exploitation are still seen as too radical or extreme.

During the 1970s and 1980s, the controversial question of whether we owe animals certain rights began to re-emerge for the first time in decades. Whilst humane societies and animal protection groups had maintained a steady presence in Canada since the nineteenth century, the idea of animals having *rights* did not. For instance, the humane slaughter debates of the 1950s addressed the topic of reducing suffering during slaughter, not the issue of whether animals should be slaughtered at all. By the 1970s, developments across animal cognition research and animal advocacy created an opportunity for animal rights discourse to return. Animal language experiments, in particular, seemed to narrow the gap between humans and other species once more. These attempts to "talk to dolphins" or "teach language" to primates received considerable public attention (de Waal 2016, 99). The idea that other animals could be capable of language introduced a further sense of urgency to animal protection efforts.

Particularly influential were Peter Singer's *Animal Liberation* (1975), Tom Regan's *The Case for Animal Rights* (1984), and Richard Ryder's work on the concept of speciesism in 1970. It is little known, however, that a group of Canadians in Oxford (England) were also crucial to the re-emergence of animal *rights* discourse specifically. Rosalind and Stanley Godlovitch (both born in Montreal) coedited *Animals, Men and Morals* (1971) with their British colleague, John Harris. Rosalind Godlovitch's (1971) chapter, "Animals and Morals," was the first significant animal rights argument since Henry Salt's *Animals' Rights* in 1892. Although these ideas had lain dormant for eighty years, they were still highly controversial. Over the next few decades, the animal rights movement would face a significant backlash as the fear of 'humanizing' animals became a growing concern once again.

Conclusion

Certain ideas about animals rise and fall throughout this book. In the 1970s, the questions of animal *minds* and animal *rights* re-emerged for the first time in decades. With the mechanomorphic thinking of the early twentieth century, both ideas had been dismissed as anthropomorphic sentimentalism. Their near-simultaneous re-appearance illustrates the reciprocal communication between science and animal advocacy. Indeed, both topics were last popular in the late nineteenth century when humane societies and comparative psychology had shared parallel developments. This is not to suggest that either idea received complete acceptance, however. The cognitive revolution and animal protection movements had not eliminated anthropocentrism or mechanomorphism. Nonetheless, they represented a crucial shift in thinking for many. As we have seen throughout this book, however, each time theories of animal consciousness or animal rights seem to narrow the human-animal divide, they meet significant resistance from those invested in human uniqueness and supremacy.

REFERENCES

Arnaquq-Baril, Alethea, dir. 2016. *Angry Inuk*. National Film Board of Canada.

Atwood, Margaret. 1972. *Survival: A Thematic Guide to Canadian Literature*. Toronto: Anansi.

Barry, Donald. 2005. *Icy Battleground: Canada, the International Fund for Animal Welfare, and the Seal Hunt*. St. John's, NL: Breakwater Books.

Carson, Rachel. 2018. In *Silent Spring & Other Writings on the Environment*, ed. Sandra Steingraber. New York: The Library of America.

Chang, Darren. 2020. Tensions in Contemporary Indigenous and Animal Advocacy Struggles: The Commercial Seal Hunt as a Case Study. In *Colonialism and Animality: Anti-Colonial Perspectives in Critical Animal Studies*, ed. Kelly Struthers Montford and Chloë Taylor, 29–49. Oxon: Routledge.

Clemens, Michael D. 2022. *Screening Nature and Nation: The Environmental Documentaries of the National Film Board, 1939–1974*. Athabasca: AU Press.

Dawkins, Marian Stamp. 2006. Animal Welfare. In *Essays in Animal Behaviour: Celebrating 50 Years of Animal Behaviour*, ed. Jeffrey R. Lucas and Leigh W. Simmons, 347–361. London: Elsevier Academic Press.

Forkey, Neil S. 2012. *Canadians and the Natural Environment to the Twenty-First Century*. Toronto: University of Toronto Press.

Gardner, Howard. 1987. *The Mind's New Science: A History of the Cognitive Revolution*. New York: Basic Books.

Godlovitch, Stanley, Rosalind Godlovitch, and John Harris, eds. 1971. *Animals, Men and Morals: An Enquiry into the Maltreatment of Non-Humans*. New York: Taplinger.

Griffin, Donald R. 1976. *The Question of Animal Awareness: Evolutionary Continuity of Mental Experience*. New York: Rockerfeller University Press.

Loo, Tina. 2006. *States of Nature: Conserving Canada's Wildlife in the Twentieth Century*. Vancouver: UBC Press.

MacDowell, Laurel Sefton. 2012. *An Environmental History of Canada*. Vancouver: UBC Press.

Mitman, Gregg. 2009. *Reel Nature: America's Romance with Wildlife on Film*. Seattle: University of Washington Press.

Russell, Charlie, and Maureen Enns. 2003. *Grizzly Heart: Living Without Fear Among the Brown Bears of Kamchatka*. Toronto: Vintage Canada.

Sorenson, John. 2010. *About Canada: Animal Rights*. Black Point: Fernwood.

Tinbergen, Niko. 1996. On Aims and Methods of Ethology. In *Foundations of Animal Behaviour: Classic Papers with Commentaries*, ed. Lynne D. Houck and Lee C. Drickamer, 114–137. Chicago: The University of Chicago Press.

de Waal, Frans. 2016. *Are We Smart Enough to Know Smart Animals Are?* New York: W. W. Norton & Company.

CHAPTER 7

1950s–1980s Texts

This chapter addresses the ways in which animal representation began to diverge in the 1960s. During this period, Canadian writers were exploring the same question of knowing other animals that had preoccupied science decades before. Many took the stance of 'unknowability' established by early twentieth-century ethologists and behaviourists. Yet the cognitive revolution's attempts to study animal language and consciousness were opening up new pathways to knowing. At the same time, animal advocacy and environmental movements created a greater sense of urgency in the need to improve our understanding of other species. These changing ideas about animals found expression in two new forms of animal representation in fiction: the *failure of knowing* the animal and the *acceptance of not knowing* the animal. This chapter offers three examples of diverging attempts to know animals through fiction from this period.

Marian Engel: *Bear* (1976)

In 1976, Marian Engel (1933–1985) published a controversial book. *Bear* did not stir debate on the scale of the Nature Fakers controversy but it did raise eyebrows both upon publication and after winning the Governor General's Award for the best English-language novel of the year. The controversy was due to the book's depictions of a woman's attempts to engage

© The Author(s), under exclusive license to Springer Nature Switzerland AG 2023

C. Allmark-Kent, *Literature, Science, and Animal Advocacy in Canada*, Palgrave Studies in Animals and Literature, https://doi.org/10.1007/978-3-031-40556-3_7

in sexual activities with a male bear. Most unusually, however, *Bear* took a seemingly ambivalent stance towards zoophilia, neither condemning nor condoning it. Instead, Engel (1976) simply presents the woman's action as misguided: a reflection of her failure to understand the bear. As a relatively famous (or infamous) book, *Bear* offers one of the clearest and best-known examples of the *failure of knowing* the animal narrative.[1]

Coral Ann Howells (1986) called *Bear* a "quintessentially Canadian" book (105). Of course, similar statements were made about the works of Ernest Thompson Seton and Charles G. D. Roberts. Margaret Atwood (1972b) characterized their stories as "distinctively Canadian" (73). Yet, Engel's approach to animal representation reflects a profound departure from their styles. This begs the question of what counts as essentially 'Canadian' to begin with. Up to this point, the books that have formed the focus of this study have engaged in a *fantasy of knowing* the animal. Within their individual differences, each author has operated from a basic assumption that animals are knowable to humans, at least to some degree. By contrast, *Bear* (1976) explores a *failure of knowing* the animal. Such texts challenge the comfortable assumption that humans can *ever* understand other animals. They reinforce the human-animal divide by emphasizing the differences between human and nonhuman brains. In essence, they explore the same problem of knowing animal minds that behaviourists and ethologists had articulated decades before.

It is worth noting that the *failure of knowing* narrative emerged during the second half of the twentieth century. This may be a result of authors, such as Engel, who grew up during the rise of behaviourism and ethology, developing a certain scepticism towards knowing other animals. They tend to reject the *fantasy of knowing* representations of previous generations as naive or anthropomorphic (particularly those written under the assumption that animals have complex minds and emotions). This position is reminiscent of the animal-sceptical academic perspective discussed in Chap. 1 of this book. Indeed, this shared scepticism may be one reason

---

[1] Other examples from this period include Robert Kroetsch's *The Studhorse Man* (1969), Graeme Gibson's *Communion* (1971), and Margaret Atwood's *Surfacing* (1972a). Interestingly, it was in 1974 that the American philosopher, Thomas Nagel (1974), published the paper "What Is It Like to Be a Bat?" concluding that animals are inherently unknowable to humans. This is similar to the points made by Margaret Floy Washburn in *The Animal Mind* (1908).

why *failure of knowing* texts tend to gain greater traction within literary animal studies than the *fantasy of knowing*.

It is important to recognize that the *failure of knowing* is not a mere adaptation of Seton's or Roberts's approaches, as we saw in Chap. 5. This is a deliberate separation—an intentional divergence—from previous methods of animal representation (and, hence, the *fantasy of knowing*). Indeed, Engel (1976) positions *Bear* in explicit opposition to the wild animal story. The protagonist, Lou, reflects that she had "read many books about animals as a child," including those of "Thompson Seton or was it Seton Thompson, with the animal tracks in the margin" and "Sir Charles Goddamn Roberts that her grandmother was so fond of" (Engel 1976, 59). Echoing the language of Seton's and Roberts's stories, she observes that "[w]ild ways and furtive feet had preoccupied that generation," yet she "had no feeling at all that either the writers or the purchasers of these books knew what animals were about" (59–60). However, Lou does not assume that she understands animals either: "She had no idea what animals were about" (60). The only thing she seems certain about is the gulf between human and nonhuman beings: "They were creatures. They were not human" (60).

Bear (1976) demonstrates the *failure of knowing* particularly well by exploring one human's attempts to understand another animal. The narrative moves us through her initial, inaccurate *fantasy of knowing* and into the sudden realization of her *failure of knowing* at the end. The book takes the perspective of Lou, a young researcher who is assigned to Cary Island in Northern Ontario to catalogue the documents of the Cary family estate for the Toronto Historical Institute. To Lou's surprise, she finds a bear chained up outside the old house when she arrives. Apparently, generations of Colonel Carys had lived on the estate and each had owned a bear: "There had always, it seemed, been a bear" (Engel 1976, 26). Lou spends a summer living and working on the island. For the most part, the bear is her only company. Whilst the book explores Lou's emotional journey during her relative isolation, the plot is driven by her attempts to know the bear. We witness her changing understanding, as well as the moments in which she questions herself. Lou's uncertainty about how to comprehend the bear preoccupies their early encounters, but soon she becomes increasingly confident that she *does* understand him.

Gradually, Lou enfolds the bear into her life on the island. She unchains the bear and invites him into the house. They swim together, sit in the sun, lie down in front of the fire, and play games. Initially, Lou treats the bear like a dog and their activities resemble a stereotypical human-canine companionship. She even uses the chain to take the bear for a walk around the island (Engel 1976, 86). As she becomes more comfortable with the bear, Lou begins to develop romantic and sexual feelings for him as well. One night, when he licks her, Lou perceives it as an initiation of sexual contact and encourages him. At the end of the novel, however, we witness Lou's *failure* to understand him. Her belief in their relationship is shattered when she attempts penetrative sexual intercourse. She gets "down on all fours in front of him, in the animal posture" (131). The bear reaches out a paw and rips the skin down her back. Lou interprets this as a rejection. Not long after, she leaves the island and returns to the city.

At the core, Lou's understanding of the bear is continually thwarted by her habit of seeing him as something other than himself. Initially, the "idea of the bear" strikes her as a spectacle or a curiosity; something "joyfully Elizabethan and exotic" (29). In the flesh, though, he becomes mundane: "a lump" (34). Upon closer inspection, he seems "piggish and ugly" (35). In his small enclosure, he looks "stupid and defeated," a "middle-aged woman" (35). Sometimes he seems to be "a pig" or a "fur coat" or "some kind of raccoon" (40, 47). Sitting in the water, he becomes "a near-sighted baby" and then a "large hipped-woman" (54, 69). Standing on two legs, he seems "a cross between a king and a woodchuck" (55). When Lou tries to dance with him, he is a "strange, fat, mesomorphic mannikin" (113). Inside the house, he appears "solid as a sofa, domestic, a rug of a bear" (70). Lying in front of the fire, "thinking his own thoughts," he seems like "a dog, like a ground-hog, like a man" (91). As Lou feels more intensely for him, the bear takes on epic proportions: "he was God," a "creature larger and older and wise than time" (118–9).

Interestingly, Lou seems aware of her tendency to see him under different guises. She reflects, "you have these ideas about bears: they are toys, or something fierce and ogreish in the woods" (34). She tells herself: "That is a bear. Not a toy bear, not a Pooh bear, not an airlines Koala bear. A real bear" (34). Yet, it seems she cannot avoid moulding him into a woman, a man, a baby, a god, another species, or even an inanimate object. All of this would seem to indicate the impossibility of seeing animals *as animals*. Rather than approaching the bear as himself, on his own terms, Lou continuously fits him into stereotypical animal roles: "lover, God or friend. Dog too" (134). She also perceives him as a violent threat, despite the bear's consistently placid behaviour. When her failed attempt at penetrative sex leaves her with deep cuts in her back, Lou suddenly fears that the "smell of blood would cause him to wound her further" (134). Their months of intimacy seem instantly forgotten. In Lou's eyes, he becomes the fierce and ogreish figure from her imagination. Fitting him into this role of the savage wild animal, she acts out an almost cliched reaction by taking a burning stick from the fire and chasing him from the house. For all her attempts to know the bear, it seems Lou cannot escape the various anthropocentric lenses that she brings to their relationship.

Inevitably, all of this impedes Lou's ability to interpret the bear's behaviour. She finds that she can "paint any face on him that she wanted" (71). In a light-hearted moment, she thinks that he "looked as if he was laughing" or else that he "definitely grinned" (49, 72). When she feels morose, she believes that "he, too, seemed subdued and full of grief" (84). By contrast, "his actual range of expression was a mystery" (71). She laughs at herself "looking for emotion" when "there was none" (72). Repeatedly, she asks herself "how and what does he think?" but her curiosity does not take her much further than this (60). Instead of attempting greater understanding, she concedes to the impossibility of knowing. Lou observes that, to a human, "a bear is more an island than a man" (60). This comparison between the difficulty of knowing both humans and other animals mirrors Margaret Floy Washburn's (1908) argument in *The Animal Mind*: "If my neighbour's mind is a mystery to me, how great is the mystery which looks out of the eyes of a dog" (2).

As part of Engel's (1976) exploration of the *failure of knowing*, there is almost a rejection of the act of interpreting animal behaviour itself. Lou imagines vaguely that other animals live "dim, flickering, inarticulate psychic lives," but reflects that this does not lead her to "presume" whether the bear "suffered or did not suffer" (60). Here, the act of labelling the animal capable or incapable of suffering seems to be the issue (not whether the animal is, indeed, suffering). Elsewhere, Lou thinks: "There was a depth in him she could not reach, could not probe and with her intellectual fingers destroy" (119). The implication is that attempting to study animal minds—probing their depths with our intellectual fingers—is inherently destructive. In other words, studying animals destroys something in their unknowable otherness. This is similar to the animal-sceptical position that *any* claims we make on behalf of other animals are inherently suspect.

Engel (1976) extends her scepticism towards all attempts to know other animals. She never lets us assume that we or Lou (or perhaps even Engel herself) know exactly what the animals in her book are thinking or feeling. It is even uncertain whether they are thinking or feeling in the first place. This rejection of almost all forms of knowledge about other animals means that, unsurprisingly, there is little engagement with science or animal advocacy. Lou's interactions with the bear explore the idea that human observations are inherently subjective, unreliable, and anthropocentric. Her work cataloguing the Cary family's library enables Engel to reinforce this further by illustrating our collective failure to know animals through other means.

Ostensibly, Lou's role is to build an archive of local history, but scraps of paper jotted with notes about bears keep falling out of books at random. The content of these slips ranges from scientific information about bears to myths and legends from various cultures. In theory, each represents a different attempt to understand bears. Collectively, however, they present a litany of anthropocentrism. Through these scraps of knowledge, we learn more about humans in specific historical and cultural contexts than we do about the bears themselves.

Only one scrap of paper offers scientific information about bears and it happens to be the first one that Lou finds:

> *In the Linnean system*, brown, beautifully curled, minute handwriting told her, *Ursus comes between Mustela and Didelphis. This order includes Arctos, the true bears; Meles, the badger; Lotor, the racoon; and Luscus, the wolverine. Walk: plantigrade; grinders: tuberculated; stature: large. Carnivorous. Frugivorous. Tail generally short. Brain and nervous system fairly developed. Claws for digging, non-retractable. Sense acute. Cylindrical bones more similar to man's than those of other quadrupeds, esp. the femur. Therefore able to rear up and dance. Tongue has a longitudinal groove. Kidneys lobed in bunches of grapes; no seminal vesicles. Bone in penis. In the female, the vagina is longitudinally ridged. Clitoris resides in a deep cavity.* (Engel 1976, 43–4, emphasis original)

Despite the somewhat sexual note upon which the extract ends, the overall implication here is that dry, anatomical details are all that the sciences can offer. Another slip of paper lists the lifespan of several species, including the brown bear: "*Ursus Arctos – 34 years*" (52). It is worth noting that the original Colonel Cary (who died in 1869) would have made these notes in the mid-nineteenth century. This means that his sources were largely limited to pre-Darwinian anatomy and zoology. Towards the end of his life, the ripples of Darwinism may have stirred public interest in animal minds, but the Colonel would have died before comparative psychology had developed. It is significant that Engel chooses to leave science in this state. She makes no other engagement with the sciences and there is no indication that research has progressed at all in the ensuing century.

Although Engel (1976) makes no acknowledgement that behaviourism or ethology exists, we can see their influence in her language. Lou "supposed" that animals' "functions" were "defined by the size, shape and complications of their brains" (60). As we have seen, her reference to the "dim, flickering, inarticulate psychic lives" of animals is particularly reminiscent of the mechanomorphic language in *Last of the Curlews* (1955) by Fred Bodsworth (60). Despite the clear influence of behaviourism and ethology shaping Engel's approach to animal minds and emotions, there is still a rejection of science overall. Ironically, of course, the same questions that she raises about knowing other animals also occupied the very sciences that she dismisses.

Ironically, perhaps, Engel's animal-sceptical approach seems to encourage symbolic interpretations of the bear. In other words, scholars rarely treat the bear simply *as a bear* (just like Lou). Graham Huggan and Helen Tiffin (2010) remark astutely:

> Bear has, for most critics and commentators, effectively disappeared from his own narrative, leaving only the limited interpretive possibilities of an avatar of the Canadian wilderness or, still more anthropocentrically, a mere catalyst for the sexual awakening of the human protagonist of the text. (197–8)

Whilst critics have engaged closely with Lou's perceptions of the bear and the impossibility of knowing animals, few have taken a close look at the bear himself.

From the off, it is worth acknowledging that *Bear* mingles a multitude of bears. Engel's (1976) lack of specificity here may be a consequence of her rejection of science. Yet, it seems reductive for us simply to discuss the book's representations of 'bears' when there is such a diversity of species and subspecies. Colonel Cary's scraps of paper record histories and traditions from both Europe and North America. His notes mention *Ursus arctos*, the brown bear, which is found throughout Eurasia and North America. In Canada, there are two subspecies of brown bears, grizzly (*Ursus arctos horribilis*) and Kodiak (*Ursus arctos middendorffi*). Grizzlies can be further divided into two subgroups: coastal and inland. As the best-known brown bear, we might expect Lou to meet an inland grizzly. Certainly, such a bear would carry suitably dangerous expectations of size and strength. Yet, all types of brown bears are more likely to be found in Western Canada than in Ontario.

Cary Island's location and Engel's descriptions of the bear would seem to suggest that he is an Eastern black bear *(Ursus americanus americanus)*. Both grizzly and Kodiak bears would be considerably larger than the bear Engel (1976) describes:

> It was only a dusky bulk of blackish fur in a doorway. It had a long brown snout, and its snout had a black, dry, leathery end. It had small, sad eyes [...] Its nose was more pointed that she had expected—years of corruption by teddy bears, she supposed—and its eyes were genuinely piggish and ugly. Now she could see that it was what Homer could call a good size: up to her hip and long with it. (34–5)

If he is an Eastern black bear, it would make Colonel Cary's research on brown bears even less relevant to Lou's attempts to understand this specific bear. Although, it is worth noting that no one knows where the bear came from: "I don't know where they got it, there aren't any bear [sic] around here" (27). This suggest that the bear could be a member of any species, even one from outside of North America. Engel's vague homogenization of different bear species not only reflects a lack of engagement with science, but a lack of engagement with bears themselves. As Kenneth Shapiro and Marion Copeland (2005) suggest, respectful animal representation includes presenting an animal not only as "an individual with some measure of autonomy" but also as "a member of a species with a nature that has certain typical capabilities and limitations" (344). Engel's lack of specificity makes it difficult for us to judge whether her bear demonstrates a "species-typical way of living in the world" (345).

To some degree, we might argue that Engel's (1976) bear refuses categorization. It is tempting to suggest that his otherness and unknowability mean that he cannot fit into the neat subdivisions of biological classification. However, this reading would be more persuasive if Engel presented an *acceptance of not knowing* the animal, in which the boundaries between species erode. Both Timothy Findley's *Not Wanted on the Voyage* (1984) and Margaret Atwood's *Oryx and Crake* (2003) explore human-animal relations through contexts in which the category of species becomes irrelevant. In Engel's *Bear*, the human-animal divide remains firmly in place.

Not only that, the gap between humans and other species seems utterly insurmountable. If Engel insists that the bear is a *real* bear—not the shape-shifting deity Lou sometimes imagines him to be—then it is important to examine what kind of bear she offers us. In arguing against our tendency to turn animals into symbols or empty vessels, we might expect Engel to present us with the opposite: a vital, living individual.

As the mind of the bear is unknowable, we must perform a kind of 'behaviourism' to interpret his representation. In other words, Engel forces us to focus on external, observable actions. Initial descriptions of the bear indicate that he is in a poor condition when Lou meets him. This is not just his physical condition—"his hindquarters matted with dirt"—but also his mental state (Engel 1976, 35). Chained to a post, he has little freedom of movement and little to keep him engaged. As a result, there are "no new tracks in the mud" outside of his "old cabin" (33). With no mental or physical stimulation, he seems to spend most of his time lying down inside the shelter. Given that the bear had "been on that chain" for "many years," it seems likely that he is in a poor emotional state (41).

Interestingly, the bear seems to be familiar with the inside of the house. Given the opportunity, he pushes the door open and heads upstairs to the fireplace: "Deliberately he walked around the far end of the chimney wall and lay down in front of the fire" (55). Not only does this indicate that he "knows his way," but it also suggests that the bear prefers to seek the warmth of the fireplace when possible (55). Indeed, he chooses to lie in this spot during subsequent visits indoors. By contrast, when Lou takes him swimming, the bear seems ambivalent: "He showed no doggish enthusiasm" (54). He is also uninterested in the "pretty stones" she finds for him, but he does toss "pinecones" at her (117). When Lou finds a ball, they roll it to each other for hours at a time (117). However, his favourite activities seem to be searching for grubs and eating raspberries (69, 86, 120).

Despite Lou's difficulties with understanding the bear, he does seem to find pleasure in her company: "The bear sat as close to her as he could at the end of his chain. She unsnapped it and he came to sit by her knee" (54). He chooses to be close to her and initiates bonding by licking: "He licked her hand once and ambled back to his byre;" "he began to run his long, ridged tongue up and down her wet back" (61, 63). Depending on where he licks Lou's body, however, she interprets him as either a dog or a lover (134). Interestingly, she never interprets him as a bear engaging in social bonding behaviours typical for his species.

It is difficult to ascertain how the bear perceives their sexual encounters. Certainly, there is evidence of male black and brown bears licking the genitals of their female partners (Bagemihl 1999, 444). Similarly, there are also observations of captive male brown bears engaging in oral stimulation together, typically initiated by the provider (Sergiel et al. 2014, 2). In Engel's (1976) novel, it might initially *seem* as though the bear instigates sexual contact with Lou. However, she directs his actions. At first, he simply grooms various places on her body, but she then "move[s] him south" and swings "her hips and make[s] it easy for him" (93). It appears that Lou chooses to turn the social grooming into something sexual. Indeed, he tends to become "distracted" and she must "cajole and persuade him" (115). She even puts honey on her body, "but once the honey" is gone, he wanders off "farting and too soon satisfied" (115). Indeed, when she mounts him, he is "quite unmoved" (122).

The bear's sudden erection during their final encounter is something of a mystery. As it was not preceded by any stimulation, it may be simply spontaneous and non-sexual. Certainly, the bear seems to look "confused" by it (131). Either way, when Lou offers penetration by getting "down on all fours" in the "animal posture," he "reache[s] out one great paw and rip[s] the skin on her back" (131). For Huggan and Tiffin (2010) this is "an apparently admonitory paw," a categorical refusal of Lou's offer (196). Given the history of their encounters, I would concur that the sexual nature of their relationship is one-sided. However, it also seems reductive for us to deny him any sexual agency whatsoever. Perhaps his paw was not a refusal. Whatever his intention, the interaction between his sharp claws and her bare skin solidifies the irrefutable incompatibility of their two bodies. Lou's *fantasy of knowing* is shattered. Finally, she recognizes her *failure* to know the bear. The human-animal divide remains as solid as ever.

Undeniably, Lou's relationship with the bear is one-sided. Not only does she fail to know or understand him, but she also fails to care about his wellbeing. The day after her failed attempt at penetrative sex, she finds the bear outside "waiting expectantly for her" (134). When she brings him food, he "edge[s] a little closer to her" (134). Afterwards, he follows her inside to lie down in front of the fire as usual. When she puts out her hand, "he lick[s] and nuzzle[s] it" (134). It seems that, from his perspective, their companionship is unchanged. For Lou, however, "[s]omething was gone between them" (134). Promptly afterwards, she leaves for the city and the bear is left behind on the island.

Bear ends with Lou driving back to Toronto. We see no more of the bear and gain no real insight into his future. Before Lou leaves the island, we witness the bear being taken away to stay with Lucy Leroy, the elderly woman who looked after him before Lou's arrival. Whilst Lucy seems to have a bond with the bear, his previous living conditions were poor and Lou does nothing to ensure that they are improved in future. Her 'love' for him is limited to checking that Lucy and her nephew will not kill him. From her perspective, the "bear was safe" and there was no need to inquire further (Engel 1976, 139). Clearly, there is no recognition that the bear has needs or interests beyond mere survival. His welfare is wholly disregarded, both by Lou and the book itself.

Engel's (1976) rejection of science, the wild animal story, and the *fantasy of knowing* all set *Bear* apart from the other books that I have addressed so far. It is further distanced by the absence of any animal advocacy message. The narrative is about Lou's emotional journey. It's not about 'saving' the bear or any other animal. At the beginning of the book, Lou reflects that she was "not fond of animals" (Engel 1976, 32). She recalls that she "had a puppy once" and was "much moved when he was run over, but had not missed him" (32). By the end of the book, Lou's position has not changed. It's safe to say that, whilst she might be temporarily 'moved' by her separation from the bear, she will not 'miss' him. In this respect, the narrative is not just about Lou's failure to know but her failure to empathize with him.

Evidently, the bear's own experiences were secondary to Lou's emotional journey. Now that her desire for renewal in 'the wild' has been fulfilled, the bear can return to his imprisonment and neglect. Lou's relationship with the bear seems to have had the same effect as the nature holidays of urban middle-class tourists to national parks (described in Chap. 4). Lou sought renewal through an 'authentic' experience with a wild animal. Yet, both scenarios are equally contrived: whether through a carefully managed national park with strictly controlled animal populations or with a domesticated bear held captive on an island. For tourists, the bodies of wild animals are attractive scenery or trophies to be hunted. For Lou, the bear's body was an object of mystery, danger, and sexual gratification. In these anthropocentric encounters, the animals involved are *objects of utility*. Neither Lou nor the book itself seems to accept the bear on his own terms as the *subject of a life*.

ANDY RUSSELL: *ANDY RUSSELL'S ADVENTURES WITH WILD ANIMALS* (1977)

Andy Russell (1915–2005) was a writer, rancher, filmmaker, trapper, tour guide, and conservationist. After years of zealously hunting grizzly bears, he began a campaign to rehabilitate their public image through film and writing. He advocated for their protection, but never condemned their hunting. He drew on science and animal advocacy to represent grizzlies sympathetically, yet openly rejected both scientists and animal advocates. He condemned scientists for not understanding the "holistic approach" to nature and referred to their need for "a reason for everything" as "utter bullshit" (quoted in Bulbeck 2005, 158). Likewise, he called anti-hunting campaigners "bambi-types" and "cultists" (quoted in Loo 2006, 20).

As a writer of wild animal stories, Russell sits as both an insider and an outsider. His collection of short stories, *Andy Russell's Adventures with Wild Animals* (1977), uses the realistic *fantasy of knowing* the animal and holds all the characteristics of Seton's and Roberts's original stories. Indeed, I see his writing as an exemplary blend of their two styles. *Adventures with Wild Animals* is the closest return to the original wild animal story that we have seen in this book. Russell (1977) even writes about animal intelligence and emotions with the same confidence that Seton and Roberts once did. In his work, we find none of the hesitancy of the post-Nature Fakers controversy writers, nor the mechanomorphism of those shaped by ethology or behaviourism (see Chap. 5). Yet, for all his similarities with Seton and Roberts, Russell's relationship with science and animal advocacy was drastically different. Whilst he engaged with the ideas and debates of both science and animal advocacy, he rejected their proponents and indicated no desire to contribute to their discussions. It seems that Russell wrote not to engage with experts or advocates, but to change the minds of ordinary people.

Russell was born and raised in rural Alberta. Growing up in the foothills of the Rocky Mountains, the landscape seemed to become part of his soul. Russell had attended school in nearby Lethbridge and left when he was fifteen years old. By then, the Great Depression had hit the area and so, like "many single young men in the '30s," his best option was to become a trapper (Loo 2006, 201). As a result, trapping provided him with an informal course in local geography, ecology, and animal behaviour. What he learnt along the way enabled Russell to be hired as a guide for an established outfitter, Bert Riggall, who helped expand his knowledge. As an amateur botanist and naturalist, himself, Riggall gave Russell a "condensed, prolonged course" in "natural history and the environment" (203). Russell's formal education may have been short, but his outdoor education was lifelong. In 1946, Riggall retired and Russell took over the business. Only a year later, however, it was all threatened when oil was discovered in Leduc, a town near Edmonton. This was the beginning of the Alberta oil boom.

Oil companies from all over the world flooded into the province. In the "dynamic decade" after the discovery of oil in Leduc, Alberta's economy was transformed from "one rooted in agriculture to one fuelled by petroleum" (Loo 2006, 203). Whilst most citizens were enjoying the economic growth, others were witnessing a swift destruction of the local environment. In 1957, Shell found a rich deposit of sour gas and began building a processing plant near Russell's home: "Roads and pipelines soon slashed through his guiding territory, surface scars that diverted attention from the deeper damage inflicted by hydrogen sulphide" (204). In small amounts it can "rust fences, peel paint, and acidify water," as well as "cause nausea, memory loss, skin rashes, and asthma" (204). In large amounts, "it can kill instantly" (204). Unsurprisingly, Russell took action and started campaigning to protect the land he loved. He had grown Riggall's outfitting operation and was now a successful business-owner, but in 1960 he gave it all up to commit himself to this new mission. As his son, Charlie Russell, and Maureen Enns (2003) put it: "Like the grizzly bear, [he] was cornered inside a shrinking habitat, and his response was to become a film producer and writer" (16).

After producing several nonfiction books and films, Russell (1977) wrote a collection of short stories. *Andy Russell's Adventures with Wild Animals* is a slim book of only seven stories. Just like Seton and Roberts, Russell wrote a preface setting out the book's purpose:

All the stories in this book illustrate the needs of animals in relation to the needs of man [...] Paramount in all of this is the obvious need for greater understanding and sympathy on the part of man. (x)

Each story contributes a specific message to this overall aim. Broadly speaking, they focus on human cruelty, wild animal autonomy, appreciation for nature, and human-animal relationships. Their narrative structures resemble common types of wild animal story: the biography, the sketch, the story of captivity, and the autobiographical anecdote. However, their endings are less tragic. Whilst Seton's or Roberts's stories almost always concluded with the protagonist's death, Russell offers more ambiguous endings. The animal's presence tends to slip away from human eyes at the end of the narrative. This is an interesting element of Russell's realistic style, which seems to add greater authenticity to his anecdotes.

As in Seton's (1898) *Wild Animals I Have Known*, Russell's (1977) *Adventures with Wild Animals* appears to describe real encounters. These range from fleeting glimpses to long companionships with rescued animals. In the traditional style of the wild animal story, Russell blends fact and fiction. Each story seems to have been constructed from anecdotes and then supplemented with fiction. The method utilizes both Seton's style of semi-autobiographical stories and Roberts's seamless blending of anecdote and invention. As a result, there is no distinguishing between the story and the real event. Omniscient narration of wild animals in nests, unseen by human eyes, transitions into first-person narration of Russell observing the animals on his property or listening to the anecdotes of other observers.

The story "Sage" begins with a mother grizzly and two cubs (Balsam and Sage) waking from hibernation. Through omniscient narration, we 'see' them inside the den and then follow their movements out into the snowy landscape. As the story progresses, the narration also tracks the activities of Old Bill, a bounty-hunter hired to kill grizzlies. This use of dramatic irony was particularly common in Seton's (1901, 1905) stories about bounty-hunting, such as "Tito" from *Lives of the Hunted* or "Badlands Billy" from *Animal Heroes*. Yet, partway through "Sage," Russell's (1977) descriptions of Old Bill shift in perspective: "One evening some time later, I sat by a campfire with him and listened while he told of that summer of bear hunting" (15). As a result, Russell's own presence in the story increases. By the end, the narrative transitions from presenting Sage's biography to tracing Russell's various encounters with the bear as an adult.

In a similar way to some of Seton's (1905) wild animal stories—particularly those in *Animal Heroes*—evidence of Sage's life is found in material signs, such as tracks. Russell (1977) describes trailing his prints as "like reading a book written in a unique kind of script, revealing and totally fascinating" (36). Eventually, Sage's presence slips out of the story entirely. We receive no omniscient narration illuminating the rest of the bear's life. Instead, we witness Russell's attempts to interpret Sage's movements: "It was the last time I would see Sage. That fall we found his tracks in new snow [...] they pointed toward the high county back among the peaks"

(41). Again, this is similar to Seton's technique of speculating about the lives of the real animals that he encountered. We might assume that the story "Sage" arcs from fiction (Russell's attempts to imagine the bear's biography) to fact (his recollections of the bear). Of course, the anecdotes and evidence may well be fabricated; the line between fact and fiction is unclear. Yet, unlike Seton and Roberts, this caused no controversy.

It is worth noting that Russell (1977) makes no direct claims of fact; nor does he attempt to contribute to the field of animal psychology. However, he does use the book's introduction to establish his own stance on animal intelligence and emotions. Even though he identifies "intelligence" as the "greatest difference between ourselves and other animal life," it might be more accurate to say that he describes metacognition rather than intelligence: "We *know* that we know, and other animals just know" (vii). He goes on to add that, whilst "intelligence varies between species and between individuals," humans do not have a "monopoly" on "thought" (vii).

This is the first confident reference to animal *thought* that we have encountered in realistic animal fiction since Seton's and Roberts's stories. Echoing the language of early comparative psychologists, such as George Romanes, Russell focuses on the ability to "adjust" to "changing conditions" and "unusual circumstances" as evidence of intelligence (vii). He adds that to "explain it away as instinct is either deliberate misconception or pure laziness" (vii). Here, we find a direct rejection of the concept of instinct, similar to those expressed decades before in Roderick Haig-Brown's *Return to the River* (1941) and Frederick Philip Grove's *Consider Her Ways* (1947).

Russell (1977) makes equally confident statements regarding evidence of animal emotions, an idea that remains somewhat controversial. He identifies a range of emotional states, including: "happiness," "sorrow," "the serenity of peace," "the trauma of fear," "stress," "love," and "joy" (viii). Russell is unequivocal in his assertions, however, even evoking his expertise as a 'outdoors man' to strengthen his claim. This is the same idea Theodore Roosevelt and John Burroughs used in the Nature Fakers controversy. In Roosevelt's (1907) piece for *Everybody's Magazine*, he wrote that when "real outdoor naturalists, real observers of nature" went "into the wilderness to find out the truth," they felt a "half-indignant and half-amused contempt for the men who invented preposterous fiction about wild animals" and for the "credulous stay-at-home people" who believed them (427).

Clearly, Roosevelt employs the rugged, hyper-masculine figure of the 'real outdoor naturalists' to dismiss Seton's and Roberts's anecdotes of intelligent, emotional animals as sentimental and childish. There is also a suggestion of softness and effeminacy in the phrase 'stay-at-home people.' Yet, where Roosevelt claimed that 'real' experiences with wild animals reinforced our differences, Russell (1977) argues the opposite. For him, it reveals our similarities. In the introduction to *Adventures with Wild Animals*, Russell writes: "When one has spent a long time in wilderness country mingling with wildlife and watching wild animals work out the patterns of their lives, one becomes increasingly aware of parallels" (vii–viii).

Alongside his confident claims about animal emotions, Russell makes equally bold statements about animal personalities. As a similarly controversial topic, he makes further references to his expertise. He asserts that his time spent observing wild animals, "literally living with them over many months in the wild country of their choice," forms the basis for his belief that it is "very evident that here are animals with just as much individual character as human beings" (viii). Russell offers an array of interesting personalities, each of which carries its own survival "advantage" (viii). These include: "timid," "bold," "cranky," "uncompromising," and "mild" (viii).

Russell's statements regarding animal intelligence, emotions, and personality are reflected in his animal representations. His approach resembles Roberts's style of representation: realistic, but somewhat distant. There is little of Seton's playfulness or speculation. As such, there are no instances of miraculous problem-solving that strain credulity or bold claims about specific abilities. This may be because, unlike Seton or Roberts, Russell is not attempting to contribute to the study of animal psychology. Hence, feats of animal intelligence are not given a spotlight as much as in earlier wild animal stories. Learning and problem-solving are woven into the animals' lives, rather than 'showcased,' as in other narratives.

The story "Misty" explores the methods used by coyotes to avoid traps and poisons. As part of the fabric of the story, there are examples of animal learning and problem-solving, as well as animal culture. This is reminiscent of the processes described in Seton's (1901, 1905) stories, "Tito" and "Badlands Billy." In both cases, Seton depicted an unusual individual who had learned to avoid traps and poisons and then shared this knowledge with her young. Decades later, Russell (1977) explores a similar process in more depth. In "Misty," he describes a group of coyotes whose culture forbids them engaging in typical coyote behaviours:

> This was Misty; part of a generation of coyotes that ate nothing they had not killed, a product of the merciless poisoning campaign that had lasted fifteen years. These animals not only shunned anything found dead, but they were silent, never advertising their presence with the vocal serenades so much a part of normal coyote behaviour [....] Misty's mother and father had been among the few who learned that only live things were safe to eat, and they had taught her well. (77)

Whilst the question of animal culture is gaining some acceptance, it remains controversial. Although Russell does not use the word 'culture,' this would seem to be the phenomenon that he is describing. He reinforces the processes through which animal knowledge spreads by depicting Misty teaching her own young. She takes them to some poisoned bait and adopts an "attitude" that "spoke of threatening danger" (81). Each time a pup attempts to move towards the bait, she gives "a sharp alarm bark" and rushes forward to "slash wickedly at its shoulder with her teeth, driving it back" (81). Afterwards, she resumes her "attitude of alertness" and repeats the process until all her young can resist the bait (81).

Interestingly, Russell seems aware of the potentially controversial nature of this scene. Misty's lesson to her young is witnessed by a local county councillor, Henry Tanner: "If he told the story of this morning's observations to his fellow councillors, they would likely not believe it. However, its meaning was unmistakeable; coyotes were learning about the deadly 1080 poison" (82). Any potential for anthropomorphism in Tanner's story is negated by his poor relationship with the coyotes. When he observes Misty and her young, it is not for pleasure or curiosity. He is investigating why the poisoned bait on his farm had not stopped coyotes from attacking his sheep. In Russell's careful construction of Tanner as a 'reliable' witness, we can see some awareness of the stigma of anthropomorphism. Despite his confident claims about animal intelligence and emotions, there is a tacit recognition that his stories could be met with scepticism or distain.

At the time, the sciences were gradually emerging from the mechanomorphism of previous decades. Yet, Russell shows no hesitancy in describing the subjective experiences of other species. Each of his stories are filled with a wide range of emotional states, although these do seem to vary between species. Whilst the grizzly bears of "Sage" experience excitement and curiosity, their predominant emotions are related to stress and aggression: restlessness, fear, alarm, nervousness, caution, hesitation, suspicion, anger, savagery, and even a "bad temper" (12, 19–20, 26, 32). However, it is worth noting that on occasion, they enjoy "delicious food," "carefree play," and stretching out "luxuriantly" (22). In contrast, Russell employs more complex, playful language to his dogs, Kip and Seppi, in the story, such as: "ruffled his dignity," "his cheerful long-nose grin," "amuse him," "passion," "privilege," "imperious aplomb," "insisted" (33–4). Although, when facing a bear, Seppi launches "a red-eyed roaring attack" (34).

The elks of "The King Elk," experience joy, satisfaction, rage, fear, alarm, play, excitement, passion, and even engage in deception (47–56, 60). In "Misty," the coyotes are alert, apprehensive, alarmed, cautious, uneasy, afraid, excited, tempted, playful, and seduced by a "beckoning odour of meat" (81–5, 89). At the hands of human cruelty, the coyote's experiences become more extreme: "tortured grimace," "a wild mad look," "nightmare of never-ending torture," "howling nightmare," "horrifying noise" (83, 91).

When the goats of "Billy's Dangerous Game" are observed from a distance, they appear "phlegmatic," "showing little fear of man," composed, deliberate, curious, and blithe (100, 108). However, when they begin to feel threatened by Russell's presence, their behaviour changes: "I detected definite anger;" "a towering rage;" "they meant business" (107–8). Curiously enough, Russell observes a playful grizzly in the same story, sliding down a snowdrift in "merry abandon" (105). The language of pleasure, play, and curiosity is particularly frequent in "The Otters." These descriptions include: revel, enthusiastic, playful, curious, satisfy, carefree, zeal, excitement, avid, ecstasy, exhilaration, secure, content (112–9, 123–5, 134–5). However, there are also instances of rage, alertness, anxiety, alarm, caution, anger, worry, nervousness, savagery, loss, and loneliness (116, 120–7, 137).

Just like the grizzlies of "Sage," the cougar protagonist of "Kleo" experiences predominantly negative states: distress, pain, discomfort, trauma, panic, fear, helplessness, suffering, confusion, nervousness, restlessness, desperation, and "an endless, grinding nightmare" (138, 142–153). The language of anger is particularly frequent: "bad temper," threatening, menace, "screech of rage and frustration," "tail waving angrily," "mask of sheer ferocity," deadly, "seething and boiling," furious, rage, "muttering and growling to himself in cougar profanity" (138–144). Interestingly,

Achilles, the protagonist of "The Friendly Owl," is described with the same playful language that Russell applies to his dogs: "When he was put out about something he chirped loudly, a querulous complaining call" (165). Achilles is described as enthusiastic, annoyed, happy, bothered, intrigued, undaunted, triumphant, impervious, fierce, gentle, excited, amused, tense, angry, and diffident (162–176). Indeed, Russell observes that Achilles had a "whole range of expressions—from extreme anger to sublime affection—according to his mood of the moment" (169).

It is perhaps unsurprising that Russell's language would become more playful when describing the animals that he knew the longest. The emotions of Kip, Seppi, and Achilles seem more varied and their idiosyncrasies more distinct. Almost all of Russell's animal characters demonstrate some unique quality. For instance, "Sage loved to eat ants" (35). In "The King Elk," Russell remarks that the "individual animals of an elk herd display characters ranging from timid to courageous" (45). Some of them are "naturally timid," regardless of age (54).

Inevitably, Russell's depictions of Kip's, Seppi's, and Achielles's personalities are richest. When describing Kip—a big, heavily furred collie— Russell offers a portrait of steadiness and protection. He has "a dignity of monumental proportions and a deeply ingrained sense of responsibility" (32). He looks after the children of the family, holding them back when they stray beyond the "invisible line" he draws around the yard, and is "never ruffled" when they protest (32–3). Although "never a trouble-hunter when it came to bears," he would "stand them off if they tried to enter the yard, but he'd never pursue them very far" (33). By contrast, Seppi is a "natural hunter" and a "canine extrovert" with a "passion" for bears (34). He is described as pursuing and attacking bears, a "master" of fighting who could "feint and dodge any lunge" and usually sent the bear "beating a scrambling retreat up the nearest tree" (34).

Unusually, Achilles the owl seems to demonstrate the greatest complexity. Even within a collection of stories dominated by mammals, his personality, emotions, and social relationships are more nuanced and distinct. As a particularly idiosyncratic character, Russell remarks that he has "a tendency to be a real clown" (167). Even more so than the playful otters, Achilles seems to seek amusement:

> he had been installed on a perch on the veranda with plenty of old newspapers spread out under him to catch the inevitable droppings. Perhaps exposure to the written word triggered some kind of desire to amuse himself

or whoever happened to be watching, but he learned to 'read.' He would
jump down on the newspaper page and closely trace the letters across the
columns with this beak in a way that was hilarious. (167–8)

This anecdote seems closer to the 'miraculous' activities described in
Seton's stories and may well have offered more amusement to humans
than to Achilles himself. Nonetheless, the owl seems to have devised other
forms of play. He "loved to tease" the cat by flying from behind and
"planing [sic] in close" so that the cat would "let out an explosive hiss and
hightail for the nearest cover," which "seemed to amuse Achilles" (169).
He also played games of hide and seek with Russell's daughter. She would
lie down in long grass while Achilles searched from the air. He would then
launch into a "fierce strike, coming down with claws fully extended as
though to kill," but his landing was "as light as thistledown" (172). He
never seemed to mark "tender skin with his fearsome claws," indicating
"an incredible degree of control" on his part (172).

As a distinctive portrait of an unusual individual, "The Friendly Owl,"
closely resembles Seton's style of animal story. Here, one animal's unique
behaviour is the focus. When John Burroughs (1903) instigated the
Nature Fakers controversy with his article, "Real and Sham Natural
History," he criticized Seton for describing unbelievable animals. He
wrote that, such animals as Seton has known, "it is safe to say, no other
person in the world has ever known" (301). Only a "real woodsman"
could "separate" the fact and fiction (301). Of course, Russell's book
caused no controversy. His position was similar to Seton's, in that both
men claimed that observation of animals in the wild increased their belief
in animal intelligence, emotions, and personality. Crucially, however, there
was no question of Russell contributing to science. By the 1970s, disciplinary boundaries were more concrete than they had been a century
before. Scientific authority was not threatened by Russell's descriptions of
what he had seen at home or in the wild.

When comparing Russell's (1977) stories with those of Seton and
Roberts, we can see the developments of the intervening decades. For
instance, some stories reveal the progress made by animal protection
movements. In the previous chapters of this book, animal welfare and
conservation were the work of minor groups. By the late 1970s, these
organizations had become established, both in Canada and worldwide. In
the story "Kleo," one character warns another: "One of these days the

S.P.C.A. is going to drop on this outfit like a ton of rock" (156). In "The Friendly Owl," Russell describes entertaining "the president and top executive officers of a famous international conservation organization" (171). The casual nature of both remarks indicates the widespread awareness of both animal welfare and conservation organizations by this point.

In the story "Otters," Russell advocates for the importance of national parks. His protagonists exist in "otter heaven" within the park (112). However, they find themselves increasingly threatened by humans when they leave the area. Russell makes the issue clear: "when furbearers like otters leave the shelter of national parks to come into a settled area, they are exposed to far greater dangers" (135). Even though they were "extremely rare," to the point of being considered "nonexistent in this region," they "enjoyed no protection in regulation" (135). Russell argues that the otters' safety only extends to the boundaries of the national park. Of course, as we know from the history of Canadian wildlife conservation, this is an oversimplification. National parks were not quite the idealized refuges imagined by tourists. Still, Russell's position reflects the overall lack of legal protections for most wild animals.

Similarly, it seems that, when it comes to bounty-hunting, little had changed since Seton and Roberts were writing. Old Bill, the bounty-hunter in "Sage," is asked to kill a grizzly bear rumoured to have attacked cattle. However, as seemed to happen in so many of Seton's stories, the hunter is far from selective:

> A black bear came snooping, and put its foot in the trap. Bill promptly killed it [...] Two days later he had another black bear—another scalp. Two black bears being equal to one grizzly, he was uncomplaining [...] Bounty was bounty and it made no difference to him what kind of bears provided the scalps for his collection. So far he had found no sign that any of the cattle had been killed by bears. (16)

Evidently, the aspects of the bounty system that encouraged indiscriminate killing were still an issue by this point. Russell's descriptions of traps are also surprisingly close to Seton's. He writes that when, "a wild free thing as big and powerful as a grizzly" suddenly "finds itself shackled in steel," the animal "fights, roaring and plunging," for "as long as life remains" (25). He concludes such traps are "an obscenity—a desecration of nature's great gift of life" (25).

Likewise, Russell's accounts of coyote poisoning from compound 1080 are close to Seton's (1901, 1905) depictions of strychnine. In the story "Misty," Russel (1977) gives a distressing description:

> her eyes turned glassy with a wild, mad look, seeing little and recognizing even less. There were only the waves of tearing, fiery pain that ripped and tore inside her. Then, half-blindly, she began to run [...] with a queer, staggering gait like a mechanical thing, in a nightmare of never-ending torture. [...] She rolled in shuddering convulsions, accompanied by the steady chattering of her teeth. (83–4)

Over the intervening decades between Seton's and Russell's writing, the poisoning of predators had not stopped. Instead, new poisons were developed. Russell makes the comparison between compound 1080 and strychnine: "1080 never killed instantly as did other poisons such as strychnine and cyanide, and its victims died slowly and in torture" (74–7). Unfortunately, it seems that the poisoning of coyotes remained a common practice. Echoing Seton's (1901) language in the story "Tito," Russell (1977) observes that "coyote signs had been almost nonexistent" in the area after a "heavy and prolonged poison campaign had almost wiped them out" (74). Yet, as soon as they returned, the poisoning resumed. As we know, the protection of predators was still a contentious issue at this time.

Writing towards the end of the twentieth century, Russell operates from a more nuanced understanding of 'nature' than Seton or Roberts did. Any myth of a pristine 'wilderness' was no longer believable. Indeed, no wild animals in his stories are untouched by human interference. Not only have their behaviours and habitats been affected, so has the ecosystem itself. In several stories, Russell echoes Rachel Carson's arguments in *Silent Spring* (1962) that human attempts to control nature have been both destructive and ineffectual. There is even a sense that something has gone 'wrong' in nature.

In "Sage," for instance, Russell (1977) references the connection between animal agriculture and the rapid spread of disease. Soon after one case of "bovine diphtheria" is found on a cattle ranch, hundreds of other individuals become sick (13). Russell describes the epidemic as a "cruel drama dictated by Man" (13). Likewise, in the story "Misty," he explores how unhealthy adaptations could grow amongst the damaged coyote population. In a "very rare relationship," developed in a "completely abnormal environment," Misty's father also becomes the "sire of her pups" (77).

In the stories "The King Elk" and "Kleo," Russell also explores the artificial production of 'nature' in wildlife films. This seems to have been a point of contention for Russell as a filmmaker. In *Grizzly Heart*, Russell and Enns (2003) describe his perspective on Disney's *True-Life Adventures* film series at the time: "We knew that, contrary to appearances, the films were made in captivity. […] The animals were coerced into violence" (16). "The King Elk" and "Kleo" both reveal different situations in which supposedly 'authentic' depictions of 'wild' animals have been carefully constructed. In "Kleo," for instance, Russell (1977) describes situations in which captive animals are pushed down steep ice-covered slopes, forced to jump off cliffs, or made to fight each other to death (154–5). Of course, the films are marketed as 'factual,' just as Disney's *True-Life Adventures* had been. Their tragic events would have been depicted as unavoidable. As a result, the people who "came in droves" to watch and "applaud" never knew of the "misery and cruelty suffered by the animals" (155).

For the first time in this book, we are gaining a wider sense of the human impact on nature as expressed through animal fiction. Seton and Roberts sometimes described the effects of species loss in an area, Haig-Brown demonstrated the impact of pollution and dam-building on salmon migration, and Bodsworth tracked the extinction of a species. Yet, Russell explores damage to 'nature' itself. What was once 'natural' has been inescapably shaped by human hands. Yet, our desire for an authentic 'wilderness' is stronger than ever. Rather than restoring ecosystems, we construct an artificial nature for consumption in films or national parks. For Russell, at least, it had become impossible to ignore these hypocrisies in our relationships with wildlife. This more interrogative approach to the concept of 'nature' is something we will find increasingly in animal fiction throughout the twentieth century. In many of the texts that follow, basic ideas about 'nature,' 'wildness,' and human-animal relations become considerably more complex.

TIMOTHY FINDLEY: *NOT WANTED ON THE VOYAGE* (1984)

In *Not Wanted on the Voyage* (1984), Timothy Findley (1930–2002) rewrites the biblical story of Noah and the Flood. A supposed 'salvation' narrative becomes an account of speciesism, violence, and mass extinction in Findley's hands. He repositions the Genesis Flood myth, as well as

Noah's covenant with God, as an origin story for human supremacy.[2] The covenant, which Findley (1984) quotes in the book, designates all nonhuman beings who survive the Flood as human property: "*into your hands they are delivered*" (285, emphasis original). To challenge these ideas, Findley retells the story of Noah's ark through a range of nonhuman voices. He constructs these complex characters using an *acceptance of not knowing* the animal.

Compared with the other texts addressed in this book so far, *Not Wanted on the Voyage* is a distinct departure. In this chapter, we have seen Engel's (1976) *failure of knowing* and Russell's (1977) realistic *fantasy of knowing*. In both cases, regardless of whether the animal was 'knowable' or not, they remained definitively *an animal* throughout. Findley's (1984) *Not Wanted on the Voyage* offers us something different. Here, the human-animal divide is blurred. Even the line between the natural and the supernatural is unclear. This is a world in which the continuity between humans and other animals is taken to its furthest point. Nonhuman animals exist alongside humans, angels, demons, mythological 'animals' (such as unicorns and dragons), and human-animal hybrids.

In essence, Findley (1984) constructs a Darwinian fantasy world: a vast tree of diverse, interrelated beings who possess sentience, emotions, and consciousness. With no clear hierarchy of intelligence, the boundaries between humans and other animals seem to be based on differences of language and culture. Nonhuman beings possess all the qualities associated with human uniqueness, as well as the potential for fantastical or magical abilities. This differs from Frederick Philip Grove's speculative *fantasy of knowing* in *Consider Her Ways* (1947). Whilst he speculated about the upper limits of ant intelligence, the boundaries between humans and animals remained rigid. In Findley's (1984) pre-Flood world, these categories are unstable. To some extent, whether one is classified as a 'human' or an 'animal' is up for debate. Thus, all questions of anthropomorphism are negated from the beginning.

In spite of all evidence to the contrary, some humans in *Not Wanted on the Voyage* (1984) choose to see themselves as unique. Dr Noah Noyes,

---

[2] The bible passage is as follows: "The fear and dread of you will fall on all the beasts of the earth, and on all the birds in the sky, on every creature that moves along the ground, and on all the fish in the sea; they are given into your hands. Everything that lives and moves will be food for you. Just as I gave you the green plants, I now give you everything" (King James Bible Online 2023, Gen. 9.2-3).

the designer of the ark, is both deeply anthropocentric and patriarchal. Through the events of the Flood, he attempts to force the world into a strict hierarchy with the god, Yaweh, at the top and himself not far behind. To do this, he implicitly divides all living beings between not-animal (gods, angels, and humans) and not-human (all other beings, including human-animal hybrids). Whether one falls into the category of not-animal or not-human has dangerous consequences; Noah and his followers make sure of it. They believe that not-human beings can be killed without consequence, whether for the purposes of vivisection, sacrifice, or simply to 'dispose' of them.

When the dying "Lord God Yaweh" despairs at "the state of the world and the human race," he instructs his friend Dr Noyes to build an ark (Findley 1984, 66, 17). This involves gathering "two" of "every animal," though it is up to the Noyes family to interpret what this means (122). Some beings, such as fairies or dragons, are excluded from the ark. Presumably, these creatures do not survive the Flood. There is a sense that by drawing the human-animal divide and acting upon it, something essential will be lost. After the Flood, there will be no mythological creatures or human-animal hybrids. Much of the vibrant diversity of the world will be gone. In choosing this covenant with Yaweh, Dr Noyes enforces human supremacy but destroys our connection with other species. Before the Flood, his wife sings hymns with her sheep. Afterwards, they can no longer understand each other: "The sheep would never sing again" (348).

Given Findley's innovative approach to animal representation, we might imagine that he writes in 'opposition' to the wild animal story as some twentieth-century authors have done. As we know, Engel's (1976) *Bear* expressed the *failure of knowing* by explicitly rejecting the stories of Seton and Roberts (59–60). Yet, this is not so for Findley (1984). As a child, he had read both Seton's and Roberts's wild animal stories. According to biographer Sherril Grace (2020) their work left a "lasting impression" on him (67). Growing up in Toronto, Findley's father would take him on walks through the Don Valley where some of Seton's early stories were set. In "Significant Others," Findley (1993) recalls his father identifying specific locations and saying: "*Here* is where Silver Spot led his band of crows to forage—here, right *here*, is where Redruff drummed on the hollow logs" (153).

Findley (1993) describes himself 'becoming' the animals of these stories: "I was [...] every kind of bird and fish, insect and animal" (152). He describes this act of empathy as "becoming *other*" through fiction (152).

Seton's stories seem to have provided particularly powerful material for Findley's imagination. He explains: "Seton's animal's, then, and Ernest Thompson Seton himself became the first of my Canadian 'others'—and their significance grew as I got older" (153). Findley notes that, as a result, these animals took up "residence" in his own writing: "Rabbits, crows, cats and unicorns—others" (153). Unsurprisingly, we do see some of Seton's animals (such as crows, foxes, and rabbits) in *Not Wanted on the Voyage* (1984), as well as individuals from Findley's own life.

In his book, *Inside Memory*, Findley (1990) collects extracts from his own journals and notebooks. Many entries include significant encounters with animals. One describes a small, white horse that Findley called "the Unicorn" because he seemed "[m]agical and not quite earthbound" (233). Another relays a distressing trip to the zoo, in which a female gorilla sat on a chair while children screamed and laughed: "I will never, never, never forget her" (129). There are traces of these encounters in *Not Wanted on the Voyage*. Findley's (1984) Unicorn becomes a gentle, flower-eating creature who dies through Dr Noyes's violence. Meanwhile, primates feature as figures of hybridity who complicate the human-animal divide. In this world, human parents may sometimes give birth to primate offspring, but Mrs Noyes sees them as no different to human children: "born of human flesh" (173). Her human son Japeth, however, kills these individuals without remorse: "After all—he'd only killed an ape. An ape was only an animal. Nothing human" (170).

Perhaps the most significant human-animal relationship in Findley's life was with Mottle, a blind female cat who wandered into his garden in 1970.[3] Findley and his partner Bill Whitehead looked after her for twelve years, along with other animals they had rescued. Indeed, the writing of *Not Wanted on the Voyage* began not with Noah, the Flood, or the ark. It began with the death of the real Mottle. She is the first on the book's list of dedicatees. Originally, the story was about her and a human companion. It was only when Findley heard his friend Phyllis Webb's poem, "Leaning," that the Genesis Flood myth entered the story. He recounts the moment in *Inside Memory* when "the whole of *Not Wanted on the Voyage* fell into place" (Findley 1990, 220). The final lines of the poem form the epigraph to Findley's (1984) book: "*Are you, are you still there / tilting in this stranded ark / blind and seeing in the dark*" (np, emphasis original).

---

[3] Note that Findley's real cat was Mottle but the fictional cat is Mottyl.

The Mottyl of *Not Wanted on the Voyage* is a "pregnant," "old," "blind," "wildwood cat" (Findley 1984, 129). She is not one of Yaweh's two "very beautiful cats" assigned to the ark (129). She is a semi-feral stowaway; the eyes of all those who were abandoned by Dr Noyes. She is the aged, visually impaired female animal 'other' who is explicitly *not wanted* on the voyage. As Mrs Noyes's companion, Mottyl roams between human and nonhuman spaces. It is her narration that bridges these elements of the story together and her perspective that offers the greatest defamiliarization. Interestingly, it is Mottle/Mottyl's radically different sensory world that seems to have stirred Findley's curiosity about animal minds in particular. Journal extracts reprinted in *Inside Memory* describe several attempts to imagine her perspective. In one anecdote, Findley (1990) describes himself crawling on the ground "cat postured" and "bum in the air," "eyes shut tight and groping for safety," to get a "cats-eye view of the world" so that he can better imagine "being Mottle" (224–5).

Evidently, just like Seton before him, Findley seems to have thought carefully about the sensory worlds of individual animals, particularly those of animals he has known. When Findley (1984) introduces Mottyl's perspective at the beginning of *Not Wanted on the Voyage*, she is sitting on the porch with Mrs Noyes. With one eye "blind from cataracts," Mottyl feels "safer" with Mrs Noyes "than any other living thing" (18). Yet, she senses her companion's agitation through "vibrations," "shudders that passed through her fingers as she leaned down to pat Mottyl's rump" (19). The cat wonders to herself whether this agitation means that Mrs Noyes is "in heat," although "there wasn't any smell of that" (19). She does know, however, that young "Emma certainly was in heat—and possibly her first" (20).

Mottyl also suspects that she is coming into her own oestrus. Findley imagines this experience as a growing irritation, a hot itch. Mottyl considers whether the "first, faint warnings along her sides and over her shoulders" could be a "fever," "illness," "something she'd eaten," or simply "the weather" (19). With these potential diagnoses in mind, she contemplates trying "an emetic—one of those grasses out in the meadow" (19). In these opening sections of the book, Findley presents the possibility of following a nonhuman train of thought. Within the reality he creates, this is a zoocentric stream of consciousness shaped by species-specific senses in combination with Mottyl's own unique perspective and experiences.

Mottyl's autonomy as a 'wildwood' cat means that she ranges from the house, over the grounds of the farm, and into the wild spaces of the forest.

Her narration offers crucial observations in both the human and nonhuman spaces. Her perspective defamiliarizes human practices, whilst also offering a glimpse into a complex nonhuman society. In the fields and woods, she engages in a variety of nuanced social interactions. These vary from hostile and curious encounters with other animals to close friendships and the trading of information with allies. In the fields, Mottyl tends to encounter wild animals in isolation. However, in the densely populated forest, the animals are more closely connected and their interactions become imbued with more cultural practices.

In the meadow, "[s]omeone had given birth" and Mottyl finds "several birds" eating the placenta (Findley 1984, 40). Although she hopes that there might be a "tasty" "tidbit of afterbirth" for herself, Mottyl knows that the "news of the event itself" is "tradeable" (40). She reflects that her friend Crowe "would enjoy" the placenta and "might well offer, in exchange, the latest news about fallen nestlings" (40). As both animals share similar diets, they exchange information about food. However, Mottyl has a different arrangement with Whistler the groundhog. Instead, they trade stories about common enemies:

> Tales of escape were like currency and everyone hoarded them. They, too, like the news of a birth or a death or an injury, were tradeable—though the trade was confined to those who shared enemies. A four-footed escape meant nothing to a bird—just as a winged escape would mean nothing to Mottyl or Whistler. (41)

Interestingly, Findley grounds these speculations in survival. Mottyl's friendships are based on cooperation and reciprocal exchange. Whistler gives her "permission" to use his "straddles" and escape routes, whilst Mottyl leads him to "drink at a pond near the Noyes's yard" during a "drought" (41). Even though Findley writes with the *acceptance of not knowing*, he clearly still engages in zoocentric speculation. In this fantastical setting, he is free to imagine complex nonhuman lives shaped by language, cooperation, and culture.

Mottyl heads towards the forest to exchange information. She is "interested in hearing the gossip of the wood and eager to hear some news of her acquaintances there" (42). Findley identifies the woods as a space of wild, nonhuman autonomy. Indeed, it even seems to assert its own agency. At the edges of the forest, any fences erected by humans are "battered by fallen branches" (42). Here, we might imagine some inspiration was taken from his childhood trips into the Don Valley. In his review of *Wild Animals I Have Known*, Findley (2003) describes the ravines as a "blessing and a haven for beasts whose lives are the echoes of those" told in Seton's stories: "the rabbits, crows, and foxes of another time" (186).

The forest in *Not Wanted on the Voyage* is densely packed with a wide variety of species, including unicorns, dragons, and fairies. Despite the diversity of this vast nonhuman network, behaviour within the woods is shaped by a loose, shared culture. Some animals believe that the "floor of the wood" is "haunted by the dead" and should be treated with "reverence and respect" (Findley 1984, 43). Some parts of the wood are "holy," serving as "sanctuary" for any "beast who was ill or injured" (43). Even serious injuries, such as broken limbs, were "known to mend in sanctuary" (43). The mushrooms growing there are "thought," "perhaps," to be the "source of healing" (43). Over time, they even came "to be thought of as the spirits of the dead, whose bones had gone down under the leaves and into the earth" (43).

Mottyl's forest-dwelling companions include the lemurs, Bip and Ringer, and the elusive Unicorn and his partner, the Lady. Bip and Ringer are useful allies for Mottyl as lemurs are "considered the guardians of the wood" (42). Indeed, "no one leaves or enters without being inspected from the lemurs' trees" (42). To the animals on the farm, who rarely venture into the wood, the Unicorn and the Lady are "only an idea," "creatures whose whole existence was told and embellished by others" (53). There are "legends" that the Unicorn and the Lady are "made of glass" or that their "hoofprints" were "good luck" and that, if water gathered there, "drinking it was meant to bring good health" (54). The flowers on which the Unicorns feed even take on their own meaning:

> Strands of columbines and clutches of wild iris took on the atmosphere of almost holy places, not unlike sanctuaries. 'Leave it for the Unicorn,' had become a universally accepted axiom regarding the rarer kinds of lily and mimosa. (54)

Whilst there may be some forms of shared culture between the animals in the novel, there are also cultural differences. The infrequent exchanges between the farm animals and the animals of the wood have resulted in different ideas and practices. Just as Findley's nonhuman characters are not homogeneous, nor are their cultures.

There are also some shared cultural practices surrounding death. Findley speculates that in the woods and fields, the "smell of death" would be "universal" since "there was always some dead creature in the process of decay" (55). Instead, it is the "sound of death," the "sound of flies," that told of a recent passing (55–6). It could be "both dreadful and noble" and "brought the victim a kind of respect" (55). When Barky the dog dies, it is the sound of flies that guides Mottyl to his body. He is not one of her friends, as her definition of "enemies" included "anything whose scat had the smell of meat or whose voice was either a bark or a yip" (43). Nonetheless, she follows the appropriate cultural practices when she finds his body. First, Mottyl sits down "as was proper" (56). Then, after "a suitable time had passed," she rises, retreats "with infinite care," and then "pray[s] for him" (56). She does this by "leaving her heat-infested traces nearby," which conveys: "*I, Mottyl the cat, have been here* […] *I knew this beast. My prayer is for his release to the buzzards*" (56, emphasis original).

In Book One of *Not Wanted on the Voyage*, Findley (1984) establishes the cognitive, emotional, social, and cultural complexity of his nonhuman characters. Each one is sentient, conscious, and the *subject of a life*. The diversity of Findley's characters and his use of the *acceptance of not knowing* offers almost limitless potential. There is a sense that more is yet to come. If we linger long enough in the woods, we might learn untold secrets of nonhuman lives. However, we know that the Flood is coming and that this rich fantasy world and its complex nonhuman beings will soon be gone.

Book Two addresses the building of the ark and the beginning of the Flood. Here, Findley identifies the reality of categorizing animals as 'wanted' and 'not wanted.' Of course, animals "do not come in pairs" and so "choosing this mare and that stallion was easier said than done" (122). Findley makes it clear that these individuals are not objects; they are unique members of complex social networks with companions, dependents, and family members who cannot be separated without consequence. All of them are "crying out" to each other in "confusion and fear" and many call out to their "abandoned young or to others of their kind who were penned or corralled or stabled" (123). The remaining animals on the Noyes family farm are burned alive in a final sacrifice to Yaweh. When Mrs Noyes confronts her husband, he responds: "It was our duty, madam, not to waste these animals—which, after all, were prime sacrificial specimens raised for that purpose" (127). From his perspective, it would have been a "great waste" if the animals were just left to drown: "Unforgivable" (127).

In these sections, Findley reveals the dichotomy between seeing nonhuman beings as *objects of utility* or as *subjects of lives*. This is a technique we have seen in several texts addressed in the previous chapters of this book. Indeed, there is some similarity between the ways in which Seton and Findley use the subject/object distinction. Both rely on the distressing contrast between the reader's knowledge of an animal's life and their treatment as disposable (such as in Seton's [1901] story "Tito"). In Dr Noyes's eyes, all not-human beings are disposable objects. Thus, the animals on his farm are treated as resources that ought not to be 'wasted.' By contrast, the wild animals are irrelevant. It is worth noting that in neither the Bible nor in *Not Wanted on the Voyage* are these animals the intended targets of the Flood. The 'sins' of humanity are being swept away; these countless individuals are merely bystanders who were not lucky enough to be saved. Interestingly, Findley chooses not to explore the perspectives of the humans who will drown. Instead, he focuses entirely on the unfortunate animals who will become the collateral damage of Yaweh's 'benevolence.'

As the waters begin to rise, the woods become "a haven for every kind of animal refugee in every kind of condition" (Findley 1984, 145). Rapid habitat loss leads an even wider range of animals—"marsh," "field," "river," and "domestic"—to move into the wood, "every one of them out of place" (145). As the animals become more densely packed, food and space become scarce. They are "all in competition" and the guardians of the woods, the lemurs, shout "*no more room!*" from the treetops (145, 131). Every "berry" and "succulent leaf" is "destroyed" (145). Frogs, mice, squirrels, rabbits, monkeys, and birds can "find no place to hide" from the predators; their "cries" and the "stench of blood and offal" are "everywhere" (145).

Mottyl's friend Whistler becomes a knowing witness to this violence. As he is not wanted on the voyage, he watches the "hordes of refugees steaming up the hill" to seek higher ground (190). To him, there seems to be "flesh" everywhere; a "whole hill of backs and scurrying feet" (190). He contemplates joining them but knows that they are "doomed" (190). Living close to the Noyes's farm, Whistler has a better understanding of what is happening than the other animals:

> It had something to do with Yaweh and Noah and the swath of death being cut as wide and deep as a person could imagine. He had heard the sounds and seen the fires of the sacrifice in the yard—and he knew these animals moving up towards the altar—unaware, for the most part, of what an altar was—all had the same hope of being saved. (190)

Whistler chooses to "sit in his favourite burrow and watch the world's last days from there" (191). Findley stops short of depicting the drowning of these individuals, but he ensures that we know their fate. The horror is left to our imagination. As the flood approaches, Findley emphasizes that the animals who are *not wanted on the voyage* are still feeling and knowing subjects. They *know* that they are going to drown, they are afraid, they are fighting to stay alive, and they know that they have been denied access to the ark. They know that they are not wanted; that they have been categorized as disposable objects.

Books Three and Four of *Not Wanted on the Voyage* reveal that the animals aboard the ark have not been 'saved' at all. Findley's (1984) inclusion of the bible verse describing Noah's covenant with God makes this clear: "*into your hands they are delivered*" (285, emphasis original). As human supremacy becomes absolute, the divide between the humans and other animals widens ever more. Dr Noyes and his supporters simply see the animals aboard the ark as "cargo" (210). Kept in the dark in the bottom of the ship, the animals are indeed treated like objects. Almost immediately, the "air" inside becomes "fetid with the stench of animals confined without windows" (197).

In short time, the animals' lives become "absolute hell" (250). They are "caged and underfed, left without air and daylight, separated from all their kind but one" (250). At best, they might have their mate for company to help ease the loss of family and community. At worst, the pairs may have been chosen at random and they are placed in a small cage with a stranger. Many of the animals come to think that this existence is "death" or "certainly something very close to death" (251). Evidently, the animals suffer physically, mentally, and emotionally in their captivity. Mrs Noyes observes a "dreadful sadness" over them all that is quite "unbearable to see" and she wonders whether this misery constitutes "*being saved*" (251, emphasis original). This seems reminiscent of the despair Findley (1990) describes in *Inside Memory* upon seeing the gorilla in the zoo: "Bewilderment—sadness and dignity shone from her eyes" (129).

Findley's (1984) zoocentric retelling of the Genesis Flood myth illustrates the violent outcome of an anthropocentric world. It reveals an empty, rather lonely, existence for humanity. Biodiversity has been significantly reduced. Only those who we force to live with us—or who can adapt to eke out an existence around us—can prosper. The wild animals who survive are those we choose to save and keep in captivity; all others are doomed to extinction. Even then, our efforts to protect the wild survivors are so woefully inadequate that their survival is as doomed as those who we abandoned. A small genetic population who are also suffering physically, mentally, and emotionally from their time in captivity do not make for a prosperous future for any species.

Clearly, Findley's *acceptance of not knowing* does not constitute a lack of concern for animals. His approach to animal representation seems guided by the same combination of curiosity and compassion as Seton's *fantasy of knowing* a century before. Findley's fantastical world is not a retreat from nature. By stepping away from the concerns of realistic representation, he can interrogate the human-animal divide itself. As indicated by his journal entries in *Inside Memory*, Findley (1990) seems to have reflected on these ideas carefully. In 1969, he wrote: "I never thought of myself specifically as animal before [...] I had failed to grasp that what we call the *human spirit* is absolutely rooted in the earth" (215). By 1972, however, he sits with Mottle and thinks "*I am her fellow animal*" (223).

From *Not Wanted on the Voyage* (1984), we can see the impact of the twentieth-century animal rights and environmental movements, as well as some concurrent developments in the sciences. These contemporary dialogues stirred a much more complex exploration of human-animal relations than we have seen in the other texts addressed in this book so far. Findley not only questions our treatment of other animals, but he also questions the human-animal divide itself. He exposes the operations of speciesism, challenges our notions about what separates us from other animals, and uncovers the violence at the heart of human supremacy. In retelling the Genesis Flood myth as a story of a mass extinction, Findley creates a mirror for the destruction of our own environment and its non-human inhabitants.

In an interview with Donald Cameron (1973) in *Conversations with Canadian Novelists*, Findley describes humanity as being "at war with nature" and he points out that we have declared this war against "a defenceless enemy" (50). Similarly, in his review of *Wild Animals I Have Known* (1898), Findley (2003) wrote that "[w]e live in a time when nature is increasingly being placed in hazard—not only by what we do out of ignorance, but what we failed to do because we have ceased to pay attention" (187). In the decades separating Seton's and Findley's writing, the range of human-created threats to other animals had grown immeasurably. Recognition of the dangers posed by humans now extended far beyond the activities of mere hunters. Findley's (1984) apocalyptic vision poses a stark contrast with the images of 'wilderness' he would have read about in Seton's stories as a child. Evidently, *Not Wanted on the Voyage* was Findley's own call for us all to pay attention. As Grace (2020) observes, the book was his "labour of writing against despair of man's inhumanity to man and all life besides" (287).

CONCLUSION

In response to a period of scientific and political turmoil, Canadian fiction developed new modes of engaging with other species. Engel's (1976) scepticism about our ability to perceive animals without anthropocentrism produced a *failure of knowing*. By contrast, Findley's (1984) desire for greater connection with nature created a fantasy world that blurred the line between humans and other species. His *acceptance of not knowing* thoroughly interrogated the validity of human uniqueness and supremacy. Meanwhile, Russell's (1977) *fantasy of knowing* replicated the core characteristics of the wild animal story almost completely. He made bold statements about animal minds, emotions, and personalities just as Seton and Roberts had done decades earlier. His stories marked the first confident return to such topics since the Nature Fakers controversy.

The books covered in this chapter all introduced a sense of 'unnaturalness' in their depictions of animals and the environment. A creeping sense of nature being artificial or 'out of balance' can be found in Russell's coyotes, Engel's bear, and Findley's flood. These are not the depictions of wild animals or wild spaces that we might have found in Seton's or Roberts's works. The 'pristine' wilderness that readers might have sought in their stories was gone. This sense of nature becoming 'unnatural' would continue throughout the following decades. As we will discover in the rest of this book, animal fiction written during the turn of the twentieth century would express growing concerns about the survival of wildlife, humanity, and even 'nature' itself.

REFERENCES

Atwood, Margaret. (1972a) 1992. *Surfacing*. London: Virago.
———. 1972b. *Survival: A Thematic Guide to Canadian Literature*. Toronto: Anansi.
Bagemihl, Bruce. 1999. *Biological Exuberance: Animal Homosexuality and Natural Diversity*. New York, St: Martin's Press.

Bulbeck, Chilla. 2005. *Facing the Wild: Ecotourism, Conservation and Animal Encounters*. London: Earthscan.

Burroughs, John. 1903. Real and Sham Natural History. *Atlantic Monthly*. 91 (545, March): 298–309.

Cameron, Donald. 1973. *Conversations with Canadian Novelists: Part One*. Toronto: Macmillan of Canada.

Engel, Marian. (1976) 1988. *Bear*. London: Pandora.

Findley, Timothy. (1984) 1996. *Not Wanted on the Voyage*. Toronto: Penguin Books.

———. 1990. *Inside Memory: Pages from a Writer's Workbook*. Toronto: HarperCollins.

———. 1993. Significant Others. *Journal of Canadian Studies*. 28 (4, Winter): 149–159.

———. 2003. Wild Animals I Have Known. In *Journeyman: Travels of a Writer*, ed. William Whitehead, 185–188. Toronto: HarperCollins.

Gibson, Graeme. (1971) 1982. *Five Legs / Communion*. Toronto: McClelland and Stewart.

Grace, Sherrill. 2020. *Tiff: A Life of Timothy Findley*. Waterloo: Wilfrid Laurier University Press.

Howells, Coral Ann. 1986. Marian Engel's 'Bear': Pastoral, Porn, and Myth. *Ariel*. 17 (4, October): 105–114.

Huggan, Graham, and Helen Tiffin. 2010. *Postcolonial Ecocriticism: Literature, Animals, Environment*. London: Routledge.

King James Bible Online. 2023. Genesis: Chapter 9. https://www.kingjamesbibleonline.org/Genesis-Chapter-9/. Accessed May 29 2023.

Kroetsch, Robert. (1969) 2004. *The Studhorse Man*. Edmonton: University of Alberta Press.

Loo, Tina. 2006. *States of Nature: Conserving Canada's Wildlife in the Twentieth Century*. Vancouver: UBC Press.

Nagel, Thomas. 1974. What Is It Like to Be a Bat? *The Philosophical Review*. 83 (4, October): 435–450.

Roosevelt, Theodore. 1907. Nature Fakers. *Everybody's Magazine*. 17 (3, September): 427–430.

Russell, Andy. (1977) 1991. *Adventures with Wild Animals*. Toronto: McClelland & Stewart.

Russell, Charlie, and Maureen Enns. 2003. *Grizzly Heart: Living Without Fear Among the Brown Bears of Kamchatka*. Toronto: Vintage Canada.

Sergiel, Agnieszka, et al. 2014. Fellatio in Captive Brown Bears: Evidence of Long-Term Effectives of Suckling Deprivation? *Zoo Biology*. 33 (4, July–August): 1–4. https://doi.org/10.1002/zoo.21137.

Seton, Ernest Thompson. 1898. *Wild Animals I Have Known*. New York: Charles Scriber's Sons.

———. 1901. *Lives of the Hunted*. London: David Nutt.

———. 1905. *Animal Heroes*. London: Constable & Company.
Shapiro, Kenneth J., and Marion W. Copeland. 2005. Toward a Critical Theory of Animal Issues in Fiction. *Society and Animals*. 13 (4): 343–346. https://doi.org/10.1163/156853005774653636.
Washburn, Margaret Floy. 1908. *The Animal Mind: A Textbook of Comparative Psychology*. New York: Macmillan Company.

PART IV

Survival

CHAPTER 8

1980s–2000s Contexts

This chapter identifies the return of certain ideas about animals introduced at the beginning of this book. Theories, debates, and concerns
established a hundred years earlier had come 'full circle' by the end of the
twentieth century. In the sciences, cognitive ethologists were attempting
to study the emotions and consciousness of other animals, just as early
comparative psychologists had done. They even embraced a limited form
of 'introspection' by accepting the utility of anthropomorphism and imaginative speculation as tools for research. Some went so far as to suggest
that animal fiction could play a role in understanding of the inner lives of
other species. Meanwhile, animal advocates made twelve unsuccessful
attempts to improve Canada's anti-cruelty legislation between 1999 and
2010. The government's resistance to even minor amendments lay in a
backlash against the animal rights movement that had begun in the 1980s.
Thus, at the turn of the twenty-first century, Canada's federal animal laws
were in almost the same state that they had been in the Victorian era.

ANTI-CRUELTY LAWS AND THE ANIMAL RIGHTS BACKLASH

A new edition of *Animal Liberation* was published in 1990. In the preface, Peter Singer reflects on the intervening years since the first edition in
1975: "Important gains for animals have already been achieved. Far

© The Author(s), under exclusive license to Springer Nature
Switzerland AG 2023
C. Allmark-Kent, *Literature, Science, and Animal Advocacy in
Canada*, Palgrave Studies in Animals and Literature,
https://doi.org/10.1007/978-3-031-40556-3_8

greater ones lie ahead. Animal Liberation is now a worldwide movement, and it will be on the agenda for a long time to come" (1990, ix). Based on the movement's trajectory, one would join Singer in anticipating significant improvements for the lives of animals during the 1990s and 2000s. This was a period in which advances in animal cognition expanded our understanding of the mental, emotional, social, and even cultural lives of other species.

Yet, Canadian federal anti-cruelty laws had not changed since the nineteenth century. The law continued to classify animals as property and view their abuse as little more than property damage. Between 1999 and 2010, there were thirteen attempts to amend the anti-cruelty provisions in the Criminal Code. Every bill failed, except one backed by industry lobbyists, which merely increased punishments for offenders. After over a hundred years of Canadian animal advocacy, the laws protecting animals had not improved. Indeed, despite evidence gathered over a century of animal psychology, the law continued to treat animals as unfeeling objects.

It is important to recognize that this resistance to improving anti-cruelty legislation is not somehow 'inherent' to Canadian society or politics. It was the result of a concentrated backlash against the animal rights movement, which began in the 1980s. Clearly, two decades of animal advocacy protests, campaigns, and international attention had had an effect. Brian Davies's crusade against seal hunting had demonstrated that media campaigns and boycotts could impact Canada's economic relationship with other nations. In essence, it proved that advocacy groups were able put the government under enough pressure to change legislation.

It also emphasized the catastrophic consequences when Indigenous peoples are excluded from legislative and policy-making processes. Animal advocates witnessing commercial hunting with large vessels created and perpetuated a homogenized image of seal hunting that excluded Inuit methods. This short-sighted approach highlighted the on-going erasure of Indigenous perspectives from mainstream conservation and animal protection campaigns. Consequently, this added to negative perceptions of animal advocates as sentimental, naive, and ill-informed. We can draw a direct link from the 1980s animal rights backlash to the failed anti-cruelty legislation of the 1990s and 2000s. By doing so, we can trace the origins of specific arguments and ideas that proved fundamental to the later parliamentary debates.

In 1983, the Fur Institute of Canada formed in response to the anti-fur movement. During the same year, CBC Radio produced a programme with fur lobbyist Alan Herscovici called "Men and Animals: Building a New Relationship with Nature." This led to Herscovici writing a book based on the programme called *Second Nature: The Animal Rights Controversy* (1985). In turn, his book influenced Sonya Dakers's 1988 report for the Research Branch of the Library of Parliament titled "Animal Rights Campaigns: Their Impact in Canada."

Both Herscovici and Dakers argued that animal rights advocacy was incompatible with the realities of life in Canada. This was true for Inuit communities and the seal-hunting ban. Yet they extended this thinking to frame the whole concept of animal rights as fundamentally at odds with 'Canadian identity' (a problematic concept in itself). At the core, their arguments were not about identity or even Indigenous sovereignty. Instead, they proposed that animal protection campaigns were detrimental to the Canadian economy because they spread misinformation about animal industries.

In 1992, the Canadian Security Intelligence Service published a paper, "Militant Activism and the Issue of Animal Rights" (Smith 1992). Then, in October 2001, Herscovici was part of the Standing Committee to discuss Bill C-15B, which proposed amendments to the anti-cruelty sections of the Criminal Code. There, he argued that animal rights were a threat to *national* security. John Sorenson (2003) points out that Herscovici not only exaggerated the scope of the amendments, but he also claimed that the bill was "attacking human rights" (389). He accused animal advocates of "terrorism" and even made comparisons with the recent 11 September terrorist attacks in New York (394–5). Clearly, these statements were "calculated" to "exploit" the panic inspired by both the attacks themselves and the media discourse around terrorism at the time (395).

By comparison, Herscovici's accusations in *Second Nature* (1985) had been relatively modest. The book positioned itself as an expansion of the "Men and Animals" radio programme, which had been an ostensibly neutral look at the animal rights movement. Although there was no mention of his role as a lobbyist or, indeed, his family's fur business, A-J Herscovici Furs Ltd. Given these interests and the on-going attempts to ban seal hunting, it is unsurprising that *Second Nature* (1985) ended up focusing on anti-fur and anti-sealskin campaigns, almost to the exclusion of any other animal welfare issue.

In the book, Herscovici (1985) gives some space to the issues of animal experimentation and factory farming because he predicts that they may become targets of future campaigns. However, he argues that they are too integral to the lives of most urban people and, therefore, "they are unlikely soon to become popular campaigns" (69). This is an astute point. As we have seen throughout this book, widespread public support for animal protection reforms tends to occur when its proponents would be unaffected by the change themselves. However, this means that he reframes the entire topic under the specific and highly complex issue of animal rights and Indigenous sovereignty. He paints animal rights advocates as "well-educated, well-meaning people" who are nonetheless "wiping out the last vestiges of traditional Inuit culture" (11, 22). Sonya Dakers's (1988) report, "Animal Rights Campaigns: Their Impact in Canada," makes the same argument.

For the most part, Herscovici's treatment of the animal rights movement in *Second Nature* (1985) is more moderate than his dire language of terrorism and human rights violations used in the Standing Committee discussions. He tends to treat advocates as misinformed sensationalists. However, he does rely on the common stereotype of concern for animals as 'feminine.' He writes: "the killing of animals has been primarily a male domain" and the "growth of the animal-rights philosophy" owes much to "the increasing economic and political power of women" (203). This leads to a rather bizarre claim that the "powerful mass appeal" of anti-sealing campaigns, particularly those that focus on "'baby' seals, which are an archetype of the infant," are a manifestation of public concern redirected from the contemporary "troubling issue" of "abortion" (203).[1]

From the 1980s to 2000s, we can trace the changing language used against animal advocates. In their publications, both Dakers (1988) and Herscovici (1985) create a gulf between the "consensus in Canadian society that the relationship between human beings and animals should be non-exploitative" and the idea of "radical animal-rights philosophy," which "calls not merely for specific reforms but for a revolution" (Dakers 1988, 1; Herscovici 1985, 19, 26). In other words, they claim that all Canadians take it as axiomatic that animals should not be exploited

---

[1] In *Survival* (1972) Margaret Atwood had argued that, "in Canada," the "nation as a whole" supported the campaign against "the slaughter of baby seals" because "Canadians themselves feel threatened and nearly extinct as a nation" (79–80). In other words, "their identification with animals is the expression of a deep-seated cultural fear" (80). Although their explanations are quite different, both Atwood and Herscovici demonstrate the common tendency to reinterpret concern for animals as something else. In both cases, animal advocacy is not about the animals *themselves*, but an expression of suppressed human anxieties.

or treated inhumanely. Yet, the idea that animals have the *right* not to be exploited or treated inhumanely is a threat to Canadian society. This means that traditional humane societies and animal welfare groups are seen as acceptable, but animal rights campaigners are not.

In *Second Nature* (1985), Herscovici describes a "split between traditional animal-welfare groups and animal-rights groups" (55). Meanwhile, Dakers (1988) appreciates "the work of animal welfare groups" to improve areas such as "humane trapping," but warns that Canada is "particularly vulnerable" to "animal rights campaigns" (7, 1). Over the following years, the increasingly sensationalized terms used to describe animal advocacy meant that, when anti-cruelty laws were debated in the early 2000s, the reforms were framed as radical, extreme, and revolutionary. In the minds of its opponents, each bill's modest anti-cruelty amendments—measures that would seem to reflect the consensus in Canadian society that animals should not be abused—had become equal with political extremism. Traditional animal welfare was now synonymous with 'radical' animal rights.

In 1998, the Department of Justice published, *Crimes Against Animals: A Consultation Paper*. The anti-cruelty sections of the Canadian Criminal Code had remained virtually untouched since they were first established in 1892. Within "Part IX: Wilful and Forbidden Acts in Respect of Certain Property," sections 444 to 447 provide the nation's only federal animal protection laws (*Canadian Criminal Code*, RSC 1985, c C.46, s.444–447). For the most part, these laws merely prohibit the wilful killing, maiming, wounding, injuring, or endangering of cattle or other animals kept in captivity for lawful purposes. Of course, 'wilful intent' is difficult to prove. Moreover, wild, feral, or other non-captive animals are entirely unprotected.

In 1999, Justice Minister Anne McLellan introduced Bill C-17, An Act to Amend the Criminal Code. It would be the first of multiple, unsuccessful attempts. The proposed amendments were modest. Changes included providing a definition for "animal" as a "vertebrate, other than a human being, and any other animal that has the capacity to feel pain," as well as moving anti-cruelty laws from "Part XI: Wilful and Forbidden Acts in Respect of Certain Property" and into an amended "Part V: Sexual Offences, Public Morals, Disorderly Conduct, and Cruelty to Animals" (quoted in Hughes and Meyer 2000, 74).

Lynne Létourneau's (2003) analysis of Bill C-10—which was virtually identical to its predecessors, C-15B and C-17—concludes that the proposed amendments "do not create legal rights for animals," nor do they "lead the way to animal liberation" (1052–4). The bill acknowledges that animals have certain interests but continues to prioritize the interests of humans first. Thus, "the basis of Bill C-10 is human-centred, not animal-centred" (1051). Likewise, Sorenson (2003) notes that, because the bills were directed at individual acts of violence, they posed no challenge to animal exploitation industries and were not motivated by animal rights philosophy (337). He observes that virtually "everyone who appeared before the Standing Committee or spoke in parliamentary debates to oppose anti-cruelty legislation indicated that they were 'animal lovers,' cared about animals or supported the idea of animal welfare" (383). Yet, at the same time they seem to have equated any increased protection for animals with the perceived threat of the animal rights movement.

According to Sorenson's (2003) analysis, animal industry lobbyists "deliberately exaggerated the amendments' effects and vilified those with genuine and reasonable concern for the welfare of animals as 'radicals,' 'extremists,' and 'terrorists'" (377). A common theme was the notion that these amendments "concealed a 'hidden agenda' that would not only 'humanize' animals but would allow 'animal rights extremists' to accomplish their goals" (337). Particularly interesting is the frequent claim that moving anti-cruelty laws from the property section of the Criminal Code into its own category of Cruelty to Animals would constitute "a fundamental, even revolutionary reconfiguration of the human/animal boundary" (385). Antonio Robert Verbora (2015) cites one MP who claimed that the bills were "not about cruelty to animals legislation" at all but were really an attempt "towards the humanization of animals in this country" (52).

The only successful bill was S-203, which merely increased the maximum penalties for offenders. As Verbora (2015) observes, this bill "left offences from 1892 untouched," which allowed "wild animals and strays to be killed for any reason, or even for no reason" and for individuals to "kill animals brutally and viciously as long as the animal dies immediately" (51). Bill S-203 was backed by animal industry lobbyists and the political opponents of the previous bills. Despite their prior claims to be 'animal lovers' concerned with animal cruelty, the only issue they found with the previous laws was that the penalties were not severe enough.

Sorenson (2003) concludes that the key factor in explaining these events is "material interests" (387). Opposition to the other bills "came directly from animal exploitation industries" who "organized to defend their financial interests" (387). Once more Canada's dichotomy between exploitation and protection led to the will to exploit overriding even the most minimal desires to protect. Verbora (2015) adds that the Criminal Code perpetuates "a form of speciesism" by viewing animals as property and, thus, offering less protection to "wild or stray animals in comparison to cattle and other working animals" (58). Ironically, this pattern of events mirrored the nine unsuccessful attempts to improve Canadian anti-cruelty legislation in the 1880s and 1890s. Even then, proponents found themselves "repeatedly frustrated by length debates" and, in the end, only one bill passed (Ingram 2013, 242).

COGNITIVE ETHOLOGY

It seems astounding that, at the same time as Canadian politicians were debating whether animals were essentially objects, the scientific community was trying to find out whether those same animals were capable of conscious thought. For decades, researchers had been discovering that many animals' cognitive abilities, emotional states, social relationships, communication methods, and even their capacities for tool use were considerably more sophisticated than previously thought. By the beginning of the twenty-first century, this mounting evidence triggered what Martin Schönfeld (2006) identifies as a paradigm shift in the sciences, in which our "basic assumptions about animals and their inner lives" had changed (354).

Colin Allen and Marc Bekoff (2007) observed that animal cognition research had been enjoying "widespread exposure" through "television documentaries and the science sections of newspapers and magazines" (300). Recent studies that had captured public attention included:

> dolphins apparently recognizing themselves in mirrors, starlings identifying recursive syntax violations, chimpanzees who appear to know what others can see, crows fashioning tools, monkeys rejecting unfair rewards, play and moral behaviour in animals, fish rubbing inflamed lips, and rats laughing when tickled. (300)

For decades, most of these abilities had been held up as the dividing line between human and nonhuman beings. Self-awareness, language, empathy, tool use, emotions, play, and altruism could no longer be treated as uniquely human attributes. By the beginning of the twenty-first century, it seemed as though the line between humans and other animals was growing thin. Perhaps the fears of some Canadian politicians about the 'humanization' of other animals had been influenced by these discoveries.

The study of animal cognition had grown considerably since the publication of Donald Griffin's *The Question of Animal Awareness* (1976). It had become a multidisciplinary endeavour addressing a range of topics from memory and decision-making to social interactions and the pursuit of pleasure. Yet, amongst the various fields of animal cognition research, only Griffin's own *cognitive ethology* remained explicitly interested in the question of *consciousness*.[2] In 1997, Allen and Bekoff defined cognitive ethology as the study of "thought processes, consciousness, beliefs, and rationality in nonhuman animals" within a "comparative and evolutionary framework" (313). For all the progress made by the cognitive revolution, however, a certain scepticism was still attached to the question of animal thought. For instance, Hank Davis (1997) has described Griffin's *Animal Thinking* (1984) as demonstrating that "anthropomorphism" was "neither a quaint nineteenth-century problem, nor confined to those without scientific training" (338).

Clearly, cognitive ethology's commitment to the study of animal consciousness was divisive. Allen and Bekoff (1997) observed that cognitive ethology faced significant "challenges to its scientific status" due to both its "subject matter and methods" (314).[3] These criticisms tend to focus on concerns about the knowability of animal minds, the unreliability of anecdotal evidence, the use of anthropomorphic language, and the preservation of the human-animal divide. Of course, these are the same issues that we have seen expressed in every chapter of this book. Underlying fears that drove the Nature Fakers controversy are the same as those faced by cognitive ethologists a century later.

In part, scepticism towards cognitive ethology has been exacerbated by its associations with Charles Darwin, George Romanes, and early comparative psychology. As stated by Allen and Bekoff (1997), cognitive ethology maintains an explicitly "comparative and evolutionary framework," just as Darwin's and Romanes's comparative psychology had done

---

[2] In "Animal Cognition and Animal Behaviour," Sara J. Shettleworth (2001) draws a clear distinction between cognitive ethology and other animal cognition research. "Except in the context of cognitive ethology," she writes, "the study of cognition is not the study of consciousness" (278).

[3] Ten years later, Allen and Bekoff (2007) note that some scientists were still unwilling to accept the label "cognitive ethologist" (305).

(313). Along similar lines, Carolyn A. Ristau (1992) described the work of cognitive ethologists as studying the "mental life of animals" in their own habitats, particularly as they solve "everyday problems in their natural world" (125). This was quite a departure from the behaviourist-style learning experiments that had been popular in North America for most of the twentieth century. Instead, cognitive ethology's approach had more in common with classical European ethology and early comparative psychology. Indeed, Ristau (1992) observes that cognitive ethology's roots in Darwin's and Romanes's work are quite "evident" (125).

Unlike most scientific fields, cognitive ethology tends to be more receptive to both anecdotal evidence and the use of anthropomorphic language as tools to aid more rigorous research. Inevitably, this can reinforce comparisons with Darwin and Romanes. However, there is a stark difference between twenty-first-century scientists who view animal anecdotes as a starting point for further research and the nineteenth-century comparative psychologists who only had access to anecdotal evidence. For instance, Ristau (1992) suggested "anthropomorphizing" could be a "useful beginning" by "suggesting potential animal capacities" (125). After all, all we can do as humans "imagining" another animal's perspective is to "anthropomorphize" (125). Along similar lines, Bekoff (2007) argued that "anthropomorphic language" was simply unavoidable: "we have no alternatives" (124). Yet even though it is a necessary "linguistic tool" to help us describe the "thoughts and feelings of other animals," we must still make "every attempt to maintain the animal's point of view" (123–5).

Cognitive ethology's stance on anthropomorphism is significant. This shift in thinking towards anthropomorphic language has the potential to be transformative. Within the context of this book, it is particularly profound. It means that the role of scientifically engaged animal fiction has changed. Indeed, it is remarkable how many cognitive ethologists are receptive to contributions from beyond the sciences. Ristau (1992) proposed "using new data" and "new methodologies in creative ways," as well as engaging with other fields at conferences and meetings (133). She also suggested "reading about other fields, beginning, if need be, in the popular media" (133). Bekoff (2000) postulated that a truly "rigorous study" of animal minds may require input from diverse sources, including "nonacademics who observe animals and tell stories" (869). Similarly, Bernard E. Rollin (2007) commented that "far more ordinary people than scientists observe animals" (113). It would be a "pity" to continue excluding such a "potentially valuable source of information" (133).

In 2003, the Canadian marine biologist, Hal Whitehead, made an astonishing recommendation that scientists should take inspiration from animal fiction. As part of his conclusion to *Sperm Whales: Social Evolution in the Ocean* (2003), he addressed gaps in the current research, such as "interactions among individual sperm whales," "the social context and function of vocalizations," and "the significance of culture in determining behaviour" (370). One possible avenue for future research could be to examine fictional depictions of animal societies first. Whitehead directs the reader to two novels written by Canadian women, Alison Baird's *White as the Waves* (1999) and Barbara Gowdy's *The White Bone* (1998). He describes both books as "remarkable" (370).

Whitehead's (2003) discussion of the two novels focused on their combination of fact, fiction, and speculation:

> Both novels use what is known of the biology and social lives of their subject species to build pictures of elaborate societies, cultures, and cognitive abilities. [...] A reductionist might class these portraits with *Winnie-the-Pooh* fantasies on the lives of animals. But for me they ring true, and may well come closer to the nature of these animals than the coarse numerical abstractions that come from my own scientific observations. [...] We need to take these constructions, note the large parts that are consistent with what we now know, and use them as hypotheses to guide our work. (370–1)

Both *White as the Waves* (1999) and *The White Bone* (1998) are speculative *fantasy of knowing* narratives. In essence, they are the literary descendants of Ernest Thompson Seton's and Charles G. D. Roberts's wild animal stories. Although they use the speculative style seen in Frederick Philip Grove's *Consider Her Ways* (1947), the creative debt they owe to the original wild animal story is undeniable. A century after the Nature Fakers controversy, a biologist who praised two works of Canadian animal fiction and took their animal representations seriously, also advocated for their value to science. Moreover, he declared that the "communication" between writers and researchers "should be reciprocal" (371). A century after the height of the wild animal story, it might be time for scientifically engaged animal fiction to fulfil its purpose at last.

CONCLUSION

The issues, debates, and concerns established at the beginning of this book were still alive more than a century later. Questions about knowing other animals, scientific authority, and human uniqueness had survived into the new millennium. Likewise, any developments in science or animal advocacy that seemed to narrow the human-animal divide continued to inspire either enthusiasm or resistance. Political debates about the legal status of animals as property focused on a fear of 'humanizing' other species. For all the campaigns and appeals of the previous century, animals were still mere objects under the Canadian Criminal Code. As had been the case when those laws were first established, economic concerns remained a deciding factor in animal protection debates. Nonetheless, a new atmosphere of interdisciplinary collaboration was beginning to emerge across literature, science, and animal advocacy. Finally, Seton's and Roberts's scientific aspirations for the wild animal story might find fulfilment in the twenty-first century.

REFERENCES

Allen, Colin, and Marc Bekoff. 1997. Cognitive Ethology: Slayers, Skeptics, and Proponents. In *Anthropomorphism, Anecdotes, and Animals*, ed. Robert W. Mitchell, Nicholas S. Thompson, and H. Lyn Miles, 313–334. Albany, NY: State University of New York Press.

———. 2007. Animal Minds, Cognitive Ethology, and Ethics. *The Journal of Ethics* 11 (3): 299–317.

Atwood, Margaret. 1972. *Survival: A Thematic Guide to Canadian Literature*. Toronto: Anansi.

Baird, Alison. 1999. *White as the Waves: A Novel of Moby Dick*. St. John's: Tuckamore Books.

Bekoff, Marc. 2000. Animal Emotions: Exploring Passionate Natures. *BioScience*. 50 (10, October): 861–870. https://doi.org/10.1641/0006-3568(2000)05 0[0861:AEEPN]2.0.CO;2.

———. 2007. *The Emotional Lives of Animals: A Leading Scientist Explores Animal Joy, Sorrow, and Empathy – And Why They Matter*. Novato: New World Library.

Criminal Code, RSC 1985, c C.46.

Dakers, Sonya. 1988. *Animal Rights Campaigns: Their Impact in Canada*. Ottawa: Research Branch of the Library of Parliament.

Davis, Hank. 1997. Animal Cognition Versus Animal Thinking. In *Anthropomorphism, Anecdotes, and Animals*, ed. Robert W. Mitchell, Nicholas S. Thompson, and H. LynMiles, 335–347. Albany, NY: State University of New York Press.

Gowdy, Barbara. (1998) 2000. *The White Bone*. London: Flamingo.

Griffin, Donald R. 1976. *The Question of Animal Awareness: Evolutionary Continuity of Mental Experience*. New York: Rockerfeller University Press.

Grove, Frederick Philip. (1947) 1977. *Consider Her Ways*. Toronto: McClelland and Stewart.

Herscovici, Alan. 1985. *Second Nature: The Animal Rights Controversy*. Toronto: CBC Enterprises.

Hughes, Elaine L., and Christiane Meyer. 2000. Animal Welfare Law in Canada and Europe. *Animal Law* 6 (23): 23–76.

Ingram, Darcy. 2013. Beastly Measures: Animal Welfare, Civil Society, and State Policy in Victorian Canada. *Journal of Canadian Studies* 41 (1): 221–252. https://doi.org/10.3138/jcs.47.1.221.

Létourneau, Lyne. 2003. Toward Animal Liberation? The New Anti-Cruelty Provisions in Canada and Their Impact on the Status Animals. *Alberta Law Review* 40 (1): 1041–1055. https://doi.org/10.29173/alr1350.

Ristau, Carolyn A. 1992. Cognitive Ethology: Past, Present, and Speculations on the Future. *PSA: Proceedings*: 125–136. https://doi.org/10.1086/psaprocbienmeetp.1992.2.192829.

Rollin, Bernard E. 2007. Animal Mind: Science, Philosophy, and Ethics. *The Journal of Ethics* 11 (3): 253–274.

Schönfeld, Martin. 2006. Animal Consciousness: Paradigm Change in the Life Sciences. *Perspectives on Science* 14 (3, Fall): 354–381. https://doi.org/10.1162/posc.2006.14.3.354.

Shettleworth, Sara J. 2001. Review: Animal Cognition and Animal Behaviour. *Animal Behaviour* 61 (2): 277–286. https://doi.org/10.1006/anbe.2000.1606.

Singer, Peter. 1990. Preface. In *Animal Liberation*, by Peter Singer. New York: Avon Books.

Smith, G.D. 1992. *Militant Activism and the Issue of Animal Rights*. Ottawa: Canadian Security Intelligence Service.

Sorenson, John. 2003. 'Some Strange Things Happening in our Country': Opposing Proposed Changes in Anti-Cruelty Laws in Canada. *Social & Legal Studies* 12 (3, September): 377–402. https://doi.org/10.1177/09646639030123005.

Verbora, Antonio Robert. 2015. The Political Landscape Surrounding Anti-Cruelty Legislation in Canada. *Society & Animals* 23 (1, February): 45–67. https://doi.org/10.1163/15685306-12341353.

Whitehead, Hal. 2003. *Sperm Whales: Social Evolution in the Ocean*. Chicago: University of Chicago Press.

CHAPTER 9

1980s–2000s Texts

This chapter demonstrates the survival of each form of literary animal representation: the realistic *fantasy of knowing*, the speculative *fantasy of knowing*, the *failure of knowing*, and the *acceptance of not knowing*. Each style is reflected in the four texts addressed in this chapter. Two *fantasy of knowing* narratives reveal that core characteristics of the wild animal story still survived a century after their creation. Likewise, perennial concerns about human uniqueness and our ability to know other animals resurface in the *failure of knowing* and *acceptance of not knowing* texts. Unusually, three out of the four books mirror contemporary cognitive ethology by depicting other animals as capable of *consciousness*. The fourth reflects a resistance to any narrowing of the human-animal divide and expresses a fear of anthropomorphism instead. All written at the turn of the twenty-first century, these four texts are united by questions of 'survival.' Unlike older examples of animal fiction, this uncertainty of survival extends beyond individuals or single species to the survival of ecosystems, humanity, and even 'nature' itself.

R. D. LAWRENCE: *THE WHITE PUMA* (1990)

Ronald Douglas Lawrence (1921–2003) published *The White Puma* (1990) a century after Ernest Thompson Seton's *Wild Animals I Have Known* (1898) and Charles G. D. Roberts's *Kindred of the Wild* (1902).

© The Author(s), under exclusive license to Springer Nature Switzerland AG 2023
C. Allmark-Kent, *Literature, Science, and Animal Advocacy in Canada*, Palgrave Studies in Animals and Literature, https://doi.org/10.1007/978-3-031-40556-3_9

Yet, his realistic *fantasy of knowing* the animal bears a striking resemblance to their original wild animal stories. His story of a rare albino puma (*Felis concolor*, also known as a cougar or mountain lion) being hunted by the same men who killed both his mother and sister could almost have come from one of Seton's or Roberts's books. Lawrence also employs a narrative structure that was particularly favoured by Seton, in which the author juxtaposes the perspectives of both the hunted and the hunter. Perhaps the best-known example would be Seton's story, "Lobo," first published as "The King of Currumpaw" in *Scribner's Magazine* in 1894.

Although *The White Puma* holds all the core characteristics of the wild animal story, Lawrence (1990) does make some changes. Most significantly, when the white puma's efforts to evade his hunters prove insufficient, he begins to hunt them. Such an act of resistance is absent from most wild animal stories. It is even absent from the other twentieth-century texts addressed in this book. For all their similarities, Lawrence resists Seton's (1898) infamous claim from *Wild Animals I Have Known* that the life of the "wild animal always has a tragic end" (12). Indeed, Lawrence's (1990) puma is one of the few protagonists to survive at the end of his story. He slips away from human sight at the end of the narrative, just like the animals of Andy Russell's *Adventures with Wild Animals* (1977). Using tracks, traces, and rare sightings, the humans attempt to monitor his movements. It is only in the final lines of the novel that we learn of a white puma kitten seen in the area, indicating that the protagonist had managed to find a mate and now had "a son or daughter just like him" (Lawrence 1990, 329).

A hundred years separate the publications of *Wild Animals I Have Known* (1898) and *The White Puma* (1990). We can see a sharp contrast between Seton's depictions of tragic animal victims and Lawrence's more optimistic narrative of survival. In the intervening century, multiple waves of animal protection movements shaped and reshaped public attitudes towards animals. I would suggest that these developments enabled Lawrence to write a more hopeful story of animal survival. The animal rights, conservation, and environmental movements were all particularly prominent in the decades leading up to the publication of *The White Puma*. Unlike most of the texts addressed here, Lawrence (1990) includes human characters who advocate for the puma's protection. The two most significant figures are Heather Lansing (a conservationist) and David Carew (a biologist), although they are also eventually joined by a hunter who undergoes an ethical transformation.

By the end of the novel, the animal advocates ensure the long-term safety of the white puma, his mate, and their offspring. These protections are not easily won, however. Lansing and Carew repeatedly face insults, such as "nature freaks," "bleeding hearts," and "bloody activists" (Lawrence 1990, 240, 250). Evidently, the continued stigma against concern for animals remained potent throughout the twentieth century. This prejudice seems to have endured, despite an increasing acceptance of human responsibility for environmental degradation and species loss. Here, we can see ripples of the 1980s and 1990s backlash against the animal rights and environmental movements. Through the two hunters, Walter Taggart and Steve Cousins, Lawrence explores the ease with which existing animal protection laws could be circumvented or even exploited. This secondary human narrative reflects the state of animal protection work at the end of the twentieth century, including its barriers, limitations, and future potential.

The optimistic ending of the *The White Puma* is highly significant. A positive ending is rare for a wild animal story. Indeed, is unusual for most protagonists of animal fiction to survive their own narrative. For those who do, the authors tend not to give any indication of their future life beyond the conclusion of the story. The ending of Marian Engel's (1976) *Bear*, for instance, is particularly abrupt. The human character, Lou, does little to ensure her companion's wellbeing, beyond asking another human not to "kill him" (138). By contrast, *The White Puma* (1990) explores the possibility of ensuring a wild animal's long-term protection through a variety of measures, including: the puma's legal protection; increased conservation officers in the region; a transformation of the hunter, Cousins, into a conservation officer; and the deployment of dedicated researchers to study the pumas. These developments suggest that the puma's ongoing protection is secured from *all* future hunters, not just Cousins or Taggart.

Naturally, this does raise the question: who is responsible for the puma's survival? Is it the puma himself or the humans who campaign on his behalf? The prologue to *The White Puma* introduces the protagonist through his resistance to victimization:

> Had he lived in a region undisturbed by human activity, the puma would never have been given cause to experience hatred. [...] He had been goaded by those men and their dogs. [...] Of late, however, the cat had begun to hunt the hunters. (Lawrence 1990, 4–6)

Importantly, Lawrence avoids reinforcing speciesist stereotypes by emphasizing that the puma is seeking two *specific* humans, not humans in general. Indeed, the puma has "good reason to remember Taggart and Cousins" (4). Even though it is "not in the puma's nature to feel hatred," an "emotion" that is "rarely experienced by any animal," these two men had "taught him to hate" (4). It is the puma's unique response to a lifetime of harassment from these two men. Thus, this is not a random act of violence from a 'savage' beast.

As we can see, Lawrence introduces his protagonist as an emotional creature. This seems to be part of the return to confident depictions of animal minds and emotions in the wake of the cognitive revolution. Of the texts addressed in this book, Russell (1977) had offered the first such representation since Seton's and Roberts's own stories. Evidently, the mechanomorphism of earlier decades had continued to subside with the waning influences of behaviourism and ethology. Lawrence (1990) maintains this return to unapologetic depictions of animal mentation, but also incorporates contemporary scientific evidence. For instance, he reinforces the credibility of animal emotions by grounding his description in biochemistry: "his emotions fired heavy charges of endocrine hormones into his bloodstream, especially adrenaline, the chemical that prepared his body for immediate and strenuous action" (4).

Interestingly, Lawrence takes his animal representation a stage further by suggesting that his puma also has a degree of self-awareness. Russell (1977) had identified metacognition as the main difference between humans and other animals: "We *know* that we know, and other animals just know" (vii, emphasis original). In *The White Puma*, however, Lawrence (1990) gestures towards puma's awareness of his own emotions. He is "inherently aware" that it is unusual for him to feel "hatred" for Taggart and Cousins (4). Although he is "not given to conscious rationalization," he sensed that "unbridled, single-minded odium was inhibiting and only rarely produced positive results" (4). It is worth remembering that, apart from Russell (1977), we have not seen such depictions of animal consciousness since the Nature Fakers controversy. For most of the twentieth century, even the suggestion of animal minds or emotions would have been laughable. Perhaps the cognitive revolution's re-examination of animal consciousness (however controversial) enabled Lawrence to make an equivalent move in realistic animal fiction.

I would suggest that some of the similarities between *The White Puma* (1990) and the original wild animal stories owe something to the fact that

Seton, Roberts, and Lawrence were not writing at the height of behaviourism or ethology. Despite the century separating them, we can see the common attitudes to animal minds that they express. In ways reminiscent of Seton and Roberts, Lawrence demonstrates the survival advantages of having emotions, long-term memories, intentionality, methods of communication, and, most importantly, the ability to learn. At all times, Lawrence integrates the ability to learn from experience or observation as a core component of animal survival. Just like Roderick Haig-Brown's (1941) 'home stream theory' thought experiment in *Return to the River*, Lawrence's (1990) biography of the white puma essentially argues that animals *require* complex minds and emotions in order to survive.

Using the perspectives of both the white puma and his mother (the tawny puma), Lawrence goes to significant lengths to explore his protagonists' different survival strategies in detail. For instance, he carefully considers the different senses involved when the tawny puma chooses a new den site. First, she uses her nose and ears to detect whether the den was already "occupied by a large and powerful animal" (Lawrence 1990, 117). She only advances inside when she is satisfied that she cannot identify any trace of another predator. Then, she spends a considerable amount of time "accustoming herself to those sounds and scents that were detectable within the den and outside, in the immediate environs" (118).

Through years of experience, the tawny puma is already aware of the "normal and unchallenging signatures of a given home site," but she knows that each has "its own special medley" (118). "Without conscious intent," she identifies and memorizes all the "olfactory and sonic characteristics" of the den so that she can check them briefly "every time she reentered the shelter" (119). In fact, she does not "relax" until she completes her "inventory" (119). Though she had "already been in the habit of routinely checking every one of the environmental influences that she detected," she had become "more cautious than ever" after being shot by Taggart (120). The "memory of the shock, pain, and fear she had experienced" remained with her long after she had "recovered from the wound" (120). As we might imagine, her emotional reaction to the pain was integral to learning from the experience.

Moreover, she is "aware" that if her kittens are to "survive," they must be "taught to be cautious, to be keenly observant, and to exercise their memories, even while engaging in routine affairs" (120). As we might expect, the descriptions of the tawny puma teaching her young are similar to those found in Seton's stories "Tito" (1901) and "Badlands Billy"

(1905), as well as "Misty" from Russell's (1977) *Adventures with Wild Animals*. In each case, the parent is intentionally teaching their young. As Lawrence (1990) writes:

> So [...] the puma led her kittens cautiously and taught them by example; patiently, and hour by hour she demonstrated the skills that would make them capable of identifying and storing a veritable cornucopia of environmental signals. (120)

Without qualification, Lawrence states that the tawny puma actively *teaches* and instructs her young. It is worth recalling, here, that the question of animal teaching drew some of the greatest criticisms during the Nature Fakers controversy. Yet, by the 1990s, the idea seems to have become acceptable once more.

In 1992, animal cognition researchers, Tim M. Caro and Marc D. Hauser, published "Is There Teaching in Nonhuman Animals?" in the *Quarterly Review of Biology*. Their paper set out a comprehensive definition of animal teaching:

> An individual actor A [the tutor] can be said to teach if it *modifies* its behaviour only in the presence of a naïve observer, B [the pupil], at some cost or at least without obtaining an immediate benefit for itself. A's behaviour thereby *encourages or punishes* B's behaviour, or provides B with *experience*, or *sets an example* for B. As a result, B acquires knowledge, or learns a skill earlier in life or more rapidly or effectively than it might otherwise do so, or would not learn at all. (Caro and Hauser 1992, 153, emphasis added)

Of course, *The White Puma* (1990) was published two years before Caro and Hauser's paper. Lawrence would not have been aware of their research. Yet, his depiction of the tawny puma's teaching methods conforms to their definition. Indeed, there are many instances in which the puma modifies her behaviour in the presence of her kittens and adjusts in accordance with their development.

When the puma judges them to be old enough, she leads the kittens away from the den to "teach them to survive in the wilderness" (Lawrence 1990, 93). At first, she uses body language—"her tail rigid and her eyes fixing a stare"—to teach them how to remain hidden (95). If they try to follow her, she disciplines them by "[s]narling loudly," then raising a "front paw, toes spread," and finally "charg[ing]" at them until they remain still (95–6). However, as they grow older and begin to demonstrate the "alert and eager sensibilities of true hunters," the tawny puma changes her behaviour and, instead, teaches them how to hunt:

> Despite her intense preoccupation with the task that lay ahead, she became aware of the change [...] As soon as she had oriented herself, she moved forward without ordering the kittens to stay behind. She was tacitly allowing them to be her partners in the hunt. [...] [T]he manner in which their mother was moving, and the fact that she was clearly allowing them to participate in the hunt further affected the behaviour of the kittens. (132)

Even though Lawrence's writing demonstrates the core elements of Caro and Hauser's definition, this is not to suggest any contact between them. It does, however, reveal the shift in late twentieth-century attitudes towards animal minds that enabled these parallel descriptions of teaching to arise.

Almost a century before, John Burroughs had ridiculed Seton's depictions of animal teaching. In his article, "Sham Natural History" (1903), he had targeted Seton's story "Silverspot" in particular: "crows do not train their young;" nor do they have "schools, or colleges, or examining boards, or diplomas" (304). Burroughs's absurd examples indicate the degree of anthropomorphism he saw in Seton's story. This is because he believed that animals were governed by instinct alone:

> Nature has instilled into them all the fear of their enemies and equipped them with different means in different degrees to escape them [...] The young of all the wild creatures do instinctively what their parents do and did. They do not have to be taught; they are taught by nature from the start. (304)

If we recall, there were no clear descriptions of animals teaching in the mid-century texts, *Return to the River* (1941), *Consider Her Ways* (1947), and *Last of the Curlews* (1955). Haig-Brown (1941) explored salmon learning through individual experience and observation of others, but not through active teaching. Frederick Philip Grove (1947) asserted that ants learn through instruction, just like humans, but gave no descriptions of the act. Meanwhile, Fred Bodsworth's (1955) curlew was almost entirely controlled by instinct.

Alongside his explorations of teaching, Lawrence (1990) also speculates about the survival advantages of complex communication. He focuses on the sensory experiences of pumas to consider the differences between communicating through body language, vocalization, and scent. As we have seen in the descriptions of teaching, the tawny puma and her kittens constantly observe and interpret each other's body movements. Likewise, she also uses particular vocalizations with her young, such as "the special purr that summoned her children" or the soft growl of the "alarm signal" (94, 98). Physical proximity between the family members means that they prioritize body language and vocalizations. Apart from the basic olfactory information that aids kin identification and bonding, they do not require the use of scent to communicate with each other.

Outside of the family, the longevity of scent enables a constant stream of information to be shared between individuals. This might involve simply cataloguing the odours left by an animal's presence, but it can also involve intentional communication. Lawrence (1990) even indicates the possibility of a basic scent 'language' shared between members of a species. He describes the various "markers" that pumas might leave for each other (147). These include "urine sprays on rocks and trees," as well as "fecal [sic] mounds" made by "raking earth and debris over their droppings" (147). Indeed, he remarks that "a dozen or more" of these "mounds" are "always present" at the "junction of puma trails" (147). I would suggest that we see intentionality in the creation and location of these urine sprays and faecal mounds.

If the tawny puma wishes to protect her food, she urinates nearby to "mark her ownership of the carcass" (96). Likewise, when "announcing her claim" to a new territory, she spends time leaving urine sprays on plants (43). At the same time, she also inspects the "messages left by her competitors" (44). In the search for a mate, the tawny puma discovers the location of a male puma through his "trails" (24). Although she detects traces of the grizzly bears, wolves, and wolverines who also use his routes, their scents carry no further significance. Instead, she follows the male's faecal mounds: the "oldest" lying "almost flat" and the "newest standing out like molehills" (24). Upon meeting each other, both pumas are cautious. To share information without close contact, the male puma sprays "urine" in the grass and backs away from it (25). This allows the tawny puma to move forward and sniff at it "intently" while keeping a safe distance (25). Evidently, these are not random deposits. Each spray or mound carries meaning, intentionality, and the desire to communicate.

Lawrence's nonhuman landscapes are densely layered with messages left by a variety of species in their own 'languages.' This is similar to Timothy Findley's depiction of complex animal networks in *Not Wanted on the Voyage* (1984). In his novel, the heavily populated forest was imbued with nonhuman meaning. Although all of Findley's nonhuman beings seemed to share a single language, they did differ in myths and cultural practices. However, these differences were based on location (such as the farm or the forest) rather than species. In Lawrence's (1990) more realistic narrative, the pumas cannot interpret the 'languages' of other species. Thus, he resists the common literary trope of all nonhuman beings communicating through one universal 'animal language.'

Whilst the pumas cannot decode the messages of other species, they can gain some limited information. For instance, the abrupt silence of otherwise noisy birds is a "signal" of danger to "all animals in the area" (Lawrence 1990, 128). The puma waits for the birds to "resume their calls" and is not "convinced" of her safety until they do (128). Of course, the birds may have little intention of communicating with the pumas. Yet this ability to observe and learn from the signals of other species is also vital for the pumas' success as predators. When the pumas see a moose with a "thin body and stiffened legs," they note the "awkward way" in which he moves and his "laboured respiration" (162). Through knowledge and experience, the tawny puma "reads" these "signals" and identifies the moose as "old" and in "poor condition" (162).

Lawrence suggests that a predator's ability to read the body language of other animals enables them to target directly the ill or injured members of the herd. Indeed, he remarks that when "given the choice of several prey animals at a time," the pumas "invariably chose the one whose behaviour and condition demonstrated physical weakness or emotional distress" (135). The moose is "twenty years old," "arthritic," and bothered by parasites (164). Although his death by the "fangs and claws of three pumas" is "violent and gory," it does release him "quickly" (164). Certainly, it seems preferable to the grim alternative that Lawrence describes, which could have taken "seven or eight days" (164). We can see that a predator's ability to choose their prey carefully could be (somewhat) beneficial to both animals involved.

This more nuanced depiction of predator-prey relationships is one of the significant differences between *The White Puma* (1990) and the original wild animal stories. Unlike Lawrence, Seton and Roberts emphasized the serendipity of predator-prey encounters. Their use of random chance for dramatic purposes meant that their predators rarely made *choices*. Instead, Lawrence's more ecological perspective indicates the potential benefits of predators to both individuals and groups. Almost every animal killed by his pumas is old, diseased, or injured. He also connects the relationship between prey, predator, and scavenger by describing all the animals able to feed from one deer killed by the tawny puma: "seven ravens," "a red fox," "two coyotes," "[t]wo weasles," "a striped skunk," and even "mice, shrews, and insects" (Lawrence 1990, 58). These sections are crucial for challenging traditional perceptions of predators as 'vermin.'

Of course, this ecological perspective would not have been fully available to Seton or Roberts. Although they would have been aware of these systems to some degree, the formal science of ecology did not emerge until the 1920s and 1930s. It was only in 1927 that Charles Elton published the first book in the field, *Animal Ecology*. However, Tina Loo (2006) points out that it took until the 1960s for the public to begin expressing the "'values for varmints' that had been articulated by ecologists a generation earlier" (152). Ecology had argued for decades that "predators should be left in peace," yet it was human sentiment that ultimately determined their fate (158). Thanks to wildlife writers and filmmakers, such as Andy Russell or Bill Mason, urban Canadians became increasingly concerned with the protection of predators towards the end of the century. By the time that Lawrence was writing *The White Puma* (1990), the predator bounty system was being phased out.

As we have seen, bounty-hunters were frequent characters in Seton's wild animal stories, as well as Russell's (1977). However, Lawrence's (1990) hunters do not operate under this system. Unlike their predecessors, Taggart and Cousins cannot kill predators indiscriminately. Taggart explains that, although they can only kill pumas during the hunting season, they are "not actually protected by law" (14). After all, they are still "pests," so "nobody really gives a darn if one of them gets to eat a nice lead pill" (14). As Loo (2006) observes, predators continued to be "feared and despised by many rural Canadians," despite the arguments of scientists or animal advocates (172). Much of the human narrative of *The White Puma* (1990) focuses on this tension between different attitudes towards pumas.

Throughout the book, Taggart and Cousins must find ways to legitimize their hunting. Both men work as guides for High Country Safaris, which caters to "rich" tourists "from a number of countries" who pay "high prices for the privilege of killing animals" (Lawrence 1990, 12). However, due to the short hunting season—"just a few weeks in autumn"—they supplement their income through illegal means (12). Over glasses of whisky, they make deals with clients to procure animal skins and heads to be turned into rugs or mounted on plaques. A New York stockbroker agrees to pay them "three hundred dollars" for a puma head and hide, "provided that the skin was not badly mutilated by bullets" (14). Smuggling these "trophies" out of Canada is "not difficult" because none of the "illegally killed animals" are listed as "endangered or threatened" (13). As such, their "importation" into other countries "not restricted" (13).

Given their economic reliance on hunting, Taggart and Cousins repeatedly find excuses to kill pumas outside of the official season. For instance, they follow puma tracks and find the remains of a moose. They report the kill to their boss and give "their opinion that unless the adult puma was not killed, she would continue taking the ungulate prey, which [...] rightfully belonged to the High Country Safaris clients" (123). Elsewhere, they fabricate a story about an encounter with the tawny puma:

> The next morning, an exaggerated report of the affair appeared in the leading daily newspaper under the headlines SAVAGE LION ATTACKS MAN. The story was quickly picked up by the wire services and flashed across the continent. The attendant notoriety turned Walter Taggart into something of a heroic figure, with Steve Cousins lauded as the 'daring rescuer.' (37)

Of course, speciesist stereotypes enable the story to escalate quickly. Their boss, Andrew Bell, uses the publicity to obtain "official permission to expand his licensed hunting area" (85). He also calls the "Victoria headquarters of the fish and game department" to ask that they "declare open season on all cougars in the region" (250, 242). He brags to Taggart and Cousins, "I've some influence there, you know" (242).

Through this secondary human narrative, Lawrence (1990) explores the complex interplay of motivations that surround animal protection efforts:

> Politically, the outfitters [like Bell] had a lot of clout [...] for they employed local people as guides and in other capacities and were thought to contrib-

ute to the economic well-being of isolated Northern regions. Besides, the hunters, especially those coming from Europe and the United States, spent a great deal of money in the province. (242)

As we have seen throughout this book, conservation was often shaped by economic concerns. This resonates with Loo's (2006) statement that rural Canadians "constituted a powerful lobby influencing wildlife management" (172). They shaped "predator policy both before and after the end of the bounty system" (172). Indeed, thanks to rural lobbyists, the predator bounty system was reinstated in Alberta in 2007 and Saskatchewan in 2009 (Proulx and Rodtka 2015, 1035).

Writing at the end of the twentieth century, Lawrence (1990) is one of the few authors addressed in this book to offer depictions of animal advocacy itself. Towards the end of the novel, he introduces Lansing and Carew as they begin "their own campaign, condemning the open season and, especially, calling for the full protection of the white puma" (243). As part of their efforts, they search for proof that the white puma exists. Eventually, however, *he* finds *them*. In contrast to Taggart and Cousins, Lansing's "body odor telegraphed neutrality" to the puma (271). Perhaps due to his specific experiences with the hunters, he perceives her as a curiosity rather than an enemy. He tracks her from a distance over several days and observes that she does not seem to be a threat.

Eventually, there is an encounter between Lansing, Taggart, Cousins, and the puma. Although the white puma escapes, Cousins shoots Lansing by mistake. After Taggart leaves, the puma returns to investigate:

> The cat was so fast, Lansing was barely aware of its leap. [...] Instinctively, she screamed at the puma. "*No! Don't do it!*" Perhaps it was the unexpected sound of the woman's now shrill voice that caused the puma to land short of his target, instead of striking Cousins in midleap. Perhaps the highly intelligent animal understood the meaning of Lansing's cry. Whatever the reasons for his subsequent actions, the cat remained crouched for a split second after he had landed, his fierce gaze fixed on the man's eyes. (Lawrence 1990, 294–5)

Here, Lawrence allows the puma's motivations to remain unknown, thereby avoiding any reassuring anthropocentric fantasies. Nonetheless, Cousins's interpretation of the events leads him to believe in the puma's consciousness:

He could've killed me, but he didn't. [...] *I saw him turn away.* But I can't believe it. Never reckoned an animal could think. [...] Reckon I'm done hunting. I just don't reckon I can go and kill animals if they can *think*. It ain't right. (304)

Thus, it is the white puma who triggers the hunter's ethical transformation. Within a week, Cousins is sworn in as a deputy conservation officer for the area and persuades Taggart to stop hunting for anything but his own consumption.

Of course, this ending rather oversimplifies the relationship between rural peoples and predators. Yet, as *The White Puma* (1990) demonstrates, the near extinction of pumas in North America is a human problem that requires a human solution. Even if campaigners like Lansing and Carew can make progress in the short term, a true change requires the participation of those who benefit from the current system. As long as some of us remain reliant on animal exploitation, their protection can only go so far. Lawrence's depiction of the difficulties in ensuring an animal's long-term wellbeing gives some insight into the state of animal advocacy—and its opponents—at the turn of the century. Multiple waves of animal protection movements separate Seton's tragic stories from Lawrence's more optimistic novel. For all the setbacks, we can see evidence of progress in the policies and programmes described in the book. As a result, the white puma is one of the few animals to survive their own story.

Barbara Gowdy: *The White Bone* (1998)

It is tempting to read *The White Bone* (1998) by Barbara Gowdy (1950–) as an allegory or anthropomorphic fantasy. The narrative focuses on a herd of elephants who share a complex culture, which includes language, myths, medicine, songs, and a religion. Gowdy's (1998) elephants possess the qualities we associate with human uniqueness, such as consciousness and self-awareness. Some are even capable of prescience and telepathy. At first glance, these conventions would seem to signal that the story is not about elephants at all. Certainly, the parallels with human societies—such as religious creation myths—appear to encourage such comparisons. Yet, as with so many of the authors addressed in this book, Gowdy's writing was inspired by the activities of real animals. For Seton, it had been the survival strategies of wolves in the Currumpaw valley of New Mexico. For Gowdy, it was the mourning practices of African elephants in Kenya.

In an interview with John Bemrose (1998) for *Maclean's* magazine, Gowdy describes watching documentary footage of elephants finding the skeletal remains of their former matriarch. She recalls feeling "shivers going up and down" her back as she witnessed the elephants tenderly touching the bones with their trunks (56). At the same time, the documentary's narrator, Cynthia Moss (a renowned elephant researcher and conservationist), explained that elephants tend to "bury the bones of their own dead" or sometimes "turn and ceremoniously pass a hind leg over the remains, as if carrying out a religious rite" (56). For Gowdy, this was not just unusual behaviour; it was evidence of consciousness itself:

> It seemed to me that if you're conscious of death, then you're conscious of life. And whatever consciousness is—awareness, sadness, dreaminess or speculative thought—the elephants had it. (56)

Gowdy's reaction seems similar to Seton's during his experiences with the Currumpaw wolves. It is the sudden realization that these individuals' cognitive, emotional, or social complexities reach far beyond our current understanding. In these encounters, the animals' surprising behaviours defy our ideas about their limitations. Of course, Seton's observations could have been dismissed as inaccurate anecdotes. By the late twentieth century, however, video footage of unexpected activities became more difficult to ignore.[1]

As with so many of the authors addressed in this book, Gowdy identifies this gap in our knowledge as a productive site for speculation. I classify *The White Bone* alongside Grove's *Consider Her Ways* (1947) as a speculative *fantasy of knowing*. Although the novel shares some characteristics with Findley's (1984) *Not Wanted on the Voyage*—such as the use of supernatural abilities—Gowdy's (1998) elephants remain *elephants* throughout. In the Bemrose (1998) interview, Gowdy acknowledges that her attempt to "write about elephants from their own viewpoint" was "going to be imperfect" (57). Nonetheless, her commitment to creating a sustained, speculative exploration of elephant life is clear. After watching the documentary and trying to read "everything she could find" about elephants,

---

[1] Whilst Gowdy may have been surprised by the footage in the 1990s, the evidence for elephant grief has since become more widely accepted. In *How Animals Grieve* (2013) Barbara King writes: "Example after example of mourning by elephants who have lost one of their tightly bonded group has been reported by scientists. It's the closest thing we have, in the nascent world of animal-grief study, to scientific certainty" (52).

Gowdy realized that she "needed" to "observe" them "in the wild" (57). In 1996, she took a trip to Africa and visited "Kenya's Masai Mara Reserve," where she encountered "elephants, cheetahs and gazelles," as well as "tens of thousands" of migrating wildebeests (57).

Of course, Gowdy goes further in her exploration of animal consciousness than most authors of animal fiction. Where Russell (1977) had suggested that animals could be capable of thought or Lawrence (1990) had subtly gestured towards self-awareness, Gowdy (1998) takes these ideas as axiomatic. Elephant consciousness and self-awareness are the basic assumptions upon which she builds her narrative. This means that her speculation extends beyond straightforward questions about cognitive or emotional complexity. Instead, Gowdy sets out to imagine the structures of an entire elephant culture. Even though the more fantastical elements of the text might risk disrupting our ability to read the elephants *as elephants*, this is clearly not a human drama dressed up in animal costume. Compared with Grove's (1947) ants undertaking a scientific expedition, Gowdy's (1998) depiction of elephants struggling to survive ivory poaching and a drought seems more grounded in the experiences of real animals.

It is worth noting that *The White Bone* (1998) is the first speculative representation we have encountered since *Consider Her Ways* (1947). As we might expect, these two texts share significant similarities. Both authors employ specific strategies to ensure that their animals are read *as animals*. For instance, paratextual features (such as appendices or footnotes) help to strengthen the connection to their subject species, whilst also reinforcing the text's scientific foundations. In *Consider Her Ways*, Grove (1947) used an introduction written by a fictional editor to list his scientific sources and to outline the various debates around ant intelligence. Likewise, in the acknowledgements section of *The White Bone*, Gowdy (1998) lists the many books that "proved helpful" in her "research" (339). She also remarks on the difficulties faced by those "tirelessly fighting" for elephant safety due to the "pressures of the ivory trade" and the "disappearance of habitat" (340).

In addition, *The White Bone* also includes elephant family trees and a map. This is reminiscent of Seton's various sketches, diagrams, and maps printed in the margins of his books. Indeed, Gowdy seems to employ a blend of Grove's and Seton's approaches. Whereas Seton sought to strengthen his scientific credentials by making his books resemble a naturalist's journal (complete with marginalia), Grove's more playful approach used footnotes to merge genuine scientific information with the imagined details of his ant societies. Whether playful or serious, each author gives their fiction a pseudo-scientific feel. Gowdy (1998) even adopts the alliterative naming system used by some elephant researchers. Members of the She-S family, for example, include the matriarch, She-Swaggers, her daughter, She-Spoils, and her grand-daughter, She-Soothes. Likewise, the She-D family contains She-Deflates, She-Demands, and She-Distracts.

Together, these features of *The White Bone* seem to imply the presence of a human researcher. This figure, akin to Grove's F.P.G. character, creates a sense of 'translation.' In one footnote, this unseen narrator mentions that 'father' is "neither a concept nor a word" for Gowdy's elephants, "since bulls are not thought to be co-conceivers of life" (1998, 20). Indeed, alongside her other paratextual features, Gowdy includes an entire glossary of elephant vocabulary. This is comparable to Grove's (1947) use of ant-centric concepts, such as "scent-trees" or "common antlengths" (31, 37). However, Gowdy goes further by creating a more extensive set of terms and phrases.

In *The White Bone* a hindlegger is a human being, a jaw-log is a crocodile, and a howler is a jackal (Gowdy 1998, 335). Some words also give insights into the elephants' perspectives. A rhinoceros is known as ghastly because it has "short unsightly legs" and its "'tusks,' or horns, are arranged one on top of the other rather than side by side" (334). It is worth noting that, although *Consider Her Ways* (1947) and *The White Bone* (1998) use 'talking' animals, both authors create this sense of 'translation' in their work. This modified language, along with various paratextual elements, invite us to accept these animals *as animals* within the specific reality they construct.

Just as Gowdy's (1998) invented language seems grounded in her attempts to think like an elephant, so, too, is her imagined elephant culture. By utilizing what we know of the social lives of elephants, she explores how these structures might impact the formation of culture. In *The White Bone* related female elephants and their infants travel together in herds led by a matriarch. By contrast, the males are largely solitary, though they may form small bachelor herds for a short time. This means that male and female elephants assist in the production of their culture in different ways.

Wandering males gather stories, geographical information, and news from other herds. Meanwhile, the females construct and maintain a matriarchal culture. The elephants worship the "She," the "mother of elephants" (Gowdy 1998, 19). They refer to themselves as "She-ones," which is a term that applies to elephants of either sex and is "comparable to 'mankind'" (337). The sun is the "eye of the She," whilst the moon is her son, the Rogue, who is "untrustworthy, mischievous and often malevolent" (19). Gowdy's imagined elephant beliefs can be read as commentary on patriarchal religious structures in human societies. Yet, they are also the logical conclusion of a society in which females remain together while males are isolated.

Another facet of elephant culture that seems rather anthropomorphic is the system of superstitions known as 'links.' At first glance, the idea of superstitious elephants feels absurd. However, the speculation is rooted in animal cognition and gives insights into the formation of the elephants' culture. A male elephant from the She-B family called Tall Time spends his life gathering knowledge and attempting to learn every 'link.' This earns him the nickname the Link Bull. Other elephants consult Tall Time's knowledge frequently, providing him with "opportunities to confirm or discount the power of certain superstitions and thereby refine his inventory of determinants" (Gowdy 1998, 50). I suggest that these 'links' might be the link between cause and effect. The superstitions seem to be based on contextual learning, shared between individuals, and occurring with sufficient frequency to be reinforced and remembered.

In the elephants' belief system, it is considered particularly unlucky to come across a three-legged hyena, a one-eyed wildebeest, or a "crazy" warthog (254). It is not difficult to imagine the pragmatic reasons behind the superstitions; the hyena and wildebeest may have been injured by a nearby enemy and the warthog may be poisoned or diseased. If an elephant in the area later becomes ill or injured, and does not correctly attribute cause and effect, a 'superstition' may be created. Although the process is not made explicit, it is presumably in this way that the elephants draw the 'links' between cause and effect as they experience the world. Furthermore, just as a 'superstition' might become part of religion, an individual's serendipitous experiment or accident could become part of medical treatment. If an elephant asks an older female why "one treatment was chosen over another," the "answer was always a variation of 'That's what works'" (107). Rather than anthropomorphic fantasy, what Gowdy presents is a speculation about the production of pragmatic nonhuman knowledge.

To explore the process in detail, we witness the learning experiences of a young elephant encountering a car wing-mirror for the first time. Initially, Date Bed thinks that the place where she finds the mirror could be "sacred" because it "yielded the amazing Thing" (Gowdy 1998, 162). Her first encounter with the mirror (or Thing) is during a confrontation with four lionesses:

> Her right foot came down on a stone. She snatched it up. Even in her terror she could feel how unnaturally cold and smooth it was. She swung it, and a pale beam of light flew over the ground. The lionesses stepped back from the beam [...] And while Date Bed continued to trumpet and brandish the stone, her assailants disappeared. (164)

A mysterious object which frightens and deters lions is an obvious advantage to an elephant, particularly one alone, weak, and wounded in a drought-stricken landscape. We can see that, just as with Tall Time's links, the creation of such superstitions is pragmatic. From Date Bed's perspective, this potentially sacred area could yield more amazing Things. It could benefit her survival to remember it in future.

As soon as Date Bed determines that the lions are a safe distance away—when she can "no longer smell them"—she examines her "weapon" (164). As with Grove's (1947) ants, Date-Bed explores the object using her own unique frame of reference:

> It was no stone. It was too cold and too symmetrical: flat on one side, curved on the other, about the size of an ostrich egg but heavier than that and more elongated; it was like an elongated egg sliced in half. The curved side shone like slime. The flat side shone like water, and like water she could see herself in it... if she held it at a certain angle, with the moonlight in her eye, and when she did that her image was so unclouded that she gasped. She pivoted the Thing and waved it where the lionesses had been. The beam appeared. (Gowdy 1998, 164)

From their zoocentric perspective, the elephants believe that vehicles are animals who carry humans in their bodies. When Date Bed recognizes "the unnatural blue of a vehicle's skin," she realizes that the Thing must have been part of the vehicle's body: "a kind of gall perhaps or extrusion of bone—and she had a moment of disgust" (165). Even though Date Bed's error is comical, it reinforces Gowdy's nonhuman perspective, whilst also providing potential insights into elephant learning.

Through this speculative *fantasy of knowing*, Gowdy (1998) attempts to embody her characters in ways that would be difficult to achieve through more realistic representation. As we have seen in other 'talking' animal texts, such as Grove's (1947) *Consider Her Ways* or Findley's (1984) *Not Wanted on the Voyage*, the authors present a defamiliarizing version of humanity as seen through nonhuman eyes. This can be used to strengthen the impression of an animal's 'alien' perspective (such as Date

Bed's perception of the wing-mirror). However, it can also offer particularly powerful ways to challenge anthropocentrism and speciesism. Such texts empower animal victims to observe, judge, and respond to humanity directly. So far, the most visceral opposition to animal exploitation that we have seen have come from the 'talking' animals in *Consider Her Ways* (1947) and *Not Wanted on the Voyage* (1984). By contrast, more realistic texts can only go so far in their exploration of the animal's perception of human violence.

Gowdy's (1998) embodiment of the elephant perspective is most vivid when she depicts a massacre of two elephant families. The herd is relaxing beside a watering hole when they catch the scent of a vehicle. They become alert but do not move away, given the rarity of water during a drought. Abruptly, a vehicle "bellows" over a bank in a "swell of dust" (86). To the elephants, it seems that the vehicle had "scented them" from afar (86). Even before the vehicle stops, "humans leap out" and the elephants hear the "rattle of gunshot" (86). With "hyena-like yells the humans gallop into the swamp, knees capering above the water, guns firing" (86). In their shock, the elephants' usual "V-formation" crumbles: "She-Scares gives a dreadful roar. She-Screams and the calves start screaming" (86). "She-Scares" is hit with a bullet and "falls onto She-Demands" and "She-Scavenges" sinks into the swamp (86).

Similar to the strange laughter of the Wheeler in *Consider Her Ways* (1947), Gowdy (1998) creates a disturbing contrast between the violence of the scene and the apparent enjoyment of the humans. The men joke and play as they kill and abuse the young elephants:

> The human that shot She-Stammers flings a rope after Blue's head [...] He yanks on the rope, and Blue trashes and squalls. Her twin sister, Flow Sticks, rushes back to her. The human jumps astride Blue and kicks her so brutally that her forelegs buckle. He goes on kicking until she bolts. Her brief, bird-like screams alternate with her sister's quivering screams, and the human rider her kicks and whoops and holds one hand high. The other human howls. (87)

From the elephant's perspective, humans are predators whose behaviour is unprecedented amongst animals. Within their experiences, the humans seem inexplicable, unpredictable, and unknowable. Indeed, Tall Time confesses to another bull, Torrent, that he had lost faith in elephant knowledge after this unprecedented destruction. He asks, "what use are the links if they do not warn of such tragedies?" (157). To which Torrent responds:

"No link with which *you* are acquainted warned of such tragedies" (157, emphasis original).

With distressing dramatic irony, we know what the elephants do not. We understand why humans hunt elephants for their tusks, we know that a car is not an animal, we recognize that the man imitates cowboy when riding Blue, and we can identify his companion's 'howl' as laughter. Yet, through the defamiliarizing effect of the elephant perspective, their actions become inexplicable to us as well. There is no answer, no excuse good enough for the deaths of so many unique individuals with whom the readers have become closely acquainted. Similar to the shock of the ants witnessing human violence in *Consider Her Ways* (1947) or the curlew's confused loneliness in *Last of the Curlews* (1955), Gowdy presents an uncomfortable situation in which we are the informed witnesses. We hold the knowledge that the other animals do not. We may sympathize with the animals yet remain uncomfortably complicit with the humans.

Amongst the constant dangers of poachers and a seemingly endless drought, Gowdy's (1998) elephants find hope in the myth of the 'white bone.' According to a legend, carried by a wandering male, the mystical white bone will lead the elephants to safety. "The Safe Place" is a "paradise," in which there are no "droughts" and no "perils" (71). There, the humans are all "entranced" and just peacefully gaze at the elephants (74). Once again, similar to Russell (1977), we find an oversimplified vision of nature reserves that reflects the expectations of tourists more than the complex histories of their creation.

The elephants who know most about the white bone seem to be the African forest elephants, known as the "Lost Ones, or the Forest Dwellers" (Gowdy 1998, 64). They are described as having "abnormally long narrow tusks," "small ears," and "sleek skin" (64). To the other elephants, they seem "beautiful" despite their "diminutive" size (64). For the most part, this seems an accurate description of an African forest elephant. Yet, not only do Gowdy's Lost Ones have "luminous green eyes," but their eyes also produce beams of "light" (64, 216). Moreover, all of them are prescient "visionaries" (65).

To some extent, we can argue that the descriptions of the Lost Ones could be based on rumours shared amongst various elephant populations. For instance, in *Not Wanted on the Voyage* (1984) animals living in distant areas (such as the farm or the forest) believe different myths and legends. Strangely enough, though, the stories about the Lost Ones prove to be true when Tall Time finds them living in a cave. Inside, the Lost Ones illuminate the cave walls with their glowing eyes and Tall Time realizes that elephant art has been scratched into the rock. The drawings are rough and barely visible, presumably having been etched using tusks, yet they cause Tall Time to experience visions: "Two Lost One cow and a calf lie on their sides. The cows have cavities where their faces should be. Nobody has tusks, feet or tails" (Gowdy 1998, 220). Looking at another piece of art, Tall Time learns the location of the white bone that could lead the elephants to the Safe Place.

These instances of magic and fantasy seem jarring against the real threats the elephants face from ivory poachers, climate change, and habitat loss. Tall Time's vision of the slaughtered cow and calf is grounded in the terrible violence experienced by actual elephants. Yet, the context is absurd. Whilst so much of Gowdy's speculative *fantasy of knowing* focuses on the realities experienced by living elephants, her depiction of the super-natural feels strangely out of place. Indeed, Onno Oerlemans (2007) com-ments that these aspects of the novel "strain credulity to such a degree" that it "undermines" Gowdy's otherwise "seemingly serious" engagement with "environmental ethics and animal consciousness" (190). Along simi-lar lines, Ryan Hediger (2013) asks: "do the fantastical elements of the book trivialize the elephants themselves?" (37).

I would suggest that, on the whole, Gowdy's use of the supernatural serves a practical purpose. For instance, her approach is different to Timothy Findley's (1984) blending of real and mythical animals in *Not Wanted on the Voyage*. Instead, it more closely resembles Grove's (1947) use of telepathic communication in *Consider Her Ways*. In both cases, these 'magical' abilities facilitate the sharing of complex informa-tion. By contrast, other plot devices may seem insufficient to explain how an ant could share her life story with a human or how elephants might find their way to a distant nature reserve. As we know from Margaret Stobie's (1978) descriptions of Grove's multiple manuscripts, he adopted the tele-pathic approach towards the end of his writing process. Initially, the ants had used ink to write in an entomologist's notebook. In the end, after multiple rewrites, Grove opted for the simplest solution, even if it was the least plausible. We might wonder whether Gowdy went through a similar process.

The use of magic in speculative *fantasy of knowing* texts seems to reveal the limits of animal representation. In more realistic texts, authors tend to restrict themselves to straightforward stories of survival or migration. Indeed, almost all of them rely on a biographical narrative structure. As we have seen, the interactions between other animals in those texts are limited to basic communication through scent, sound, or body language. These animals engage with each other as rivals, companions, mates, or family members. Any sharing of information is generally restricted to parental teaching or observational learning. By contrast, the social networks and communication methods explored in 'talking' animal narratives are considerably more varied. Speculative *fantasy of knowing* texts, such as *Consider Her Ways* (1947) and *The White Bone* (1998), construct intricate plots that would be difficult to achieve through more realistic representation. For animal fiction, a complex plot seems to necessitate complex communication. In most cases, this may well require the use of unlikely abilities.

Despite Gowdy's use of the supernatural, *The White Bone* stirred no controversy. Whilst Oerlemans (2007) may have called it "the most extreme and sustained example of anthropomorphism I have encountered," other critics have defended Gowdy's approach (184). John Sandlos (2000) argues that to label the work as anthropomorphic is to "miss the point;" instead we are challenged to "accept the *idea* that 'real' biological animals may have cultural experiences similar in kind to those of human beings" (88). Likewise, Rebecca Raglon and Marian Scholtmeijer (2007) note that the purpose is not to claim that elephants have mystical visions, it is to "challenge human 'knowledge' by imagining other possibilities" (135).

Evidently, Gowdy goes further in her exploration of animal consciousness than most authors addressed in this book. Her imaginative work extends beyond straightforward speculations about mental or emotional capacities. She envisages elephants capable not only of abstract thought, language, culture, and religion, but also telepathy and prescience. Perhaps, as Raglon and Scholtmeijer (2007) suggest, this use of the supernatural is merely an acknowledgement that animals may possess specialized senses or abilities that we do not. Whatever the case, for biologist Hal Whitehead (2003), Gowdy's fictional elephants still "ring true" and may well "come closer to the natures of these animals" than the "coarse numerical abstractions" of scientific research (371).

Significantly, Whitehead (2003) does identify the science behind Gowdy's speculations. Even though she imagines "elaborate societies, cultures, and cognitive abilities," her "constructions" are "built upon" our current understanding of the "biology and social lives" of elephants (371). Indeed, he remarks that only a "reductionist" would class the novel with *Winnie-the-Pooh* (371). Instead, Whitehead recommends that scientists "note the large parts that are consistent with what we know" and use the speculations as "hypotheses to guide our work" (371). It might be possible that nonhuman cultures "encompass abstract concepts, perhaps even religion," but "we won't find out if we don't look" (371).

As we might expect, the aftermath of the cognitive revolution was crucial to both the writing and the reception of *The White Bone* (1998). The documentary footage of elephant mourning, Gowdy's reaction to it, her subsequent approach to elephant representation, and Whitehead's response to the novel were all shaped by the shifting discourse around animal consciousness at the end of the twentieth century. As a result, *The White Bone* emerged into an atmosphere that was already becoming more open to the idea of animals as thinking, feeling beings. Bemrose (1998) quotes the observations of Sara Bershtel (Gowdy's editor) that there were "waves of intense interest" at the time around the "discovery of consciousness in animals" (57). Admittedly, Bershtel may overstate the case slightly, considering that the scientific community was not entirely unified on the idea of animal consciousness. Nonetheless, we can certainly see a clear shift in attitudes towards animal minds, emotions, and thoughts at the turn of the twenty-first century.

From this example, the complex relationship between science and speculative animal fiction is clear. Gowdy's initial curiosity about elephant minds was sparked by the research of Cynthia Moss and others. She sought out further information by reading a variety of scientific texts. From there, she imagined what the furthest developments of elephant minds might look like. She envisaged the constructs produced by such minds, including language, myths, and a complex culture. In so doing, she opened up a space of possibility in which scientists, such as Whitehead, could make their own speculations and discover new avenues for research. Interestingly, Whitehead's (2003) recommendation for reciprocal communication between scientists and storytellers came a century after John Burroughs's (1903) article, "Sham Natural History," initiated the Nature Fakers controversy. Where Burroughs had helped to widen the divide between researchers and writers, Whitehead made a remarkable gesture by reaching across that gap a hundred years later.

Yann Martel: *Life of Pi* (2001)

Yann Martel's (1963–) *Life of Pi* (2001) stands out amongst the works addressed in this book. With an acutely animal-sceptical perspective, it seems to argue that all human-animal relations are inherently one-sided. As such, Martel (2001) presents an unusually thorough exploration of the *failure of knowing* the animal. Most of the narrative is preoccupied with a teenage boy's attempts to know a Bengal tiger. Yet, the novel seems to show little interest in the tiger himself. Overall, *Life of Pi* tends to present animals as *objects of utility*, rather than the *subjects of lives*. The novel seems to challenge anthropocentrism, yet fiercely reinforces the separation of humans and other animals. It advocates for the power of animals and gods to remedy anthropocentric solipsism but offers a strikingly mechanomorphic depiction of animals. In spite of the book's message of belief, any faith in the complexity of nonhuman experiences is quashed.

As we might expect, the concerns and anxieties expressed in *Life of Pi* are the same as those raised during the Nature Fakers controversy. The novel shares common ground with several *fantasy of knowing* texts addressed in this book, including the wild animal stories of Seton and Roberts. At the same time, however, Martel (2001) replicates the language used by Burroughs (1903) and Theodore Roosevelt (1907) to ridicule those same stories. He also employs some of the literary devices used by Grove (1947) and Bodsworth (1955) to guard against questions of accuracy. Consequently, *Life of Pi*'s relationship to the fear of anthropomorphism more closely resembles the work of these mid-twentieth century authors than any of Martel's contemporaries in this chapter.

Similar to other texts addressed in this book, *Life of Pi* presents itself as an autobiographical animal anecdote, albeit a fictionalized one. It is Piscine 'Pi' Molitor Patel's 'true' account of spending 227 days alone in a lifeboat with a Bengal tiger called Richard Parker (who was given the name due to a clerical error). Clearly, this echoes Seton's semi-autobiographical stories of encounters with wild animals. In a similar way to Grove (1947), however, Martel (2001) disrupts the novel's sense of realism and, thus, subverts any questions of accuracy. Both *Life of Pi* and *Consider Her Ways* include author's notes written by fictionalized versions of Martel and Grove. Both blend fact and fiction to describe the authors meeting the fictional characters whose 'true' stories they transcribe. Grove (1947) depicts the ant Wawa-quee telepathically transmitting her story to the book's fictional author. Part One of *Life of Pi* interweaves Pi's biography set in India in the 1970s with 'interviews' between Pi and Martel in Canada in the 1990s.

In both *Life of Pi* (2001) and *Consider Her Ways* (1947), this layering of narration creates a distance between the author and their animal representations. The descriptions of animals in *Life of Pi* are translated firstly through Pi's perspective, secondly through the passing years between the 1970s and 1990s, thirdly through his conversations with the fictional Martel, and finally through the author's translation of that conversation into the finished novel. Martel adds to this technique in the final chapters of the book.

Whilst Part Two is devoted to Pi's 'true story' of the sinking of the *Tsimtsum* and his experience of being stranded in the Pacific Ocean on a lifeboat with a small collection of zoo animals, Part Three is the transcript and final report of his interview with two officials investigating the shipwreck. The interview offers something akin to the accusations made during the Nature Fakers controversy in which the veracity of Pi's animal representation is called into question. The interviewers doubt his animal anecdotes to such a degree that he offers them a second, more anthropocentric, account of the events. The first story describes Pi's experiences onboard a lifeboat with a zebra, hyena, orangutan, rat, several cockroaches, flies, and a tiger. Each of these animals die until only Pi and the tiger remain. They survive in the Pacific Ocean for 227 days. However, there are some rather fantastical elements to this story, including an island of carnivorous plants inhabited by meerkats who sleep in trees to avoid the dangerous plants on the ground.

The second story excludes the fantastical island and replaces the animals on the lifeboat (apart from the rat, cockroaches, and flies) with human characters: the zebra becomes a sailor, the hyena the ship's cook, the orangutan Pi's mother, and Pi himself becomes Richard Parker. The interviewers are more satisfied with a human story of murder and cannibalism than of a sixteen-year-old boy and a tiger. Yet, all agree that the "story with animals is the better story;" to which Pi replies, "so it goes with God" (Martel 2001, 317). In the end, they choose the first story and their report concludes: "few castaways can claim to have survived so long at sea as Mr. Patel, and none in the company of an adult Bengal tiger" (317–9).

The message that "the story with the animals is the better story" and, hence, "so it goes with God," implies that animals and gods hold some remedy to anthropocentric solipsism (317). Yet, *Life of Pi* continually reinforces the gulf between humans and other animals. In the novel, Pi learns that "an animal is an animal, essentially and practically removed from us, twice: once with Father and once with Richard Parker" (31). On the lifeboat, Pi yearns to know and bond with Richard Parker. When they reach land, however, the tiger leaves abruptly, seemingly without giving Pi a second thought. We can read the entire book as Pi's gradual realization of his failure to know the animal. Indeed, *Life of Pi* articulates this idea more fully than any other book addressed in this volume. It ties the *failure of knowing* the animal into an idea of inescapable anthropocentrism: "We look at an animal and see a mirror" (31).

Throughout the novel, Martel (2001) reinforces the message that anthropomorphism is irresistible, yet also must be resisted. Pi's father teaches him that the most dangerous animal on earth is the "*Animalus anthropomorphicus*, the animal as seen through human eyes" (31). As a result, much of the narrative is dedicated to Pi's efforts to resist anthropomorphism. A similar preoccupation with resisting anthropomorphism can be seen in *Last of the Curlews*. In both cases, it seems to manifest in reductive descriptions of animal minds. Bodsworth (1955) often referred to the curlew's "instinct-dominated" mind or his "tiny, rudimentary brain" (9, 25). Likewise, Martel (2001) describes animals as thinking "dimly" or having "undeveloped mind[s]" (43, 85). In attempting to write compelling animal protagonists, both texts occupy the contradictory space of striving to convey an individual as the *subject of a life*, whilst simultaneously using reductive, mechanomorphic language to avoid accusations of anthropomorphism.

It is clear, however, that Pi's impulse is to see animals as complex, fellow beings. He grew up surrounded by other animals in the Pondicherry Zoo, which was run by his father. Pi describes himself as a "strict vegetarian" to whom all "sentient life is sacred" (Martel 2001, 197, 183). As a child, he "shuddered" when snapping open a banana because it "sounded" like "the breaking of an animal's neck" (197). But he also refers to his reluctance to kill a fish as "ridiculous" "sentimentalism" (183). Evidently, Pi's nature is to see another animal as the *subject of a life*. However, his father and his experiences on the lifeboat teach him to see animals as objects.

Despite being cast as the 'benign' zookeeper, who runs Pondicherry Zoo according to "the most modern, biologically sound principles," Pi's father undoubtedly treats animals as objects (12). He seems to see goats, in particular, as disposable. Mr. Patel teaches Pi the dangers of anthropomorphism by forcing him to watch a tiger kill a goat. Ostensibly, the goat is being used to demonstrate to Pi that predator animals are dangerous: "Better a goat than him, no?" (36). The real lesson is that animals are *objects of utility*. Mr. Patel had previously demonstrated this instrumentalized approach to animals when choosing companions for a lonely rhino. Interestingly, he recognized the rhino as a complex individual capable of loneliness yet saw the goats as interchangeable objects: "If it worked, it would save a valuable animal. If it didn't, it would only cost a few goats" (26). There is a clear difference here between the few, valuable animals and the abundant, disposable animals.

The distinction between valuable and disposable animals is something that Pi replicates in his relationship with Richard Parker. After the shipwreck, Pi sees himself and Richard Parker as the only valuable individuals remaining. Pi is "glad" and "grateful" for the tiger's companionship, even with the danger he seems to pose (164). The value Richard Parker held in the zoo (as a charismatic mammal) even carries over on to the boat:

> What a stunning creature [...] I counted myself lucky in a way. What if I had ended up with a creature that looked silly or ugly, a tapir or an ostrich or a flock of turkeys? That would have been a more trying companionship in some ways. (175)

After considerable time together, Pi finally declares: "I love you, Richard Parker. If I didn't have you now [...] I would die of hopelessness" (236). For the most part, the other animals Pi encounters become disposable objects. Initially, he uses the bodies of other animals to placate Richard Parker, preventing himself from being eaten. However, this soon slips into Pi killing other animals to tend for the one animal he sees as his only companion. When they are both close to starvation, Pi becomes distressed that he could "no longer take care of Richard Parker" and that he had "failed as a zookeeper" (242).

The first time Pi kills a fish for Richard Parker, he weeps "heartily" over the "poor little deceased soul" (183). As the first fish he encounters, he sees them as an individual *subject of a life*: "I never forget to include this fish in my prayers" (183). Yet, even in the next sentence, he begins to see the dead fish as an object: "After that it was easier. Now that it was dead, the flying fish looked like a fish I had seen in the markets of Pondicherry" (183). Indeed, after killing the flying fish, it becomes easier to kill other fishes too. With the next fish he catches, Pi feels an exultant "hunter's pride" and finds that killing is "no problem" (185). Indeed, he describes himself "gleefully bludgeoning" the fish to death (185). The apparent abundance of these fishes makes them just as disposable as Mr. Patel's goats. In fact, when there are plenty of fishes to be caught, Pi hunts "far beyond" his need (196). Clearly, he no longer kills out of necessity or survival; it has become entertainment: "Fishing was surely a better way of passing the time than yarn-spinning or playing I Spy" (186).

Eventually, Pi becomes so comfortable with seeing animals as objects that he exploits them with little justification. When he and Richard Parker encounter the island of carnivorous plants, Pi tests whether the plants on the forest floor are dangerous by dropping a meerkat from a tree. After he touches the ground himself and experiences the same "searing pain" the meerkat must have felt, he shrieks and seeks relief by soaking his feet in water and wiping them with leaves (Martel 2001, 281). When this does not work, he kills two meerkats and tries to "soothe the pain with their blood and innards" (281). Before escaping the island, he kills and skins countless meerkats for Richard Parker: "as many meerkats as would fit in the locker and on the floor of the lifeboat" (283). Without a doubt, Richard Parker holds more value to Pi than the abundant, disposable meerkats and fishes. Yet, this very tendency to see animals as objects inevitably harms his attempts to know and bond with Richard Parker.

In Part One, Martel (2001) uses the concept of zoomorphism to establish the potential for companionship between Pi and Richard Parker. He writes that there are "many examples of animals coming to surprising living arrangements" (84). These are all instances of "zoomorphism," the "animal equivalent of anthropomorphism," in which "an animal takes a human being, or another animal, to be one of its kind" (84). Interestingly, this would seem to imply that there is always some form of *failure of knowing* across species boundaries. Martel cites a range of examples, including relationships between 'prey' and 'predator' species. Of course, most of these occur in confined situations, such as zoos, in which the animal's social network is limited. The lifeboat is just such an enclosure.

Given that Richard Parker was taken into captivity at three months old, it seems plausible that a tiger so accustomed to humans might seek companionship when trapped alone with one. Indeed, we might consider Richard Parker's use of prusten as an indicator. Martel (2001) describes prusten as "the quietest of tiger calls, a puff through the nose to express friendliness and harmless intentions" (163–4). In a manner reminiscent of Seton (1898), Martel lists a range of tiger sounds and their meanings,

including: the "full-throated *aaonh*" roar, "usually made during the mating season;" the "*woof* when they are caught unawares;" or sometimes
even a "*meow*, with an inflection similar to that of domestic cats, but
louder and in a deeper range" (163). Growing up in the zoo, Pi hears a
variety of tiger vocalizations; but he admits to never having heard prusten
until Richard Parker makes the sound on the lifeboat.

At first Pi is astonished and doubts his own hearing. Then Richard
Parker does it again, "this time with a rolling of his head," looking "exactly
as if he were asking me a question" (164). This repetition seems to confirm to Pi that Richard Parker is using prusten intentionally. In theory, this
might suggest the tiger's expression of "friendliness and harmless intentions" (164). The sound gives Pi hope. Yet, he does not seem to embrace
the possibility of a 'zoomorphic' relationship. For instance, Pi makes no
attempt to recreate the prusten sound himself. Instead, Richard Parker's
attempts to communicate lead Pi to a different realization: "I had to tame
him" (164).

When reframed in this way, Pi immediately adopts the power dynamic
of the circus trainer and the tiger. Abruptly, he reimagines their environment as a "perfect circus ring, inescapably round, without a single corner
for him to hide in" (Martel 2001, 164). In turn, the lifeboat's shrill emergency "whistle" becomes "a good whip with which to keep him in line"
(164). Pi seems to experience a thrill at the idea of exerting power over
Richard Parker, just as he revels in his "hunter's pride" when "gleefully
bludgeoning" a large fish to death (185). Playing the role of a circus ringmaster, Pi shouts to Richard Parker:

> Ladies and gentlemen, boys and girls, hurry to your seats! […] Here
> it is, for your enjoyment and instruction, for your gratification and
> edification […] THE GREATEST SHOW ON EARTH! […] THE
> PI PATEL, INDO-CANADIAN, TRANS-PACIFIC, FLOATING
> CIRCUUUUUSSSSSSSSSSSSS!!! (165)

Pi's language takes a playful, humorous tone and it is clear he takes much
"pleasure" in this new role (165). He even names the imagined circus after
himself.

After shouting his ringmaster's speech, Pi blows on the loud safety
whistle, which Richard Parker seems to find distressing. While he cringes
and snarls at the sound, Pi rejoices: "Ha! Let him jump into the water if
he wanted to! Let him try!" (165). Eventually, Richard Parker backs away

and cowers under a tarpaulin. Pi considers this "first training session" a "resounding success" (166). Subsequently, he devises a "training program" (186). This involves blowing the whistle while rocking the boat to make Richard Parker feel seasick. As the imaginary training programme states:

> Treatment should be repeated until the association in the animal's mind between the sound of the whistle and the feeling of intense, incapacitating nausea is fixed and totally unambiguous. Thereafter, the whistle alone will deal with trespassing or any other untoward behaviour. (205)

Interestingly, Pi's approach to training seems to mimic behaviourist models of animal learning. In essence, his strategy relies on the fundamentals of conditioning: using punishment (or reward) and repetition to create a new connection between a novel stimulus and a desired response.

When they reach the carnivorous island, Pi and Richard Parker live independently for a while. Consequently, their time apart means that Richard Parker begins to reassert his agency and autonomy. This leads Pi to realize that he "had to step into the circus ring again" (273). Despite Pi's playful circus imagery, his initial 'training programme' on the lifeboat had served a practical purpose. If Pi needed to access something on the other side of the boat, he had a basic tool with which to move Richard Parker into a different area. This time, however, Pi opts for pointless tasks, which merely offer him amusement.

Now, Pi fully casts himself in the role of a circus performer: "I trained him to jump through a hoop I made with thin branches" (Martel 2001, 274). He creates a "simple routine of four jumps," each of which earns Richard Parker "part of a meerkat" (274). This routine includes a test of Pi's control, a "nerve-racking experience," in which he kneels and holds the hoop above his head so that Richard Parker can jump over him (274). The final part of the "act" involves the unnecessarily difficult task of Pi rolling the hoop and Richard Parker attempting to run through it, which he is "never very good at" (274). These activities serve no purpose other than to demonstrate Pi's dominance and control over Richard Parker.

It is worth noting Pi's complex and contradictory relationship with Richard Parker's autonomy. When Richard Parker does something unexpected—such as making the prusten sound—Pi seems to recognize the tiger's agency as a unique individual. As we have seen in many texts addressed in this book, when an animal acts in an unexpected way, it can challenge human expectations and prompt a temporary acceptance of the animal as the *subject of a life*. In essence, these moments appear to offer behavioural evidence of the individual's complexity. However, for Pi there seems to be an oscillation between a desire to connect with Richard Parker as a fellow *subject of a life* and the impulse to control him as an *object of utility*. As much as Pi seems to respect, perhaps even crave, these moments in which Richard Parker asserts his agency and autonomy, he also feels the contradictory need to limit and suppress such behaviour.

One crucial aspect of Pi's attempts to dominate Richard Parker is the belief that he knows and understands the tiger. For instance, the circus tricks rely on Pi's knowledge that Richard Parker will jump over him without attacking. When he behaves unexpectedly, though, it forces Pi to recognize his own *failure of knowing*. Thus, despite his intense desire to know and bond with Richard Parker, Pi is nonetheless compelled to prove to himself that even this intimidating tiger can, eventually, become an *object of utility*.

Whilst assertions of agency and autonomy might increase the tiger's charismatic appeal, they also threaten Pi's sense of supremacy. Consequently, his ultimate failure to know Richard Parker is due, in part, to his inherently anthropocentric approach to their relationship. When Pi realizes that their survival is not a "question of him or me, but of him *and* me," his answer is to dominate the tiger (Martel 2001, 164). Alone on the ocean, Pi's solution is to re-establish human supremacy. To some extent, we might argue that he must do this to ensure his own survival. Yet, the excessive 'circus' tricks would seem to suggest that Pi also rather enjoys controlling his companion.

Pi's failure to know the tiger becomes clear when they reach Mexico at the end of the book. After 227 days together, Richard Parker leaps over Pi and out of the boat. On weak legs, he makes his way up the beach towards a jungle. Without ever looking back at his human companion, Richard Parker heads into the trees and disappears:

> At the edge of the jungle, he stopped. I was certain he would turn my way. He would look at me. He would flatten his ears. He would growl. In some such way, he would conclude our relationship. He did nothing of the sort. He only looked fixedly into the jungle. Then Richard Parker, companion of my torment, awful, fierce thing that kept me alive, moved forward and disappeared forever from my life. (Martel 2001, 284–5)

This moment of realization is a common feature of *failure of knowing* texts. As we have seen, it happens in Engel's *Bear* (1976) when Lou attempts sexual intercourse with the bear. We also find similar examples in Robert Kroetsch's *The Studhorse Man* (1969) and Graeme Gibson's *Communion* (1971).

Although the moment is less dramatic than in other *failure of knowing* novels, Richard Parker's departure still produces considerable distress and confusion, nonetheless. Pi reflects that he "wept like a child" because Richard Parker had left him "so unceremoniously" (Martel 2001, 285). Pi longs for a sense of culmination, a moment of communication that a human could recognize as proof of their relationship: "I wish so much that I'd had one last look at him on the lifeboat, that I'd provoked him a little, so that I was on his mind" (285).

Of course, we only receive Pi's interpretation of the event. Does Richard Parker's departure mean that he felt no companionship at all? Did he give signals that Pi could not recognize? Perhaps he expected Pi to follow him into the jungle? On the other hand, it could be that Richard Parker left "unceremoniously" because he had endured months of Pi's "psychological bullying" (285, 211). We might ask: what does Richard Parker owe to the man who 'tamed' him? Evidently, Pi feels that he is owed something: "That bungled goodbye hurts me to this day" (285). Ultimately, Richard Parker's own perspective remains unknown to us. It is clear, however, that Pi still misunderstands him. This ending is particularly reminiscent of *Bear* (1976). In both cases, the animal's motivations are left unknown to both characters and readers. What is unmistakable, though, is the human's *failure of knowing*.

Regardless of Pi's own anthropocentrism, I would suggest that there is never any chance of knowing Richard Parker. As readers, we also fail to know him. We receive no explanations for his actions, no insight into his perceptions. His perspective remains as inaccessible to us as it is to Pi. Indeed, *Life of Pi* demonstrates little interest in the minds of the animals depicted. Just as Mr. Patel teaches Pi, Martel (2001) teaches his readers a crucial lesson: "an animal is an animal, essentially and practically removed from us" (31). In essence, this approach to human-animal relations is shaped by the fundamental belief that the minds of other animals are always unknowable to humans.

Here, it is important to recall the relationship between behaviourism and the knowability of animal minds. In the early twentieth century, behaviourism helped to introduce the idea that animal minds were fundamentally unknowable. Its founder, John Watson (1925), had argued that the "real field of psychology" must be "what we can *observe*" (6). As a result, behaviourists restricted themselves to the observation of external behaviour. They did not attempt to interpret the content of an animal's mind, nor did they take it for granted that animals had 'minds' to begin with. One consequence of this approach was the use of increasingly abstract, mechanistic terms to describe the activities of animals, such as 'stimulus' and 'response.'

As we have seen, Pi's approach to animal learning relies on behaviourist models. In one section, he describes it in detail:

> The major difficulty in training animals is that they operate either by instinct or by rote. The shortcut of intelligence to make new associations that are not instinctive is minimally available. Therefore, imprinting in an animal's mind the artificial connection that if it does a certain action, say, roll over, it will get a treat can be achieved only by mind-numbing repetition. (Martel 2001, 273)

Martel's references to both instinct and rote-learning suggest dual influences of behaviourism and classical ethology. Both fields originated at the beginning of the twentieth century and were known to employ mechano-morphic language to describe nonhuman animals.

It is interesting that, whilst Martel (2001) does cite real scientific sources, he only uses early-to-mid-century research: "Beebe (1926) [...] Bullock (1968) [...] Tirler (1966)" and "Hediger (1950)" (4, 44). Of course, most of the narrative is set in the 1970s. Yet, the retrospective narration does leave room for acknowledgement of more recent scientific works, particularly in the 'interview' sections between Pi and Martel set in the 1990s. Interestingly, however, the text does not engage with contemporary scientific debates. This is something we also found in *Bear*, in which Engel (1976) referenced only nineteenth-century scientific sources.

Of course, the point here is not that Martel and Engel are out-of-date. It is to illuminate the relationship between behaviourism and animal-scepticism. Decades after the decline of behaviourist ideas in the sciences, the question of animal minds seemed to find re-expression in the arts and humanities. Articles, such as Thomas Nagel's "What Is It Like to Be a Bat?" (1974), reintroduced the same topics that had stirred the sciences at the beginning of the century. Nagel concludes that animals are inherently unknowable to humans, just as Margaret Floy Washburn had done in *The*

Animal Mind in 1908. Meanwhile, in the sciences, Donald Griffin's *The Question of Animal Awareness* (1976) was arguing in favour of the scientific study of animal minds and consciousness—precisely the opposite of earlier behaviourists.

It is worth noting that a sense of nostalgia runs throughout *Life of Pi*. On a basic level, most of the narrative takes place in the past. However, there is also a self-aware preference for tradition. When describing the benefits of zoos, Pi remarks: "I know zoos are no longer in people's good graces. Religion faces the same problem" (Martel 2001, 19). Along similar lines, he claims: "Well-meaning but misinformed people think that animals in the wild are 'happy' because they are 'free'" (15). This tone is particularly reminiscent of Burroughs's (1903) and Roosevelt's (1907) articles during the Nature Fakers controversy. Once more, we find an association between concern for animals, sentimentality, and naivety.

Despite the century separating their lives, Martel (2001), Burroughs (1903), and Roosevelt (1907) all express some resistance to animal advocacy. Whilst they may favour mainstream efforts, such as wildlife conservation, each also challenges those they see as going 'too far.' As we know, Burroughs and Roosevelt were central figures in the Nature Fakers controversy. Interestingly, Martel has also criticized a fellow contemporary writer for 'humanizing' animals. His words were considerably less harsh than those of Burroughs or Roosevelt (and certainly caused no controversy), but they express similar concerns.

In an interview with Christian Kriticos (2016) for *The Millions*, Martel remarks on the animal advocacy of South African author, J.M. Coetzee:

> I've never met him, but he's a weird man, J.M. Coetzee. He is preoccupied with the way we treat animals. But my preoccupations are somewhat more conventionally human than his. [...] I think Coetzee's gotten to the stage now where, you know—man and animal, eh it's all the same! [...] Which I don't share—push comes to shove, I'll chose [sic] a human over any animal. (np)

Admittedly, the parallels with Burroughs's and Roosevelt's articles are limited. Martel does not take direct aim at Coetzee's writing, nor the accuracy of his animal representations. However, we can see Martel's concerns about the 'humanization' of animals. This issue shapes almost every aspect of *Life of Pi* (2001), a narrative that is uniquely preoccupied with the human-animal divide. As we discovered in the previous chapter, these same fears were pervasive throughout the debates around amendments to anti-cruelty laws during the 1990s and 2000s (discussed in Chap. 8).

In essence, the plot of *Life of Pi* provides the space for Martel (2001) to explore hypothetical survival scenarios in which animal rights arguments fail. Pi might describe himself as a "strict vegetarian" to whom all "sentient life is sacred," but when facing threats to his own survival, he discovers: "a person can get used to anything, even to killing" (197, 183–5). In a short time, he goes from "weeping over the muffled killing of a flying fish to gleefully bludgeoning to death a dorado" (185). Initially, Pi hopes he might be able to leave Richard Parker alone in a separate section of the lifeboat, but later he chastises himself for under-estimating the danger: "You fool and idiot! You dimwit! You brainless baboon. [...] You will *die!* IS THAT CLEAR?" (161). Even if Pi might "love" Richard Parker, he knows he must "tame him" through "psychological bullying" to survive (236, 164, 211).

In Martel's (2001) stance, we can see some evidence of the turn of the century backlash against animal rights. In articles and interviews, he expresses concern for animals, particularly in terms of welfare and conservation (Martel 2002; Kriticos 2016). Yet, we can see some resistance to more progressive ideas. Unlike most of the authors addressed in this book, Martel is not an animal advocate. He did not write *Life of Pi* to convey a specific message on behalf of tigers; nor, indeed, does he write on behalf of any nonhuman animal. In an interview for *The Telegraph* in India, Shrestha Saha (2019) asked Martel why he wrote about animals and his response was simple: "Just because they are a good symbolic vehicle" (np).

Interestingly, *Life of Pi* (2001) does explore topics that are relevant to animal advocates, such as equality, communication, companionship, and the human-animal divide. In the survival scenario aboard the lifeboat, however, Martel exposes these ideas to the light and finds them wanting. Just as the turn of the twenty-first century animal legislation debates claimed that animal rights were incompatible with Canadian society, Martel demonstrates that Pi cannot coexist with Richard Parker as equals. When push comes to shove, the human chooses a human over any animal—even the one he loves.

The novel declares that the story with the animals is the better story and, by extension, that our world is better with animals in it. Yet Martel (2001) also presents a strikingly pessimistic view of animal-human relations. This is not despair at the horrors of exploitation or animal cruelty. Instead, it the inherent impossibility of knowing animals because we can only ever see them as mirrors of ourselves. By following this line of thinking, all animals become symbolic to us. At the same time, the book also depicts a painfully intense desire to *know* a specific individual animal.

Life of Pi (2001) presents the *failure of knowing* more fully than most novels. It celebrates animals and religion as offering us a better story—and a better world—as a remedy to the emptiness of anthropocentrism. Simultaneously, however, the human-animal relationships in the book are strikingly anthropocentric and often utilitarian. The book's animal representations seem torn between presenting animals as unique *subjects of lives* and disposable *objects of utility*. This raises the question of *why* the story with animals is the better story. Is it because they are our fellow inhabitants of the earth? Or is it because they are useful to us?

MARGARET ATWOOD: *ORYX AND CRAKE* (2003)

Margaret Atwood (1939–) describes *Oryx and Crake* (2003) as speculative fiction. This is different from my own use of the phrase speculative representation to describe *fantasy of knowing* texts, such as *Consider Her Ways* (1947) or *The White Bone* (1998). Instead, Atwood uses the word to distinguish her work from traditional science-fiction. Atwood (2004) argues that where "science fiction proper" describes things "we can't yet do or begin to do," such as talk to aliens, "speculative fiction" takes place on earth and employs technologies "already more or less to hand" (513). In *Oryx and Crake* Atwood (2003) depicts a future that feels nearby. As a result, the issues she explores—such as extreme genetic engineering and rapid mass extinctions—feel correspondingly imminent.

As the final text addressed in this book, *Oryx and Crake* enables us to reflect back on the topics we have encountered so far. It is a piece of speculative fiction that extrapolates from the state of human-animal relations at the turn of the twenty-first century. Atwood (2003) addresses familiar concerns—species loss, climate change, factory farming, and genetic engineering—and takes them to an extreme. In her speculative future, the familiar divide between humans and other animals begins to break down. Rampant genetic engineering means that distinctions between species become less relevant. As a result, Atwood destabilizes the concerns that preoccupied most of the texts we have addressed in this book. Questions of accurate animal representation, for instance, become muddled when DNA from humans, other mammals, fishes, and molluscs can coexist in the same genetically modified individual.

Oryx and Crake offers a particularly strong example of the *acceptance of not knowing* the animal. As we saw in *Not Wanted on the Voyage*, Findley (1984) presented a fantasy world inhabited by humans, angels, demons, mythological creatures, animals, and human-animal hybrids. This diversity of beings disrupted conventional categories of human and animal or even natural and supernatural. In this fantastical setting, Findley illuminated the contradictions of speciesism and the hypocrisies of human supremacy. In *Oryx and Crake*, Atwood (2003) explores these issues through genetic engineering. The advanced techniques used in her speculative future disrupts species boundaries, the human-animal divide, and even the definition of 'nature' itself. In this not-so-distant future, even the distinction between the artificial and the natural is unclear. Species created through the natural processes of evolution are more-or-less extinct. Now, genetically engineered 'bioforms' shall inherit the earth.

Oryx and Crake (2003) is set between two timeframes that are both narrated by the same human character. In the post-apocalyptic 'present,' humanity is near extinction after the release of a genetically engineered virus that causes a global pandemic. Apparently, the sole human survivor of this disaster is Jimmy who now calls himself 'Snowman.' As he struggles to find food and shelter amongst the ruins, Jimmy/Snowman recalls the events leading up to the release of the virus. In particular, he reflects on his adolescent friendship with Glenn, who later renames himself 'Crake.' As an adult, Glenn/Crake becomes a talented geneticist. Amongst other innovations, he designs a new species of humanoid to replace *Homo sapiens*, known as the Children of Crake (or Crakers). Through Jimmy/Snowman's reflections, Atwood reveals that it was Glenn/Crake who intentionally designed and released the virus that destroyed humanity. To help establish the Craker community, however, he secretly vaccinated Jimmy/Snowman against the virus so that he could become the last surviving human.

In both the 'past' and the 'present' of *Oryx and Crake*, Atwood (2003) mirrors and exaggerates the concerns of the early twenty-first century. Before the apocalypse, the world was controlled by mega-corporations. The elite lived and worked in corporate-run Compounds, which held everything from schools and hospitals to malls and golf courses. These gated communities were protected by high walls, flood lights, and CorpSECorps private security. Their faux-historical houses were filled with reproduction furniture. Their parks and gardens were constructed from artificial rocks and genetically engineered plants. They ate synthetic food and altered their minds and bodies through unregulated pharmaceuticals and extreme biotechnologies. Meanwhile, outside the Compounds, the rest of the population struggled through poverty, crime, addiction, and disease in densely packed and under-resourced cities, known as *pleeblands.*

The world of Jimmy/Snowman's youth was excessively anthropocentric. It was also almost entirely artificial. Glenn/Crake reflected the attitude of the time when he remarked: "I don't believe in Nature […] Or not with a capital N" (Atwood 2003, 242). In the 'present,' after the pandemic, this carefully constructed society has collapsed. The division between human and animal spaces no longer exists. Birds roost in offshore towers that rise like trees out of the ocean, while below them lies a reef of rusted car parts, bricks, and rubble (3). Meanwhile, Jimmy/Snowman sleeps in a tree to protect himself from the "wildlife" below (4). Now, the Compounds offer no safety. Their streets are patrolled by packs of predators and the ruined buildings are overrun by plants and other animals. All the while, the future of 'humanity' lies with the Crakers whose superior genetic material was taken from other species. As Glenn/Crake commented: "*Think of an adaptation, any adaptation, and some animal somewhere will have thought of it first*" (194, emphasis original). Ironically, the Crakers give humanity the greatest chance of survival because they are not 'human' at all.

As part of Atwood's (2003) disruption of the human-animal divide, the genetically superior Crakers straddle the line between human and animal. To ensure a peaceful species will inherit the earth, Glenn/Crake removes the "destructive features" of the "ancient primate brain" (358). Thus, he attempts to sever their connection to our branch of the evolutionary tree. His intention is that there would be no more "killing" and "no more human predation" (116). As a result, his nonviolent, herbivorous Crakers eat only "leaves and grass and roots and a berry or two" (358). To do so, Glenn/Crake equips them with specific digestive mechanisms taken from "hares and rabbits" (187). The Crakers produce "caecotrophs," which are "semi-digested herbage, discharged through the anus and reswallowed two or three times a week" (187). Jimmy/Snowman finds the idea "revolting," but it means that food sources for the Crakers are "plentiful and always available" (187, 358–9). Meanwhile, Jimmy/Snowman struggles to find any food at all. When he does eat a fish in front of the Crakers, they "keep their distance and avert their eyes" (117).

Glenn/Crake equips his new species with the best survival strategies evolution can offer. They protect their territory from predators using scent-marking chemicals in their urine, inspired by "the canids and mustelids" (Atwood 2003, 182). They also emit a citrus smell to "ward off mosquitoes" (117). From the felines, Glenn/Crake borrows "purring" as a "self-healing mechanism," based on the idea that cat purrs occur at "the same frequency as the ultrasound used on bone fractures and skin lesions" (184). He also constructs an elaborate mating system to ensure population control. Perhaps the most notable contribution is "variable pigmentation" from baboons and "expandable chromosphores" from octopi to create genitalia that turn blue to indicate fertility (194). Consequently, it is only "the blue tissue and the pheromones released by it that stimulate the males," which means there is "no more thwarted lust" (194). Moreover, sex is "no longer a mysterious rite;" instead it is "more like an athletic demonstration, a free-spirited romp" (195).

The Crakers offer an optimized, shortcut to evolution. As the next stage in 'human' development, they are an entirely artificial species full of the characteristics of an impossibly wide variety of other animals. Despite Glenn/Crake's assertions that they are humanity's future, they are not *Homo sapiens* at all. They are *"sui generis,"* a unique species (356). Instead, humanity's prospects lie with the lonely figure of Jimmy/Snowman: "the last *Homo sapiens*" (263). In this post-apocalyptic future, Atwood upends the current state of human-animal relations. Now, for the first time in this book, we find humanity in the role of endangered species. We have seen explorations of population loss in Haig-Brown's (1941) *Return to the River*, Bodsworth's (1955) *Last of the Curlews*, and Gowdy's (1998) *The White Bone*. We even saw an initial recognition of species decline in some of Seton's wild animal stories. A century later, however, Atwood was considering the unsettling possibility that one day *Homo sapiens* could join the endangered species list.

In the unnatural world of *Oryx and Crake*, genetic engineering invariably trumps the slow, incremental work of evolution. *Homo sapiens* are far from the only endangered species. Indeed, most of the world's wild animals are extinct. In this near-future context, mass extinctions have become so mundane that they feature in a guessing game called Extinctathon. As a trivia game of extinct animals, the aim is to identify the species being described:

> *Begins with, number of legs, what is it?* The *it* would be some bioform that had kakked out within the past fifty years—no T-Rex, no roc, no dodo, and points off for getting the time frame wrong. Then you'd narrow it down, Phylum Class Order Family Genus Species, then the habitat and when last seen, what had snuffed it. (Pollution, habitat destruction, credulous morons

who thought that eating its horn would give them a boner) [...] It helps to have the MaddAddam printout of every extinct species, but [...] it was a couple of hundred pages of fine print and filled with obscure bugs, weeds, and frogs nobody had ever heard of. (Atwood 2003, 92, emphasis original)

In Atwood's speculative future, the question of knowing animals has become a question of remembering whether they ever existed. Wild animals no longer hold the awe or mystery we have seen expressed in other texts. Now, they have been reduced to half-forgotten trivia.

Yet, the world of *Oryx and Crake* (2003) remains highly populated with animals, especially after Glenn/Crake's virus reduces the human population. Although these genetically engineered species were created as *objects of utility*, they each regain their autonomy after the fall of humanity. In effect, they become self-determined *subjects of lives*. As Jimmy/Snowman learns, these animals are now far beyond human control. Ultimately, all surpass the expectations humanity sets upon them and all resist the anthropocentric purposes for which they were created. Through this process, these animals reveal humanity's collective *failure of knowing*.

As a child, Jimmy/Snowman had a pet 'rakunk,' a genetically engineered blend of a racoon and a skunk. He named her Killer. She shared his bed, licked his nose, and became his "secret best friend" (Atwood 2003, 67). Later, he reflects that she was "the only person he could really talk to" (67). As a 'tame' animal with genetic material from two wild species, rakunks straddle the line between the wild and the domesticated. Indeed, Jimmy/Snowman's mother felt that Killer would be "*happier living a wild, free life in the forest*" (69, emphasis original).

When his mother released Killer outside, Jimmy/Snowman worried about her survival. Seeing her as a "tame" and "helpless" pet, he believed she "wouldn't know how to fend for herself" (69–70). Killer's fate remains unknown. As an adult, however, Jimmy/Snowman acknowledges his failure to know her:

But Jimmy's mother and her ilk must have been right, thinks Snowman, and Killer and the other liberated rakunks must be able to cope just fine, or how else to account for the annoyingly large population of them now infesting this neck of the woods? (70)

Even though the rakunks were intended as pets, they inevitably become 'pests.' Indeed, after the pandemic, rakunks become a persistent "nuisance" to Jimmy/Snowman (49). In the 'past' he may have enjoyed Killer licking his feet in bed, but in the 'present,' he resents the rakunks "sniffing at his toes" as if "he were already garbage" (42).

Despite the differences in the way that Atwood, Seton, and Roberts represent animals, all utilize the trope of animals 'returning' to a state of 'wildness.' In Atwood's post-apocalyptic landscape, however, it is the genetically engineered animals who assert this wild autonomy. Created in laboratories, there is no *returning* to the wild for them. Nonetheless, they all seem to thrive and demonstrate a degree of wild autonomy they were not intended to have. Particularly ironic are the "bobkittens" created as a method of "control" after genetically engineered green rabbits became a "prolific" pest (Atwood 2003, 192). Inevitably, the bobkittens get "out of control in their turn" and begin attacking small dogs, babies, and people (193). Though these animals were created as *objects of utility*, their irrepressible autonomy now becomes the greatest threat to humanity.

Packs of 'wolvogs' created for protection in a BioDefences laboratory routinely hunt Jimmy/Snowman. They were "bred to deceive" and there is "no way of making pals with them" (241). Whilst they might look and behave like dogs, "they'll take your hand off" (241). Not only do the wolvogs assert their agency and defy human expectations, their appearance and deceptive behaviours highlight their unknowability. Atwood emphasizes their uncanny qualities by playing on stereotypes of canine loyalty. Initially believing them to be dogs, Jimmy/Snowman assumes that they are all "gazing" at him "with eyes of love" and friendly "wagging" tails (241). When he learns that they are wolvogs, however, he feels as though "some line has been crossed, some boundary transgressed" (242). By contrast, Atwood continues to represent real dogs as utterly devoted to humans. Indeed, after the pandemic, the few remaining dogs beg with "bewildered eyes" to be "taken in" by "some human, any human" (125–6).

To some extent, Atwood (2003) is illuminating the ways in which domestication creates dependence. However, we have also seen the genetically engineered, domesticated animals in the book adapt to life without humans. The canine stereotypes employed flatter humans while undermining the autonomy of dogs. They also reinforce the assumption that domesticated animals lack agency. Jimmy/Snowman reflects that these dogs "never stood a chance" against the wolvogs who simply killed and ate "all those who'd shown signs of vestigial domesticated status" (125). It is this domesticated status that dooms the dogs. Atwood reinforces this point when Jimmy/Snowman witnesses a wolvog "advance to a yapping Pekinese in a friendly manner, sniff its bum, then lunge for its throat, shake it like a mop, and canter off with the limp body" (125). It is significant that, in this moment, Atwood chooses a small dog stereotyped for vulnerability and dependence on humans.

By contrast, Jimmy/Snowman's interactions with wolvogs highlight their unknowability. Indeed, he demonstrates a solid *acceptance of not knowing* them. He reflects that it "hasn't taken much to reverse fifty thousand years of man-canid interaction" (Atwood 2003, 125). With rueful sarcasm he asks the wolvogs: "Who wants to be man's best friend?" (125). In response, they make deceptive "supplicating whine[s]" and "playful puppy leaps" as they hunt him (125). The unsettling behaviour of the wolvogs exemplifies *Oryx and Crake*'s engagement with the *acceptance of not knowing* the animal. With even greater irony than the bobkittens, the wolvogs defy expectations by hunting the humans they were created to protect.

Even more than the bobkittens or wolvogs, 'pigoons' are the most dangerous animals Jimmy/Snowman encounters. Yet, his realization of his *failure of knowing* is slower with the pigoons. Perhaps this is because he first saw them as a child: "He especially like the small pigoons, twelve to a sow and lined up in a row, guzzling milk. Pigoonlets. They were cute" (29). When his father warned him that the pigoons would eat him if he fell into their pen, he did not believe it: "'No they won't,' said Jimmy. Because I'm their friend, he thought. Because I sing to them" (30). He was also distressed when his father joked about eating the pigoons at lunch: "This would upset Jimmy; he was confused about who should be allowed to eat what. He didn't want to eat a pigoon, because he thought of the pigoons as creatures much like himself" (27). In this *fantasy of knowing*, Jimmy/Snowman thought of the pigoons as his "pals" (34).

Nonetheless, even as a child, Jimmy/Snowman was unsettled by the older pigoons. He found them "slightly frightening" and when they looked at him, he felt "as if they saw him, really saw him, and might have plans for him later" (30). Here, he begins to sense that there is more at work behind the pigoon eyes than he had assumed. Pigoons offer Atwood's (2003) deepest exploration of the *acceptance of not knowing* the animal. They were created to "grow an assortment of foolproof human-tissue organs in a transgenic knockout pig host" (25). The pigoons could grow multiple extra organs—"five or six kidneys at a time"—and have a "rapid-maturity gene" so that the organs could be "ready sooner" (25–6). Thus, the pigoons were "much bigger and fatter than ordinary pigs" to "leave room for all of the extra organs" (29). Most disturbingly, they could be "reaped" of these organs and then "keep on living and grow more" (26).

Of course, the use of pigs for organ transplants is not new. As Helen Tiffin (2007) observes, proponents of xenotransplantation often appeal to its long history. Some argue that it goes back as far as the "sixteenth century," though the first recorded attempt to transfer a pig organ into a human body was in France in 1906 (258). Pigs have been the favoured species for this process for two important reasons. Firstly, humans and pigs are so physiologically similar that, in some cases, they can be more suitable for xenotransplantation than other primates. Secondly, there are fewer ethical objections to the use of pigs for transplants. As we also eat pigs, we are more willing to accept their exploitation, despite the unique similarities that we share with them. Tiffin (2007) points out that the contradictions of speciesism, made clear when we eat the flesh of pigs, are further complicated by pig organ transplants. Moreover, this troubling of the species divide is set to become even more unsettling when the "transfer of human genetic material to pigs to facilitate organ acceptance by the recipient" becomes routine (259).

In *Oyrx and Crake*, Atwood (2003) takes these ideas to an extreme. Not only has human DNA been used to enable the pigoons to grow organs, in some cases it has been used to create pigoons capable of growing human brain tissue. As the name suggests, the "neuro-regeneration project" grows "genuine human neocortex tissue" inside pigoon brains (63). It is unclear how this impacts the pigoons themselves, although it undoubtedly adds an unpredictable element to their unknowability. Based on the ways in which the pigoons hunt Jimmy/Snowman after the pandemic, we might assume that the human neocortex tissue has increased both their intelligence and their violence. Certainly, description of the pigoons as both "brainy and omnivorous" is something they share with *Homo sapiens* (276). Jimmy/Snowman also senses a dangerous cunning in their similarity with humans: "Some of them even have human neocortex tissue growing in their crafty, wicked heads" (276). Perhaps this is the destructive element that Glenn/Crake attempted to remove from the brains of the Crakers.

We do not witness Jimmy/Snowman's realization of his *failure* to know the pigoons. As he suspected, though, the pigooons do indeed "have plans for him" (30). In the post-pandemic wasteland, he soon reaches an *acceptance of not knowing*. Though he no longer thinks of them as his "pals," he respects (and fears) their intelligence (30). Over several encounters, it becomes increasingly clear that the pigoons are planning traps for him. They seem capable of future planning, sophisticated communication, and complex social organization. Similar to Gowdy's (1998) speculative elephant representation, Atwood's (2003) exploration of pigoon intelligence operates from an assumption of consciousness. Indeed, without conscious thought, they would not pose such a threat.

Each interaction with the pigoons reveals a new insight into the complexity of their communication and social organization. At first, Jimmy/ Snowman encounters five pigoons in a ruined Compound. They sniff in his direction, "as if puzzled," but do not attack (Atwood 2003, 276). For a moment, the male sways "uneasily" back and forth while "making up its mind" (276). When the others move away, "the boar thinks better of it and follows them" (276). Jimmy/Snowman remains suspicious, though, knowing that the pigoons are "clever enough to fake a retreat, then lurk around the corner" (276). The next day, seven pigoons seem to materialize "from nowhere" and he wonders whether some of them are the "same as yesterday's" (313). They start following him and Jimmy/Snowman realizes: "They have something in mind, all right" (313). Then, he spots another group ahead, cutting him off:

> It's as if they've had it planned, between the two groups; as if they've known for some time that he was in the gatehouse and have been waiting for him to come out, far enough way so that they can surround him. (314)

> Clearly, the pigoons are working as a collective. As they pursue him, "twenty or thirty" more appear (314).

The pigoons seem to learn and adapt quickly as they hunt Jimmy/ Snowman. When their path is blocked, they cooperate: "two boars [...] move side by side to the door, bumping it with their shoulders" (Atwood 2003, 314). Jimmy/Snowman observes ruefully that the pigoons are "[t]eam players" (314). He infers that, if he tries to wait them out, they will "take it in relays, some grazing outside, others watching" (314). In fact, he does spot a group of pigoons "posted outside" the door "on the lookout" (317). Meanwhile, other pigoons find Jimmy/Snowman's bag of supplies. When he goes to retrieve the bag, "something lunges" at him (319). He discovers that the pigoons were "waiting for him, using the garbage bag as bait" because they "must have been able to tell there was something in it he'd want" (319). "Cunning," he thinks to himself, "so cunning" (319).

The complexity and swift adaptability of the pigoons' strategies would seem to suggest some form of language. When Jimmy/Snowman sees a lone pigoon, he feels he must shoot them because they are certainly a "scout" who "would have told the others" (Atwood 2003, 416). His suspicions could well be correct, as knowledge does spread rapidly through the pigoon population. Early on, Jimmy/Snowman scares away pigoons by waving a stick because "sticks look like electroprods" and "pigoons have long memories" (276). Later, however, this strategy no longer works. The pigoons already know that he is bluffing: "this time they stand their ground" (276). Evidently, the pigoons are not static in their behaviours. They share knowledge, cooperate, problem-solve, adapt, and develop new tactics. These are all crucial indicators of their cognitive and social complexity. As we have seen in other texts addressed in this book, it would also suggest the formation of a shared culture.

Of course, this unpredictability increases our impression of the pigoons' unknowability. We have no access to *their* experiences or perspectives. Just like Jimmy/Snowman, we can only make conclusions based on external observations of their actions (as a behaviourist might). From what we have seen, however, they seem capable of almost anything. Even though *Oryx and Crake* (2003) presents animal minds as unknowable, it does so through an *acceptance of not knowing*. This distinction is important. Previously in this book, we have seen an association between belief in the unknowability of animal minds and scepticism about the very existence of animal minds. In such instances, a writer might prevent accusations of anthropomorphism through reductive representation. They might use mechanomorphic language or portray animals as acting through instinct alone. For Atwood, however, this is not the case.

Whilst Atwood (2003) writes about animals as unknowable, she does not treat them as though they have no minds. Instead, she errs on the side of animal intelligence. We cannot access the minds of the animals in *Oryx and Crake*, yet Atwood's animal representations are built upon the assumption of sentience. Indeed, most of the animals with whom Jimmy/Snowman interacts seem capable of consciousness. Given the complexity of pigoon behaviour, it is fair to assume that they also possess some form of language and the beginnings of a complex society. Moreover, at the end of the book, it is unclear whether the Crakers or the pigoons will become the next dominant species. Certainly, the pigoons are the better strategists. As Jimmy/Snowman reflects: "if [pigoons] had fingers they'd have ruled the world" (314).

Obviously, *Oryx and Crake* is a work of speculative fiction. Questions of accuracy and anthropomorphism bear less weight than in some of the other texts addressed in this book. Yet, within the heightened context of Atwood's (2003) speculative future, she takes a realistic approach. The pigoons do not stand on two legs and speak, for instance. Even if many of the animals depicted have been genetically modified, they are still based on real-world species. With this in mind, I suggest that Atwood's assumption of animal sentience and consciousness is significant. Here, we can see the impact of the shift towards animal cognition in the sciences. Evidently, this was an atmosphere in which a writer could speculate (somewhat realistically) about animal intelligences that equalled or surpassed those of humans without causing a controversy. Of course, whether intentionally or not, Atwood certainly played into contemporary fears of 'humanizing' other species. Whatever one's stance on the topic, *Oryx and Crake* (2003) presents a vision of the future in which the gap between humans and other animals has all but disappeared.

CONCLUSION

Each book in this chapter deals with the question of survival. Indeed, most of the protagonists in these texts face extinction. For many authors addressed in this book, the topic of species loss had to be explained or justified. By the turn of the twenty-first century, however, the evidence of species loss was overwhelming. In essence, mass extinction had become a given. Lawrence (1990) and Gowdy (1998) deal with the literal survival of animals, both as individuals and populations. However, Atwood's (2003) post-apocalyptic future expands the topic to question the survival of *Homo sapiens*, as well as that of 'nature' itself. Although Martel (2001) does not engage directly with ecology or conservation, there is a sense that we are 'all in the same boat' at least. Pi's and Richard Parker's ability to survive together is uncertain. Yet there is still the message that human existence is better off *with* other species.

For most of the texts in this chapter, we can also see the continuing impact of the cognitive revolution. Although these novels deal with questions of survival and extinction, they also make solid speculations about the topic of *animal consciousness*. In these texts, we find confident statements regarding animal minds and emotions, similar to those made in Seton's, Roberts's, and Russell's stories. Even though Martel (2001) continues to express a fear of anthropomorphism, he does acknowledge the potential for subjective inner states. Indeed, all the books covered in this chapter make at least *some* reference to animal minds or emotions.

Writing at the turn of the twenty-first century, these authors use the language of subjective experiences, intentionality, and consciousness. They make statements that would have been dismissed as anthropomorphic nonsense decades before. Of course, some of these authors use fantastical or speculative literary techniques. Yet, the external behaviours of their animal characters are not unrealistic. They do not stand up and talk or wear clothes. Observed from the outside, these animals would appear no different to their real-world counterparts. Inside, though, each inhabits a rich subjectivity. Questions of animal thought, consciousness, reason, and language had lain dormant throughout most of the twentieth century. Now, thanks to the work of animal cognition research—and cognitive ethology in particular—we can start to consider them again.

REFERENCES

Atwood, Margaret. (2003) 2008. *Oryx and Crake*. London: Virago.

———. 2004. *The Handmaid's Tale* and *Oryx and Crake* 'in Context'. *PMLA*. 119 (3, May): 513–517.

Bemrose, John. 1998. Elephantine Fantasies. *Maclean's*, September 14: 56–57.

Bodsworth, Fred. (1955) 1956. *Last of the Curlews*. London: Museum Press.

Burroughs, John. 1903. Real and Sham Natural History. *Atlantic Monthly*. 91 (545, March): 298–309.

Caro, T.M., and M.D. Hauser. 1992. Is There Teaching in Nonhuman Animals? *The Quarterly Review of Biology*. 67 (2, June): 151–174. https://doi.org/10.1086/417553.

Engel, Marian. (1976) 1988. *Bear*. London: Pandora.

Findley, Timothy. (1984) 1996. *Not Wanted on the Voyage*. Toronto: Penguin Books.

Gibson, Graeme. (1971) 1982. *Five Legs / Communion* Toronto: McClelland and Stewart.

Gowdy, Barbara. (1998) 2000. *The White Bone*. London: Flamingo.

Grove, Frederick Philip. (1947) 2001. *Consider Her Ways*. Toronto: McClelland and Stewart.

Haig-Brown, Roderick. (1941) 1984. *Return to the River: A Story of the Chinook Run*. Oshkosh: Willow Creek.

Hediger, Ryan. 2013. Our Animals, Ourselves: Representing Animals Minds in *Timothy* and *The White Bone*. In *Speaking for Animals: Animal Autobiographical Writing*, ed. Margo DeMello, 35–47. New York: Routledge.

King, Barbara. 2013. *How Animals Grieve*. Chicago: University of Chicago Press.

Kriticos, Christian. 2016. Animals Emoting: The Millions Interview with Yann Martel. *The Millions*, February 29. https://themillions.com/2016/02/in-the-present-momentthe-millions-interviews-yann-martel.html. Accessed September 6 2021.

Kroetsch, Robert. (1969) 2004. *The Studhorse Man*. Edmonton: University of Alberta Press.

Lawrence, R.D. 1990. *The White Puma*. New York: Henry Holt.

Loo, Tina. 2006. *States of Nature: Conserving Canada's Wildlife in the Twentieth Century*. Vancouver: UBC Press.

Martel, Yann. (2001) 2012. *Life of Pi*. Edinburgh: Canongate.

———. 2002. A Giraffe in a Cage Is Worth Two on the Box. *The Spectator*, August 10. http://archive.spectator.co.uk/article/10th-august-2002/37/a-giraffe-in-a-cage-is-worth-two-on-the-box. Accessed September 6 2021.

Oerlemans, Onno. 2007. A Defence of Anthropomorphism: Comparing Coetzee and Gowdy. *Mosaic* 40 (1, March): 181–196. https://www.jstor.org/stable/44030165.

Proulx, Gilbert, and Dwight Rodtka. 2015. Predator Bounties in Western Canada Cause Animal Suffering and Compromise Wildlife Conservation Efforts. *Animals*. 5: 1035–1046. https://doi.org/10.3390/ani5040397.

Raglon, Rebecca, and Marian Scholtmeijer. 2007. 'Animals Are Not Believers in Ecology': Mapping Critical Differences Between Environmental and Animal Advocacy Literatures. *ISLE*. 14 (2, Summer): 121–140. https://doi.org/10.1093/isle/14.2.121.

Roberts, Charles G.D. 1902. *Kindred of the Wild*. Boston: L. C. Page & Co.

Roosevelt, Theodore. 1907. Nature Fakers. *Everybody's Magazine*. 17 (3, September): 427–430.

Russell, Andy. (1977) 1991. *Adventures with Wild Animals*. Toronto: McClelland & Stewart.

Saha, Shrestha. 2019. Why Yann Martel Relies on Animal Characters. *The Telegraph Online*, February 9. https://www.telegraphindia.com/culture/books/why-yann-martelrelies-on-animal-characters/cid/1684089. Accessed September 6 2021.

Sandlos, John. 2000. From Within Fur and Feathers: Animals in Canadian Literature. *TOPIA: Canadian Journal of Cultural Studies*. 4: 73–91. https://doi.org/10.3138/topia.4.73.

Seton, Ernest Thompson. 1898. *Wild Animals I Have Known*. New York: Charles Scriber's Sons.

———. 1901. *Lives of the Hunted*. London: David Nutt.

———. 1905. *Animal Heroes*. London: Constable & Company.

Stobie, Margaret. 1978. Grove and the Ants. *Dalhousie Review*. 58 (3): 418–433.

Tiffin, Helen. 2007. Pigs, People and Pigoons. In *Knowing Animals*, ed. Laurence Simmons and Philip Armstrong, 244–265. Leiden: Brill.

Watson, John B. 1925. *Behaviorism*. New York: W.W. Norton & Co.

Whitehead, Hal. 2003. *Sperm Whales: Social Evolution in the Ocean*. Chicago: University of Chicago Press.

CHAPTER 10

Conclusion

One purpose of this book has been to improve our understanding of the historical forces shaping human perceptions of other species. To do so, I have focused on the relationship between three specific methods of communicating on behalf of nonhuman beings: literary representations of nonhuman characters, the scientific study of animal minds, and the theoretical and practical work of animal advocacy. Until now, these contexts have not been brought together in this way. Nor have they been examined with a Canadian focus.

Over the previous eight chapters, I have charted a history of certain ideas about animals in Canada. This began with the publication of Charles Darwin's *On the Origin of Species* (1859), which stirred a new era of interest in animal minds and concern for animal protection. As a result, Canadian developments in comparative psychology, animal protection, and wildlife conservation occurred almost simultaneously. This was also the period in which Ernest Thompson Seton and Charles G. D. Roberts co-created the wild animal story. Yet, when it came to writing the Canadian Criminal Code, anti-cruelty laws were placed under the property section. This established the legal status of animals as human property in Canada.

Next, I explored the professionalization of the sciences, the early twentieth-century Nature Fakers controversy, the rise of ethology and behaviourism, and the introduction of ecological approaches to wildlife

© The Author(s), under exclusive license to Springer Nature Switzerland AG 2023
C. Allmark-Kent, *Literature, Science, and Animal Advocacy in Canada*, Palgrave Studies in Animals and Literature, https://doi.org/10.1007/978-3-031-40556-3_10

management. By drawing these different contexts together, it was clear that across science, conservation, and animal fiction there was a significant shift towards more mechanistic perceptions of animals. To remedy the perceived anthropomorphism and sentimentality of previous decades, mechanomorphic language dominated descriptions of animals for most of the twentieth century. In many cases, this produced a curious tension for Canadian authors attempting to write on behalf of other animals.

More than a century after the publication of *On the Origin of Species* (1859), the cognitive revolution created another shift in public thinking. Research into animal minds and emotions gradually returned to the sciences. Meanwhile, the animal rights and environmental movements were refocusing our attention on human-animal relations. In this period of debate and transition, Canadian authors explored the complexities of knowing other animals. This led to the development of new forms of animal representation, some of which expressed a distinct pessimism about our ability to connect with other species.

During the turn of the twentieth century, an age of ecological crises challenged human-animal relations, as well as ideas about 'nature' itself. Canadian authors continued to produce innovative responses to understanding other species, while campaigners concentrated their efforts on improving the nation's outdated anti-cruelty laws. However, a backlash against the animal rights movement had been developing since the 1980s. This led to several failed attempts to move anti-cruelty laws from the property section of the Canadian Criminal Code into its own heading.

Strangely, even as Canadian politicians held firm to the idea of animals as human property, the sciences were expanding our understanding of the cognitive, emotional, social, and even cultural complexities of other species. Even the question of animal consciousness was returning to the sciences. Astonishingly, some of these researchers challenged a century of disciplinary boundaries by suggesting that science could benefit from the input of writers and amateur observers. A hundred years after the Nature Fakers controversy, the stories of Seton and Roberts could now contribute to our understanding of animal minds after all.

Through practical zoocriticism, I have uncovered the threads of certain issues and ideas running throughout this history. Scepticism about the 'knowability' of animals can be found in science, literature, and philosophy, yet they became popular at different times. As belief in animal minds and emotions fluctuated throughout the decades, our definitions of anthropomorphism and 'human uniqueness' varied significantly. Academic stances on intellectual exchange and interdisciplinarity swung wildly from the nineteenth century to the twenty-first. Indeed, as debates around scientific authority subsided, writers who blended fact and fiction became less controversial. Meanwhile, public concern for wildlife waxed and waned, yet attitudes towards individual species transformed dramatically. All the while, a profoundly entrenched anthropocentrism repeatedly resisted and dismissed concern for animals as childish, effeminate, and sometimes even 'dangerous.' Although some ideas about animals may have changed, speciesism itself remains as ubiquitous as ever.

By drawing these interdisciplinary contexts together, we can identify a discrepancy between *animal representation* and *animal protection* in Canada. Although the issues with Canada's anti-cruelty laws have been well-documented, they have not yet impacted our understanding of animal fiction. Until now, approaches to Canadian animal representation have presupposed a continuity between sympathetic fiction and a sympathetic population. The only existing theories of animal representation in Canada are those proposed by James Polk (1972) and Margaret Atwood (1972). These frameworks have been repeated, so that scholars in other fields, such as Canadian environmental history, take them as a given (Loo 2006, 2).

As this book has demonstrated, the notion that the 'Canadian psyche' has an inherent affinity for other animals is problematic. Of course, any concept of a national psyche is suspect, particularly for a distinctly multicultural nation such as Canada. Fundamentally, though, the whole theory overlooks the reality of Canadian law. Atwood (1972) argued that Canadians wrote about animals in a unique way because they held a more sympathetic relationship with animals than their British or American neighbours. Yet, the animal protection movements in Great Britain and the United States were significantly more successful—and far more radical—that those in Canada. Without understanding the interdisciplinary histories involved, these interpretations of Canadian animal fiction can only go so far.

Ultimately, the 'animal victim' theory negates the possibility of some Canadians writing sympathetically about other animals precisely *because* they do not seem to be valued by the law. As we have seen in this book, the style of zoocentric representation shown by Seton, Roberts, and others has been relatively rare within the Canadian canon. English-Canadian culture has produced a variety of responses to nonhuman beings, only some of which constitute robust or respectful representations.

Practical zoocriticism enables us to produce analyses of animal representation that do not rely on concepts such as a national psyche or a timeless relationship with other species. Our perceptions of other animals are not 'natural' or fixed. They are built through the ceaseless interplay of countless forces, be they scientific, political, cultural, philosophical, or religious. By focusing on the contexts in which a piece of work was written and received, practical zoocriticism yields analyses that take account of our complex, fluctuating relationships with nonhuman beings. We can glean much from knowing that an author wrote *with* or *against* contemporary scientific knowledge of a species or whether they engaged with issues of animal protection. The specificity of this approach means that we can avoid reductive or oversimplified conclusions. Instead, we can testify to the complexity of our interactions with the nonhuman beings with whom we share the Earth.

Much of what I have described here is not unique to Canada. Anthropocentrism and speciesism thrive globally. In many places animals are implicitly seen and treated as human property, whether that is their official legal status or not. In other words, these issues are not limited to Euro-Canadian settler-colonial culture. Nor is practical zoocriticism restricted to this context. As an analytical framework, practical zoocriticism is applicable to many different ways in which we discuss or depict animals. I have chosen literature, science, and advocacy as the dominant forces shaping our perceptions of other species, but these could be adjusted to account for different contexts. For instance, a greater emphasis could be placed on religion or philosophy. By focusing on perceptions of animals in a specific time and place, practical zoocriticism can be adapted in a multitude of ways.

This framework can also facilitate cross-disciplinary exchanges by drawing out pertinent analyses and revealing the shared common ground. Such work may illuminate new issues that need to be addressed. In the sciences, we can challenge the use of reductive or objectifying language. For animal advocates, we can stress the importance of storytelling, particularly in ways that emphasize the experiences or personal histories of individual animals. A recent example of such representation can be found in Gabriela Cowperthwaite's (2013) documentary *Blackfish*, which influenced the banning of cetacean captivity in Canada.

LOOKING AHEAD

In the time it took to research and write this book, Canada banned the captivity of whales, dolphins, and porpoises. Bill S-203 (the *Ending the Captivity of Whales and Dolphins Act*) was passed in 2019 and ensured that cetaceans could no longer be caught or bred for display in aquariums or marine parks in Canada.[1] This means that, 150 years after the original *Cruelty to Animals Act* of 1869, it is the first federal legislation to protect animals not as 'property,' but *as animals*. Not only is it also the first anti-cruelty law to protect wild animals, it is the only law that specifically prevents animals from becoming human property. By recognizing the inherent cruelty of captivity, the *Whales and Dolphins Act* acknowledges that (at least some) animals deserve autonomy, freedom of movement, and a certain quality of life. It protects animals for their *own* sake, not as *objects of utility*, but as fellow *subjects of lives*. As the preceding chapters have demonstrated, Bill S-203 represents a profound shift in the history of Canadian animal protection.

At present, the rest of the Criminal Code continues to view animals as 'objects,' only to be protected insofar as it serves human interests. Despite repeated attempts to update the law, the animal cruelty sections of the code remain largely unaltered since they were established in 1892. This means that all animal protection laws—including those introduced by the *Whales and Dolphins Act*—remain under the 'property' section. Regardless of all the theories, debates, discoveries, arguments, and appeals over the past century, there have been few substantial changes to Canadian animal protection laws since Ernest Thompson Seton (1898) asked "Have the wild things no moral or legal rights?" (357). It remains to be seen whether the success of the *Whales and Dolphins Act* will trigger any further reforms of Canada's animal protection laws.

We must recognize that Bill S-203 passed because it targeted a highly specific, highly visible, form of animal cruelty. It is hard to make the case that Canadian society relies on cetacean captivity in the same way that had been argued for animal agriculture or fur farming (see Chap. 8). Moreover, those who would benefit from the continued exploitation of whales,

---

[1] It is worth noting that, unfortunately, the new law does not extend to whales, dolphins, and porpoises who were held captive before the passing of Bill S-203. The decision to release these animals to marine sanctuaries lies with the humans still recognized as their legal 'owners.' Thus, these individuals are not protected from being human property until the human who currently 'owns' them agrees to let them go.

dolphins, and porpoises lack the strong lobbyists of these other industries. Even so, opponents of the bill chose a well-worn path by associating the proposed amendments with more radical, hypothetical, changes to the law.

In a House of Commons debate on 10th June 2019, Blaine Calkins (Conservative MP for Red Deer-Lacombe, Alberta) argued that, because the "organizations that are publicly and vocally expressing support for the bill," such as "Animal Justice and some SPCAs," call for "the end of things like rodeos, fishing, eating animals, and raising animals on a farm," Bill S-203 should be rejected in case it set a dangerous precedent (Canada 2019, 28784). This is the same line of argument that was used against the attempts to amend the Criminal Code described in Chap. 8, in which modest animal protection legislation was mischaracterized as a slippery slope towards the complete 'humanization' of animals, along with a set of imagined, more extreme, changes to the law.

Ultimately, it was public pressure that made Bill S-203 successful. After repeated obstructions made it seems as though the bill would die from procedural delay, both politicians and animal advocates appealed to the public for support. The overwhelming response from Canadian citizens flooded the email and voicemail inboxes of senators with requests for Bill S-203 to be passed (Sykes 2019, 362). Whilst social media was crucial to this mass mobilization of the public, one factor cannot be overlooked: the 'Blackfish effect.' E.C.M. Parsons and Naomi A. Rose (2018) describe this as the "genuine social phenomenon" in response to the documentary Blackfish (2013) that led to "substantive corporate, legislative, and regulatory changes" (75). Given that Senator Wilfred Moore (Nova Scotia) introduced the bill after watching the documentary in 2015, there is no denying the role of Blackfish in the banning of cetacean captivity (Sykes 2019, 354).

The power of Blackfish lies in director Gabriela Cowperthwaite's (2013) storytelling. She exposes the cruelty of all cetacean captivity by focusing on the life of a single whale: a male orca known as Tilikum who killed three of his human trainers. To some extent, the film mirrors much of the zoocentric literature described in this book. It provides information about the cognitive, emotional, and social complexity of the species. It supplements this information with anecdotes about the unusual activities of specific individuals. It explores the protagonist's biography from his distressing capture as a juvenile in 1983 to his fatal attacks on humans in 1991, 1999, and 2010. It investigates his relationships with both humans and other orcas, first at Sealand of the Pacific (British Columbia) and then at

SeaWorld (Florida). It challenges perceptions of the species by focusing on the unusual or unpredictable behaviours of individuals. And, as with so many of the texts discussed in previous chapters, *Blackfish* treats both its protagonist and secondary nonhuman characters as unique, distinct, *subjects of lives*.

Clearly, *Blackfish* galvanized the public in much the same way that the wild animal stories of Seton and Roberts had done a century before. As we have seen, changing public attitudes requires stories that emphasize the individuality, personality, and personal histories of the animals depicted. *Blackfish* defamiliarized public perceptions of orcas by presenting the suffering of specific, named individuals. It communicated their individual stories in a way that impressed upon viewers the fact that they were not entertaining 'objects,' but complex, experiencing, *feeling* beings. This type of representation is vital for animals who face speciesist prejudices or with whom we have little contact. It is particularly important for wild animals who tend to be discussed in broad, collective terms.

When we discuss animals collectively, the conversation (and, therefore, the legislation) stops at the protection of the group. The goal is the preservation of the species. When we speak about wild animals as *individuals*, the conversation becomes about the animal's sentient experiences. Our goal becomes the protection of the individual. Wild animals may continue to be excluded from anti-cruelty laws until we are able to see them for what they are: separate individuals who are just as unique and irreplaceable as ourselves. By representing so-called 'killer' whales as individuals, *Blackfish* laid the path for the *Whales and Dolphins Act* to make a crucial step forward: protecting wild animals as individuals for the first time in Canadian history.

At the beginning of this book, I identified a discrepancy between how animals are celebrated in Canadian culture and how they are protected by its laws. In the relationship between *Blackfish* and the *Whales and Dolphins Act*, we find a rare alignment of animal representation and animal protection. Both the film and the law treat cetaceans as *subjects of lives*. This is an example of Graham Huggan and Helen Tiffin's (2010) point that animal protection legislation tends to "depend on public response to representation rather than to the animals themselves" (139).

The relationship between *Blackfish* and the *Whales and Dolphins Act* also demonstrates the crucial engagement between the sciences, animal advocacy, and storytelling. During the senate hearings for Bill S-203, the Committee on Fisheries and Oceans received evidence from scientists,

Lori Marino and Hal Whitehead. Marino was also one of the scientists interviewed for the film *Blackfish*. As a neuroscientist and founder of The Whale Sanctuary Project, she contributed crucial scientific information about the effects of captivity on cetaceans.

Whitehead is a marine biologist who is well-known for his book, *Sperm Whales: Social Evolution in the Ocean*, in which he made the case for reciprocal communication between scientists and storytellers. He wrote that scientists should look to animal representations, "note the large parts that are consistent with what we know" and "use them as hypotheses to guide our work" (2003, 371). These examples demonstrate how this reciprocal communication works. Both scientists advocated for animals by providing evidence in support of Bill S-203. One aided the storytelling power of a documentary by contributing to its scientific foundations. The other identified the imaginative, empathetic power of storytelling to provide a foundation for scientific research.

One of the books described by Whitehead is Barbara Gowdy's (1998) *The White Bone*. It was published a century after Seton's (1898) first collection of wild animal stories, *Wild Animals I Have Known*. Whilst their styles may differ, they share core aims and characteristics. Indeed, both Seton and Gowdy were inspired to write based on the activities of real animals. Even a century apart, they each attempted to know the animals in question through writing fiction.

Comparing Seton's and Gowdy's work illuminates the importance of the contexts in which they were created and received. One was written during the early days of comparative psychology, just as the old 'introspective' method and its belief in animal minds was beginning to be questioned. The President of the United States called its author a "nature faker" and an "object of derision to every scientist" (Roosevelt 1907, 428). The other was written in the wake of the cognitive revolution, which overturned behaviourism's legacy of detachment from animal minds and re-established the scientific study of animal sentience, consciousness, and emotions. This book was celebrated by a prominent biologist as a "remarkable" piece of work, which may "come closer to the natures of these animals" than the "coarse numerical abstractions" of his own observations (Whitehead 2003, 370). He even called upon fellow scientists to pay closer attention to similar works of animal fiction.

In their wild animal stories, Seton and Roberts attempted to blend animal advocacy, comparative psychology, and storytelling. Unfortunately, whilst the idea was sound, the timing was not. The professionalization of the sciences meant that their anecdotes of animal behaviour had lost credibility. Moreover, the study of animals' minds itself was undergoing a profound transition. Seton's and Roberts's amateur observations and introspective methods were thoroughly out of favour within the scientific community.

Yet, more than a century later, we can see that there is hope for the likes of Seton and Roberts. Interdisciplinary frameworks, such as practical zoocriticism, enable us to re-evaluate their representations. Meanwhile, the multidisciplinary endeavour of animal studies gives new relevance to their work. Researchers, writers, and advocates alike seek out better methods of communicating on behalf of other species. Even the scientific study of animal minds is opening itself up to interdisciplinarity once more. Thus, their greatest potential to influence human-animal relations lay not in the nineteenth or twentieth centuries. It exists here and now. Today, our current writers of zoocentric fiction have the same opportunity. It just requires the rest of us to set aside our discomfort and, finally, begin to take those imaginary animals seriously.

REFERENCES

An Act Respecting Cruelty to Animals, Statutes of Canada 1869, c. 27.

Atwood, Margaret. 1972. *Survival: A Thematic Guide to Canadian Literature.* Toronto: Anansi.

Canada, Parliament. *House of Commons Debates*, 42nd Parl, 1st Sess, Vol 148, No 430 (10 June 2019).

Cowperthwaite, Gabriela, dir. 2013. *Blackfish.* Magnolia Pictures.

Criminal Code, SC 1892, c C.29.

Gowdy, Barbara. (1998) 2000. *The White Bone.* London: Flamingo.

Huggan, Graham, and Helen Tiffin. 2010. *Postcolonial Ecocriticism: Literature, Animals, Environment.* London: Routledge.

Loo, Tina. 2006. *States of Nature: Conserving Canada's Wildlife in the Twentieth Century.* Vancouver: UBC Press.

Parsons, E.C.M., and Naomi A. Rose. 2018. The *Blackfish* Effect: Corporate and Policy Change in the Face of Shifting Public Opinion on Captive Cetaceans. *Tourism in Marine Environments.* 13 (2–3): 73–83. https://doi.org/10.1002/pan3.10221.

Polk, James. 1972. Lives of the Hunted. *Canadian Literature.* 53: 51–59.

Roosevelt, Theodore. 1907. Nature Fakers. *Everybody's Magazine.* 17 (3, September): 427–430.

Seton, Ernest Thompson. 1898. *Wild Animals I Have Known*. New York: Charles Scriber's Sons.

Sykes, Katie. 2019. The Whale, Inside: Ending Cetacean Captivity in Canada. *Canadian Journal of Comparative and Contemporary Law*. 5 (1): 349–405. https://canlii.ca/t/skr4.

Whitehead, Hal. 2003. *Sperm Whales: Social Evolution in the Ocean*. Chicago: University of Chicago Press.

Appendix: Questions for Practical Zoocriticism

- Is the animal presented through objectifying language, such as 'it' or 'something,' instead of 'she' or 'someone'?
- Is the animal treated as an object in a human-centred narrative? Or are they the subject of their *own* story?
- Is the animal presented *as an animal*? Do they possess characteristics typical of their species?
- Is the animal a unique individual? Do they have a biography?
- What are the animal's sensory experiences? Do they have a subjective quality? Do they experience pain and pleasure?
- Does the animal have emotions? What types of emotions do they experience?
- Does the animal act intentionally? Do they have agency? Do they make decisions?
- Is the animal capable of learning? Can they learn through social observation? Are they actively taught by others?
- Does the animal have social relationships? How do they communicate?
- Does the animal exist within a wider social group? How complex are their interactions?
- Does the animal have a culture? Is it specific to that species? Or is it based on a human culture?
- How does the animal interact with other species? Are there interspecies companionships?

© The Author(s), under exclusive license to Springer Nature Switzerland AG 2023
C. Allmark-Kent, *Literature, Science, and Animal Advocacy in Canada*, Palgrave Studies in Animals and Literature,
https://doi.org/10.1007/978-3-031-40556-3

- How does the author depict nonhuman sexuality? Are there any non-reproductive acts? Are there any same-sex pairings?
- Does the author engage with any specific scientific fields, such as behaviourism or cognitive ethology? Do they use up-to-date information?
- Does the author challenge our expectations of the species? Do they rely on stereotypes?
- Does the author engage with any forms of animal advocacy, such as animal welfare or conservation debates? Do they write about a specific real-world issue?
- Does the author focus on individual acts of cruelty? Do they explore systems of animal exploitation?
- How does the author present human-animal relations? What roles do humans play in the animal's life?
- Do any animal protection laws exist in the time and place that the text was written? If so, are nonhuman animals protected as 'objects' or living beings? Do they grant any rights? Which species are included or excluded?
- Does the author challenge anthropocentrism? Do they disrupt notions of human uniqueness? Do they confront the topic of human supremacy?
- Does the author explore the intersection between human and nonhuman oppressions?

INDEX[1]

A

Acceptance of not knowing, 15, 17, 21–23, 145, 152, 168, 172–174, 177–178, 195, 231, 236–239

Accuracy, 6, 21, 127, 218, 228, 230, 240

Adaptations, *see under* Wild animal story

Advocacy, *see* Animal advocacy

Advocacy-orientated, 11–13, 41

Agency, *see* Animal agency

Allegories, 9, 14, 15, 40, 106, 116, 207

Altruism, *see* Animal altruism

Amateur, 30, 62, 86, 253
  botanist and naturalist, 39, 116, 157
  ichthyologist, 98
  myrmecologist, 107, 116
  observers, 98, 191, 246

American Progressivism, *see under* Conservation

Anecdotal, 87
  cognitivism, 32
  evidence, 32, 48, 62, 86, 190–191

Anecdotes, 12, 30, 57, 65, 86–87, 136, 157–160, 164, 191, 208, 218–219, 250, 253

Animal advocacy, 7, 9, 16, 45, 48, 61, 73, 122, 136, 145, 156, 193, 248, 252

Animal advocates, 23, 136, 197
  backlash (*see under* Animal protection)
  depictions of, 206
  and human rights, 185
  negative perceptions, 184, 187
  as terrorists, 185

Animal agency, 14, 18, 38, 154, 224–225, 235

Animal agriculture, 5, 34–36, 90–91, 114–115, 137, 166, 174–175, 185–186, 189

[1] Note: Page numbers followed by 'n' refer to notes.

© The Author(s), under exclusive license to Springer Nature Switzerland AG 2023
C. Allmark-Kent, *Literature, Science, and Animal Advocacy in Canada*, Palgrave Studies in Animals and Literature, https://doi.org/10.1007/978-3-031-40556-3

Animal altruism, 59, 189
Animal anecdotes, *see* Anecdotes
Animal as human property, *see*
   Property
Animal autonomy, 14, 51, 58, 152,
   157, 171–172,
   224–225, 234–235
Animal awareness, 89, 92, 121, 125,
   198–199, 201
   of death, 174, 208
   of self, 31, 189, 198, 207, 209
Animal biography, 15, 38–39, 41,
   49–50, 54, 70, 73, 96, 99, 112,
   119, 125, 157–159, 199, 250
Animal choice, 69, 105, 120, 153
   predators, 203–204
   preferences, 69, 105, 153
Animal cognition, 190, 211, 240, 241
Animal communication, 40–41, 54,
   68, 72, 115, 135–136, 199–203,
   223, 229, 238
   body language, 105, 115, 200,
      202–203, 216
   intentional, 202
   language, 135, 141, 145, 168, 172,
      189, 203, 207, 210, 216–217,
      239, 241
   scent, 115, 202, 216
   touch, 115
   vocalization, 202, 222–223
   See also Talking animals; Translation
Animal companionship, 101, 105,
   138, 173–174, 221–222
   with humans (*see* Human-animal
      relationships)
Animal consciousness, 20–22, 88,
   133–136, 142, 183, 189–191,
   246, 252
   in fiction, 17–19, 38, 120, 145,
      168, 171, 174, 195, 198–199,
      206–209, 215–217, 238–241
Animal cooperation, 172, 238–239

Animal culture, 56, 56n3, 160–161,
   168, 172–174, 207, 209–211,
   216–217, 239
   definitions, 56n3
   differences, 173
   myths, 173, 207, 214
   practices, 172–174, 203
Animal emotions, 4, 67, 75, 81, 133,
   138, 189, 246–247, 252
   in fiction, 5–16, 68–72, 75,
      100–101, 104–105, 111,
      117–120, 126–128, 149, 153,
      156, 159–164, 168, 174–178,
      198–199, 208–209, 216–217
   in science, 20, 30–33, 81, 92, 133,
      136, 183, 189
Animal-endorsing, 10, 11, 13–15
Animal exploitation
   as acceptable, 141
   in science, 114, 185
Animal grief, 117, 126, 149, 207,
   208n1, 217
Animal instinct, 30, 50, 65–66, 88–89,
   98, 134, 201, 227
   in fiction, 53–54, 56, 65–66, 70–71,
      95, 98, 100, 110–112,
      118–121, 125, 201, 220,
      227, 240
   rejection of, 100, 110–112,
      118, 159
Animal intelligence, 30, 33, 54, 70,
   75, 110, 136, 156, 159–160,
   164, 206
Animal intentionality, 31, 89, 92, 98,
   105, 120, 135–136, 199–200,
   222–223, 241
   See also under Animal
      communication
Animal knowledge, 53–56, 161, 176,
   211, 239
   models, 54, 70
   sharing, 54, 172, 215–216

Animal language, *see under* Animal
    communication
Animal language experiments, 141
Animal laws, *see under* Animal
    protection
    See also Canadian Criminal Code
Animal learning, 31, 50, 88–89,
    135, 191
    in fiction, 40–41, 52–56, 62, 69–71,
        105, 107, 111, 119, 121, 125,
        160–161, 164, 199–201, 203,
        211–212, 216, 224, 227, 240
    teaching (*see* Animal teaching)
Animal legislation debates, *see under*
    Canadian Criminal Code
    See also Animal protection
Animal memory, 68–71, 120, 199
Animal minds, 4–6, 50, 75, 151,
    246–247, 252–253
    difficulties knowing, 31, 146, 149,
        153, 227
    in fiction, 41, 54, 65–66, 111–112,
        117, 127, 153, 156, 159, 171,
        178, 198–199, 201, 208–209,
        217, 239–240
    indifference to, 16, 38, 41,
        220, 226–228
    interest in, 34, 65, 112, 149, 171,
        217, 225
    in science, 20, 30–31, 33, 50,
        87–89, 133–136, 189–191
Animal networks, 40, 173, 174,
    203, 216
Animal pain, 54–57, 67, 69–71, 90,
    101, 103–105, 114–115,
    162, 199
Animal personality, 15, 49, 66, 108,
    118, 138, 160, 163–164,
    178, 251
Animal perspectives, 6, 15, 40–41,
    52–55, 58, 68–69, 71–74,
    104–107, 110, 112–115, 154,
    171–172, 191, 199, 210,
    212–214, 226, 239
    imagining, 40, 41, 72, 171
    perception, 14, 53, 69, 72, 171,
        199, 202, 216
    species-specific, 72
Animal play, 69–71, 100, 105,
    162–164, 189
Animal pleasure, 15, 67, 69–71,
    100–103, 105, 153, 162, 190
Animal protagonists, 6, 17, 40, 220
Animal protection, 21, 140, 186, 245,
    247, 251
    backlash against, 3, 22, 141,
        183–187, 197, 229, 246
    laws, 34, 90, 140, 197, 249
    movements, 34, 91, 136, 140–142,
        164, 185
    policies, 1, 140
    rights, 36, 41, 60–61, 73, 91,
        141–142, 177, 183–188, 196,
        197, 229, 246
    See also Canadian Criminal Code
Animal psychology, 30, 41, 49–50, 62,
    66–67, 87–88
    See also Behaviourism; Cognitive
        ethology; Comparative
        psychology; Ethology
Animal reasoning, 31, 65, 68, 70–72,
    87, 111, 117, 121, 241
Animal resistance, 51, 53,
    196–197, 234–240
    See also Animal unpredictability
Animal rights, *see under* Animal
    protection
Animals *as animals*, 9, 40,
    209–210, 249
Animals as individuals, 6, 14–15,
    38–39, 49, 58–60, 138, 174, 251
    uniqueness, 105, 138, 160,
        163, 224
    See also Animal personality

Animals as objects, 15–16, 39, 45–46,
    51–52, 58–59, 69, 107, 126,
    148, 155, 174–176, 184, 189,
    193, 218, 220–222, 225, 230,
    234–235, 249, 251
    See also Objects of utility
Animals as subjects, see Subjects
    of lives
Animal-scepticism, 10–12, 15,
    18, 31, 146, 149, 151,
    218, 227
Animal societies, 22, 106–109, 112,
    117, 172, 192, 210–211,
    216, 239
Animal studies, 7, 8, 12, 253
Animal teaching, 54–56, 70, 71, 161,
    199–202, 216
Animal thinking, 120, 135–136, 159,
    171, 189–190, 207, 209,
    216–217, 237, 238
Animal unpredictability, 11, 152, 164,
    207–208, 224–225, 235–236,
    239, 251
Animal welfare, 21, 36, 104, 139,
    164–165, 185–188, 229
    science, 136
Anthropocentrism, 16–18, 73–75,
    126, 178, 218–220, 225–226,
    230, 232, 246–248
    challenges to, 74, 114–115,
        168–169, 176, 206–207,
        213, 234
    in fiction, 52, 57, 61, 74–75, 112,
        149–152, 155, 178,
        218–226, 230
    in literary studies, 8–9, 11–12
    in nature writing, 39–40
Anthropomorphism, 11, 18, 86–89,
    109, 126–127, 168, 207,
    220, 247
    accusation of, 62, 75, 117, 121,
        126, 201, 216

    fear of, 18, 20, 32, 43, 61, 75, 81,
        86, 95–98, 118, 127–128, 195,
        218, 220–221, 238, 240–241
    in fiction, 9, 11, 15–16, 39, 45,
        168, 201, 207, 211 (see also
        Humanization of animals)
    sentimentalism, 142
    in science, 22, 31–33, 86–89, 127,
        142, 190–191, 246
    stigma, 4, 42, 49, 61–62, 161
    as a tool, 11, 183,
        190–192, 216–217
Anti-cruelty, 34, 184–188, 245–251
    bill, 35
    laws, 3, 20, 81, 104, 184, 187
    legislation, 2, 22, 61, 183, 184
Anti-sealing, see Seal hunting
Artificial/artificiality, 138, 232–233
    and the natural, 231
    production of 'nature,' 167
Attempts to know, see
    Knowing animals
Atwood, Margaret, 2, 18, 23, 45–47,
    140, 146, 152, 186n1,
    230–240, 247
    Oryx and Crake (2003), 230–240
Authentic 'wilderness,' 167
Autobiography, 50–52, 55, 108–109,
    138, 157–158, 218
Autonomy, see Animal autonomy
Awareness, see Animal awareness

B
Backlash, see under Animal protection
Behaviourism, 20–21, 31–33, 81,
    86–89, 92, 133–136, 226, 227,
    245, 252
    in fiction, 95, 98, 117, 145–146,
        151–153, 156, 198–199, 224,
        226–228, 240
Biography, see Animal biography

Blackfish (2013), 250–252
Bodsworth, Fred, 20, 95, 116–127,
    151, 167, 201, 218, 220
  Last of the Curlews (1955),
    116–127
Body language, *see under* Animal
    communication
Bounty-hunting, 37, 51, 57–58, 62,
    83, 137, 158, 165, 204, 206
Burroughs, John, 20, 41, 42, 74, 201,
    217, 218, 228

C
Candian anti-cruelty legislation, 89
Canadian attitudes to animals, 2,
    46, 247–248
Canadian Criminal Code, 3, 34–36,
    89–90, 184–185, 187, 193,
    246, 249–250
  amendments, 34, 90, 186, 229, 250
  unsuccessful bills, 189
Canadian Federation of Humane
    Societies, 91
Canadian identity, 185
Canadian literary canon, 42, 45, 83
Canadian psyche, 3, 19, 46, 247
Canadian Society for the Prevention of
    Cruelty to Animals
    (CSPCA), 34, 50
  See also Society for the Prevention of
    Cruelty to Animals (SPCA)
Captivity, 3, 35, 50, 74, 74n8, 90,
    113, 154–155, 157, 167,
    176–177, 222, 248
  whales and dolphins, 249–252
Carson, Rachel, 138–139, 166
Children's animal stories, 38, 39
Choices, *see* Animal choice
Climate change, 230
Cognitive ethology, 12, 21–23,
    135–136, 189–192, 195, 241

Cognitive revolution, 21, 75,
    133–136, 142, 198, 217,
    246, 252
Colonization, 2, 10, 37–40,
    119n12, 122–124
  See also under Science
Communication, *see* Animal
    communication
Companionship, *see* Animal
    companionship
  See also Human-animal relationships
Comparative psychology, 19–20,
    30–33, 45, 48–49, 62, 65–67, 75,
    81, 86–89, 92, 136, 142, 159,
    183, 190–191, 245, 252–253
  introspective method, 32, 62, 66,
    72, 75, 81, 86–87, 112,
    183, 252–253
Concern for animals, 61
  as feminine, 186
  stigma, 75
Consciousness, *see* Animal
    consciousness
Conservation, 1, 13, 37–38, 73, 81,
    83–86, 91, 133, 137–139,
    184, 246
  American Progressivism, 85
  animals as commodities, 85, 137 (*see
    also* Bounty-hunting)
  in fiction, 41, 60, 73, 99, 101–105,
    117, 123, 164–165, 196–197,
    206–207, 228–229, 240
  non-intervention, 137–138
  organizations, 165 (*see also*
    Sportsman's creed)
  wise use, 85
Contradictory representation, 96, 105,
    118, 220
  See also Reductive representation
Cooperation, *see* Animal cooperation
Criminal Code, *see* Canadian
    Criminal Code

Cruelty to Animals Act, 34, 249
Culture, *see* Animal culture
Currumpaw wolves, 51, 53,
    59, 207–208

D
Darwin, Charles, 19, 29–31, 42, 48,
    60, 65, 190–191
Death, *see under* Animal awareness
Defamiliarization, 59, 59n4, 72–74,
    114–115, 171–172, 212–214, 251
Desire to know, *see* Knowing animals
Domesticated animals, 7, 34–36, 39–41,
    60, 90–91, 114–115, 137, 166,
    174–175, 185–186, 189, 234–235
Dramatic irony, 119, 158, 214

E
Ecology, 20, 60, 85, 135–137, 166,
    204, 240
Emotions, *see* Animal emotions
Empathy, 6, 52, 68–69, 73, 99,
    103–104, 112, 116, 169, 189, 252
Endangered species, *see* Species loss
Engel, Marian, 18, 21, 23, 117,
    145–155, 168–169, 178,
    197, 226–227
    Bear (1976), 145–155
Environmental, 137–139, 157
    destruction, 102, 133, 139, 157,
        167, 177
    movements, 133, 139, 177,
        196–197, 246
Ethology, 20, 81, 86–89, 92,
    133–136, 189–191, 227
    in fiction, 95, 98, 117–118, 146,
        151, 156, 198–199
Evolution/evolutionary, 29, 30,
    101, 134
    continuity, 29–30, 168
    theory, 92

Experimentation, 32–33, 86–87, 99,
    113–114, 135
Extinction, *see* Species loss

F
Fact and fiction, 21, 45, 47–49, 109,
    126–127, 158–159, 164, 167,
    192, 218
Failure of knowing, 15–18, 21–23,
    145–150, 154–155, 178, 195,
    218–222, 225–228,
    230, 234–237
    See also under Knowing animals
Fantasy of knowing, 16–21, 40–41,
    45, 50, 107, 110, 114, 146–147,
    154–156, 168, 177–178, 195,
    218, 236
    realistic, 16, 20, 22, 46–47, 95–96,
        117–118, 127, 156–158,
        195–196, 203
    speculative, 16, 20–22, 95,
        109–110, 116, 195, 207–210,
        212, 215–217
Federal animal protection laws, *see*
    Canadian Criminal Code
Filmmakers, 138, 204
Films, 137–138, 167
Findley, Timothy, 18, 21, 23, 152,
    167–178, 203, 208, 215, 231
    Not Wanted on the Voyage
        (1984), 167–178
Frisch, Karl von, 134

G
Game, 38, 73, 84–85, 91, 122, 124
Gowdy, Barbara, 22, 192, 207–217,
    238, 240, 252–253
    The White Bone (1998), 207–217
Greenpeace, 139
Grief, *see* Animal grief
Griffin, Donald R., 135, 190

Grove, Frederick Philip, 20–21, 68,
    95, 105–116, 118, 127–128,
    159, 168, 192, 201, 208–210,
    212–213, 215, 218–219
    Consider Her Ways (1947), 105–116

H
Haig-Brown, Roderick, 20, 68,
    96–105, 109, 111, 114,
    117–119, 127, 159, 167,
    199, 201
    Return to the River (1941), 96–105
Historical, 101, 102, 123
    context, 59, 122
    materials, 122, 124–125
    sources, 123
Hudson's Bay Company, 122–123
Human-animal divide, 18, 146–147,
    152–154, 176–177, 188–190,
    193, 195, 218, 220,
    228–229, 240
    blurred, 168–170, 177,
        230–233, 236–237
Human-animal hybrids, *see* Hybridity
Human-animal relationships, 157,
    170, 230
    between individuals, 145, 154,
        163–164, 221–222, 225, 229
    pessimism, 17, 149, 155, 229, 246
Humane movements, 40, 61,
    104, 136
Humane slaughter, 91, 115n10,
    137, 141
Humane societies, 20, 36, 37, 81, 91,
    117, 141, 187
Humanization of animals, 109, 188,
    190, 228, 250
    fear of, 141, 193, 240
    See also Anthropomorphism
Human supremacy, 11, 17–18, 23,
    112, 142, 169, 176–178, 225

Human uniqueness, 142, 168, 178,
    189, 193, 195, 207
Hunters, 58, 59, 62, 124, 204,
    207, 213
    subsistence, 83
    as tourists, 84–85, 204–206
    See also Bounty-hunting
Hybridity, 22, 23, 168–170, 231

I
Indifference to knowing, 16–17,
    40–41, 45, 106–107
Indigenous, 18, 37, 83–84,
    123, 184–186
    authors, 18
    sovereignty, 140
Individuality, *see* Animals as individuals
Instinct, *see* Animal instinct
Intelligence, *see* Animal intelligence
Intentions, *see* Animal intentionality
Interdisciplinarity, 3–5, 7–8, 10–17,
    30, 32–33, 81–82, 109, 164,
    189–193, 208, 216–217,
    247–249, 253
    authors and science, 6–7, 17,
        41–42, 45, 47–48, 52, 60,
        65–67, 75, 81–83, 96, 98–100,
        105, 109–110, 117–118,
        126–128, 156, 164, 192, 198,
        207–210, 227, 248–253
    authors and scientific credibility, 41,
        48–49, 66, 75, 82, 97–98
    authors indifferent to science, 41,
        150–151, 155, 227
    science and animal protection, 32,
        85–86, 102, 123,
        136–138, 252
    scientists and fiction, 23, 66, 66n6,
        99, 127, 192, 216–217,
        247, 252–253
Inuit, 21, 140, 184–186

K

Knowing animals, 4, 10, 15–16, 112,
  147, 226, 234
  attempts, 17, 147, 149, 218, 222,
    225, 252
  difficulties, 31, 146, 148–149, 151,
    229, 246
  failure, 17, 146, 148, 150,
    154–155, 220, 226, 237
  indifference to, 16, 39, 226
  as individuals, 230
  through fiction, 6, 50, 145, 252
  See also Unknowable animals
Knowledge, *see* Animal knowledge

L

Language, *see under* Animal
  communication
Language experiments, 135
Lawrence, R.D., 22, 195–207,
  209, 240
  The White Puma (1990), 195–207
Learning, *see* Animal learning
Life history, *see* Animal biography
Literature and science, *see*
  Interdisciplinarity
Lorenz, Konrad, 88, 134
Love, Glen, 11–13

M

Magic, 23, 95, 112, 121, 168,
  208, 215–216
  telepathy, 107, 112, 116, 207
Martel, Yann, 18, 23, 98,
  218–230, 240
  Life of Pi (2001), 218–230
Mason, Bill, 138, 204
Mechanomorphism, 16, 16n6, 20, 33,
  81, 85–86, 89–90, 92, 117, 133,
  136, 141–142, 218, 246

in fiction, 75, 95–96, 98, 101–102,
  105, 111–112, 117–120, 128,
  151–156, 161, 198, 218, 220,
  227, 240
Memory, *see* Animal memory
Mentation, *see* Animal minds
Migration, 100, 119, 124–125
Mills, Thomas Wesley, 49, 50
Minds, *see* Animal minds
Morgan, Conwy Lloyd, 32,
  33, 88
Mourning, *see* Animal grief
Mythological creatures, 168, 169
Myths, *see under* Animal culture

N

National parks, 37, 84, 137, 155,
  165–167, 214
National Parks Service, 82
National 'psyche,' 3, 46, 247–248
Natural resources, 37, 38, 85–86, 137
Nature-endorsing, 10, 13
Nature Fakers controversy, 20, 41–42,
  45–47, 61, 63–64, 66, 74–75,
  81–83, 109, 117, 156, 159, 164,
  178, 190–192, 198–200,
  217–219, 228,
  246–247, 252–253
  impact, 42, 82–83, 92, 95–98, 105,
    109, 127
Nature faking, 62, 82, 95–97,
  117, 127
  accusations, 97
  avoidance, 97–98, 108–109
Nature reserves, *see* National parks
Nature-sceptical, 10, 11, 13
Nature writing, 39–40, 46, 48, 108
Networks, *see* Animal networks
New Ecology, 85–86, 102, 137
Non-intervention, *see under*
  Conservation

O

Objectification, 16, 18, 61, 71, 75, 89, 248
Objectivity, *see under* Science
Objects, *see* Animals as objects
Objects of utility, 15–16, 58–59, 106, 155, 175, 218, 221, 225, 230, 234–235, 249
Observation, 81, 88–89, 99, 164, 199, 203, 227, 239
Oil, 157

P

Pain, *see* Animal pain
Paratextual, 210
Perception, *see under* Animal perspective
Personal histories, *see* Animal biography
Personality, *see* Animal personality
Perspective, *see* Animal perspective
Play, *see* Animal play
Pleasure, *see* Animal pleasure
Poison, 51, 53–57, 59, 90, 103, 113–114, 137, 160–161, 166, 211
Polk, James, 42, 46, 247
Popularizing science, 42, 47–48, 60, 62
Population loss, *see* Species loss
Practical zoocriticism, 5, 7, 13, 247–248, 253
Predator, 59, 62, 83, 137–138, 166, 207, 232
  benefits, 203–204
  control, 137, 206 (*see also* Bounty-hunting)
  prejudices, 57, 73
  prey choice (*see under* Animal choice)
  protection, 133, 166, 204
  as 'vermin' (*see* Vermin)

Predator-prey relationships, 73, 203, 222
Preferences, *see under* Animal choice
Professionalization of the sciences, 32, 41, 48, 62, 85, 246, 253
Property, 3, 18, 34–36, 61, 90, 168, 184, 187–189, 193, 246, 248, 249
Psychology, *see* Animal psychology

R

Real, 41, 50–51, 55, 98, 110, 158, 170, 215, 216
  animals, 6–7, 9–10, 12–14, 49, 125, 159, 170, 207–209, 215, 252
Realism, 20, 45–47, 110, 117, 158–160, 203, 240
  disruption, 110, 177, 212–216, 218
  See also Fantasy of knowing; Wild animal story
Reason, *see* Animal reasoning
Reductive representation, 104, 118, 135, 220
  See also Contradictory representation
Regan, Tom, 14, 141
Rejection of science, *see under* Interdisciplinarity
Relationships between 'prey' and 'predator' species, 222
Resistance, *see* Animal resistance
Roberts, Charles G. D., 19–23, 45, 62–75, 82–84, 92, 95–97, 108, 119, 126, 156–160, 164–167, 169, 178, 192–193, 195–196, 198–199, 203–204, 218, 235, 240, 247–248, 251–253
  animal advocacy, 72–75, 105
  conservation, 83
  creation of wild animal story, 39–42, 45–46, 63–64, 146, 192, 249

Roberts, Charles G. D. (*cont.*)
  nature faking, 41–42, 63,
    81–83, 127
  range of species, 67–68, 72
  rejection, 147, 169
  reputation, 42, 63, 82
  and Seton, 63–64, 66–75
  science, 65–67, 70, 75, 99, 105,
    111–112, 245, 253
  stories, 62–75
  See also True stories; Wild
    animal story
Romanes, George, 30–32, 48–49,
  54, 60, 65, 68, 70–71,
  159, 190–191
  table of emotions, 72
  table of intellectual and emotional
    development, 67
Roosevelt, Theodore (President), 20,
  41, 98–99, 159–160, 218,
  228, 252
Russell, Andy, 22, 138, 156–167, 178,
  196, 198, 200, 204, 209,
  214, 240
  *Andy Russell's Adventures with
    Wild Animals* (1977),
    156–167

S
Salt, Henry S., 36, 36n3, 60–61, 141
Scent, *see under* Animal
  communication
Science, 7, 9, 12–13, 29–34, 86–89,
  133–136, 189–193, 253
  and animal protection (*see under*
    Interdisciplinarity)
  authority of, 32–33, 65–67, 75, 82,
    85–87, 164, 190–193
  and colonization, 39, 122,
    199n12
  and literature (*see under*
    Interdisciplinarity)

and objectivity, 20, 32–33,
  61, 81, 86–89, 92, 98,
  109, 127
  professionalization, 19, 32–33, 41,
    48, 62, 85
Seal hunting, 21–22, 139–140, 184–186
Self-awareness, *see under* Animal
  awareness
Semi-autobiographical, *see*
  Autobiography
Senses, *see under* Animal perspectives
Sentimentality, 43, 61, 98, 102, 160,
  184, 220, 228, 246
Seton, Ernest Thompson, 19–23,
  45–62, 92, 104–105, 107–109,
  119, 121–122, 124–126, 138,
  156–160, 164–167, 171, 173,
  175, 177–178, 192, 195–196,
  198–201, 203–204, 207–209,
  218, 233, 235, 240, 247, 251–253
  animal advocacy, 3–4, 60–61, 251
  conservation, 83
  creation of wild animal story, 39–42,
    45–46, 51–52, 63–64, 146,
    192, 247
  nature faking, 41–42, 81–83,
    95–97, 117, 127, 147, 164,
    201, 245
  rejection, 147, 169
  reputation, 42, 61–62, 116–118,
    147, 169–170
  and Roberts, 63–64, 66–75
  science, 47–50, 60, 105, 111–112,
    192–193, 245, 253
  stories, 45–62
  See also True stories; Wild
    animal story
Settler-colonial culture, 2–3, 38, 45
Sexual encounters, *see* Zoophilia
Singer, Peter, 36n3, 141, 183
Social relationships, *see under* Animal
  societies
  See also Animal companionship

Societies, *see* Animal societies
Society for the Prevention of Cruelty
    to Animals (SPCA), 139,
    164, 250
    See also Canadian Society for the
        Prevention of Cruelty to
        Animals (CSPCA)
Speciesism, 16–17, 16n5, 57–58, 68,
    137, 141, 167, 177, 189, 213,
    231, 248
Species loss, 39, 60, 83–84, 123, 167,
    197, 230, 240
    extinction, 5, 121–127, 167,
        175–177, 230–233, 240
    of *Homo sapiens*, 231–233
    human role in, 122–124, 177, 207
Species stereotypes, 57, 137, 235
Speculation, 5–6, 50, 54–55, 59,
    68–69, 99, 109–110, 114–116,
    119, 125, 159, 172, 174, 183,
    192, 201, 211, 217,
    238, 240–241
    See also Fantasy of knowing
Sportsman's creed, 84
Stimulus and response, 87, 89, 134,
    224, 227
Subjective experiences, 58, 69, 89,
    100, 103, 136
    See also Animal perspectives; Animal
        emotions
Subjects of lives, 14–15, 51–52,
    58–59, 105, 107, 155, 174–175,
    218, 220–221, 225, 230, 234,
    249, 251
Supernatural, *see* Magic

T
Talking animals, 52n2, 116, 210,
    212–213, 216
    See also Translation
Teaching, *see* Animal teaching
Telepathy, *see under* Magic

Thinking, *see* Animal thinking
Thought experiments, 54, 99,
    105, 119
Tinbergen, Niko, 88–89, 134
Touch, *see under* Animal
    communication
Tourists, 37, 84, 91, 137, 155, 165,
    205, 214
Translation, 115, 210
Traps, 51–54, 56–57, 59, 137,
    160, 165
True stories, 41, 46–47, 49
    as literary device, 46, 107–109,
        125–126, 218

U
Unknowable animals, 11, 17,
    23, 81, 87
    in fiction, 145, 146n1, 149,
        152–153, 206, 213, 226–227,
        235–237, 240
    See also Knowing animals
Unpredictability, *see* Animal
    unpredictability
Utilitarian view of animals, 39, 86,
    221, 230

V
Vermin, 38, 57, 84, 122, 204
Vision, *see under* Animal perspective
Vocabulary, *see* Translation
Vocalizations, *see under* Animal
    communication

W
Watson, John B., 86–88, 227
Welfare, *see* Animal welfare
The Wheeler, 108, 113, 213
Wheeler, William Morton,
    108, 111–114

Whitehead, Hal, 66, 99, 192,
216–217, 252
Wild animals, 50, 60, 234, 249
in captivity (*see* Captivity)
as individuals (*see* Animals as
individuals)
in national parks, 137
as natural resource, 84
Wild animal story, 73, 84, 92, 111,
156–160, 178, 192–193,
195–198, 203–204, 218, 233
adaptation of, 20, 95–97, 102,
118, 126–127
as Canadian, 46, 146, 177,
247–248
creation, 6–7, 19, 39–42, 45–48,
62–67, 246
as innovation, 46, 63–64, 116–117,
169, 177, 250–253 (*see also*
Nature Fakers controversy)

rejection, 21, 145, 147, 155, 169
reputation, 42, 46, 62, 75, 82–83,
97, 169, 246, 250–253 (*see also*
Roberts, Charles G. D.; Seton,
Ernest Thompson)
as tragic, 53, 126, 196–197, 207
See also True stories
Wildlife documentaries, *see* Films
Wise use, *see under* Conservation
Wolves, *see* Currumpaw wolves

Z
Zoocentrism, 13–15, 17–18, 53, 110,
115, 171–172, 176, 212,
248, 250–253
and anthropocentrism, 75, 107
and mechanomorphism, 96–97,
103–105, 118
Zoophilia, 146, 148, 154

Printed by Printforce, the Netherlands